TRANSFORMING CORRECTIONS

DAT

Carolina Academic Press
Criminal Justice and Psychology Series

Bruce A. Arrigo
Series Editor

Criminal Competency on Trial
The Case of Colin Ferguson
Mark C. Bardwell and Bruce A. Arrigo

The Myth of a Psychiatric Crime Wave
Public Perception, Juror Research, and Mental Illness
Corey J. Vitello and Eric W. Hickey

Police Corruption and Psychological Testing
A Strategy for Pre-employment Screening
Natalie L. Claussen-Rogers and Bruce A. Arrigo

Transforming Corrections
Humanistic Approaches to Corrections & Offender Treatment
David Polizzi and Michael Braswell

TRANSFORMING CORRECTIONS

HUMANISTIC APPROACHES TO CORRECTIONS AND OFFENDER TREATMENT

David Polizzi

INDIANA STATE UNIVERSITY

Michael Braswell

EAST TENNESSEE STATE UNIVERSITY

CAROLINA ACADEMIC PRESS
Durham, North Carolina

Library of Congress Cataloging-in-Publication Data

Transforming corrections : humanistic approaches to corrections and offender treatment / David Polizzi, Michael Braswell.
    p. cm.
  Includes bibliographical references and index.
  ISBN 978-1-59460-452-2 (alk. paper)
  1. Corrections--United States. 2. Corrections--Philosophy. I. Polizzi, David.
II. Braswell, Michael. III. Title.

  HV9471.T73 2009
  365'.9730684--dc22

                                    2009022605

Carolina Academic Press
700 Kent Street
Durham, North Carolina 27701
Telephone (919) 489-7486
Fax (919) 493-5668
www.cap-press.com

Printed in the United States of America

This book is dedicated to the memory of Mike Arons and Richard Asarian.

CONTENTS

Section II • Humanistic Perspectives in Corrections

FOREWORD

One of the most convincing testimonials to human obduracy is the care most of us take to preserve our repertoire of off-putting stereotypes—our conscious and unconscious assumptions about persons and groups who we have concluded ought to be condemned, shunned, rejected, or repudiated. Unfortunately, unflattering preconceptions have a way of being reciprocated by their targets. The result in the aggregate is a world divided into factious enclaves from which we warily scrutinize each others' camp fires in the twilight separated by protective moats.

Few human borders are more assiduously patrolled than that between incarcerated offenders and their keepers. Among the best-selling offerings of the American Correctional Association (ACA)—proudly listed under their *Management Resources*—are a "Con Games Inmates Play (Second edition)" video, a "Working with Manipulative Inmates" course, and assorted books with titles such as "Games Criminals Play," "The Art of the Con," and "Strategies for Redirecting Inmate Deception." The ACA as a rule does not market managerial books or videos by inmates, but if it did, these would no doubt bear titles such as "Initiating Prison Litigation (in Five Easy Lessons)," "Coping with Guard Sadism, Corruption, and Brutality," and "Why You Can Never Trust a Screw."

A sure-fire prescription for engendering reciprocal mistrust is to avoid disconfirming information by refraining from human contacts by preventing their occurrence. The consummate application of this strategy happens to be imprisonment, and its crowning achievement is that of "special housing" or segregation units (up to and including the "supermaxes" described in chapter seven) with regimes that completely isolate prisoners and separate them from prison staff members. These contemporary high-tech dungeons are environments designed to ensure the perpetuation of prisoner-staff estrangement. The inmates who survive such settings emerge seething with righteous resentment, while the guards who have been monitoring the prisoners feel confirmed in the view (which they volubly assert) that incarcerated men or women are the lowermost scum of the earth.

The perpetuation of offender stereotyping in prisons must not be considered the domain of correctional officers. Despite predictable disclaimers to the contrary, mental health workers can function as prime sources of rejection for prison inmates. In fact, psychiatrists, psychologists, social workers, or nurses who work in detention facilities are particularly well situated to act as agents of dehumanization. "Therapeutic" encounters with inmates can be experiences almost calculated to reinforce the denunciatory message of confinement or to accentuate the deprivations of imprisonment. As a case in point, delivering "mental health services" through the door of an isolation cell can nicely convey indifference to pain and suffering. As an example of an even less ambiguous communication, I know of no more effective way to advertise paranoia than to demand that some inmate be shackled while one builds "rapport" with him across a solid bullet-proof plastic partition.

For clinicians to pay homage to the demands of custody while they engage in custodial overkill may be a deception that adds insult to injury. The evidence suggests that most professionals in prisons are accorded a measure of respect and authority in their domain—if nothing else, to preempt litigation—and thus have more discretion in doing their work than they elect to exercise. The hesitance to take ameliorative initiatives is often a matter of choice or policy, and the mantra "custody made me do it" can be an alibi. Assigning blame to custody or the administration becomes a convenient way to preserve self-respect while one colludes to keep anxiety-provoking offenders at a distance. The avoidance behavior is apt to be transparent and it can cement the cynicism of the offenders one has avoided. Rejection happens to be the response offenders mostly expect and they have learned to react in kind. This response of the offenders can be self-servingly deemed to be "ingratitude," and one can of course point to their resistance as evidence of their imperviousness to treatment (chapter twelve). The offenders thus conveniently become the bad guys in the transaction, and this adds buttressing to one's anxieties in dealing with them. Along the way, correctional staff has made sure that no change could possibly occur: no reappraisals will have been called for, either on the staff member's own part, or on the part of the offenders the staff has taken exquisite care not to engage.

Psychological reappraisal in general becomes an issue in human intercourse where encounters with previously stereotyped "others" provide intimations of the shared humanity we have been schooled to ignore or suppress. At such serendipitous (and discomfiting) junctures, there are potential opportunities for discovery, growth, and development. Unsurprisingly, in real life (unlike in some fiction), such opportunities are rarely utilized. What mostly takes place

is a salvaging operation in which miniscule adjustments are enacted to preserve one's endangered world view. In other words, challenges to stereotypes
tend to be responded to with exercises in remedial tweaking.

The need for remedial tweaking is particularly acute where the "other"—e.g.,
the offender who looks to be human—also appears to be an impressive, congenial, or likable human being. To deal with this eventuality the safest course
of action is to invoke the principle of exceptionality. A staff person admits that
the offender is an interesting and attractive person, and further credits him
with the fact that he is interesting and attractive despite the fact that he is an
offender. The fact that the offender is a distinctive offender can then be used
to argue that he is an obvious exception to the rule.

If a correctional staff member wishes to relate to an offender as a gesture of
humanistic good will, the safest candidate for adoption is one who stands out
in some non-offense-related fashion, which facilitates his differentiation from
other offenders. If the staff member then needs to defend against the charge
that it is elitist to single out an offender-novelist, inmate-poet, or prisoner-
playwright for sponsorship, it is helpful if one's protégé has a long prison sentence, and has thus been certified by authorities as an offender of substance.
To be sure, hybrids are wildly unrepresentative in both their worlds, but being
exceptions they are safe to adopt—at least, until they re-offend.

Humanism is a broadly encompassing category—the approach comprises
a great deal of activity, as a reading of the ensuing chapters demonstrates. It,
at a minimum, connotes the effort (and capacity) to fully understand others
in the sense of intuiting the world as others perceive it. The skill is one that Carl
Rogers consistently prized and labeled as the capacity for accurate empathy.
The capacity is not a tool designed to serve one's predilections or convenience.
To know a person in this sense means to know the whole person rather than
select congenial attributes. Accurate empathy is in fact best deployed where it
is most difficult to exercise, where the distance to be bridged is greatest. It is
of least consequence where the experience of knowing others is most inviting,
where we deal with the amenable or familiar, as in caseloads of hand-picked
clients.

It is preliminarily enticing to suggest that one should distinguish between
the offender and his or her offense; however, an offense-less offender is fiction
and an offense committed by others becomes a different offense. Lastly, the
offender's offense-related dispositions must be the subject of our professional
concern, and they must certainly be a subject of concern for the offender. In
some (restorative) paradigms, the offender's motives are also of interest to
those who have been victimized (chapter nine).

Humanistic approaches ideally are open minded and ecumenical. What should matter is the achievement of consequential relationships (chapter ten), not the technology whereby they are achieved. To accentuate or belabor sectarian distinctions strikes me as unhelpful. For me, for example, the embodiment of a humanistic approach happened to have been that of Fritz Redl, who was a Freudian psychoanalyst. Redl had a regulation Viennese accent, with which he colloquially described the doings and perspectives of Detroit juvenile gang members. No one I know worked with institutionalized delinquents more skillfully and authoritatively, and with more insight and love.

For my money, Redl was the Complete Humanist. He may or may not have imbibed the requisite philosophical sources (he did have a doctorate in philosophy), but Fritz Redl walked the walk. And what Redl had in spades is Rogers' third desideratum, which is that of genuineness. It is difficult to precisely define genuineness—it was so even for Rogers—but we know it when we see it. More to the point, the offenders with whom we propose to deal know genuineness when they see it. This matters, because when we approach an offender—no matter how highly we may rate the nobility of our intentions—we embark on an act of intrusion. To earn access we must gain trust, and we earn trust by making ourselves genuinely accessible and having the offender respect what he sees.

A book subtitled *Humanistic Approaches to Corrections and Offender Treatment* manifestly does not mirror prevailing practices in corrections, nor reflect the dominant ethos of the times. Such a book instead gives some of us heady sustenance and support in the goals that we secretly aspire to—it gives us a sense of what might be achieved in the distant future, and what might already have been accomplished. The book is an invitation for us to "hang in there" and persevere. "If you are not quite burned out, have not given up, and are still fighting the odds," the message of these chapters is, "you are not nearly as alone as you sometimes feel out there on your limb." The reassuring fact is that there are enclaves of humanistic activity in correctional settings, and as these experiments demonstrate their effectiveness, they are bound to ensure the long-term survival of the approach.

Hans Toch
University at Albany
State University of New York

ACKNOWLEDGMENTS

We would like to thank our contributors for including their work in this volume. We also appreciate Bruce Arrigo, the Series Editor; Bob Conrow, the Acquisitions Editor and Beth Hall at Carolina Academic Press, for their encouragement.

We would also like to thank David Skelton, Chair of the Department of Criminology and Criminal Justice at Indiana State University, for his support and encouragement.

Finally, a special thanks goes to Kristin Wells for her tireless effort on this volume and to James Bailey for his assistance.

Dave Polizzi
Mickey Braswell

TRANSFORMING CORRECTIONS

CHAPTER ONE

INTRODUCTION

David Polizzi, Indiana State University
Michael Braswell, East Tennessee State University

Hans Toch (1997) begins his text, *Corrections: A Humanistic Approach*, with the following observation:

> Prisons have been called garbage bins of society, but the phrase is less than apt. Few offenders who are in prison today have been permanently "discarded"; most will at some juncture be released from prison to rejoin the outside world. "Garbage bins" is also not an apt appellation for settings in which men and women labor mightily to preserve meaning or self respect. (p. 1)

Toch's observation is valuable because it speaks to one of the more inconvenient truths facing the practice of corrections in the United States today: the large majority of inmates who are currently housed in penitentiaries across this country will eventually return to the community. Some lawmakers have attempted to manufacture a political resolution to this problem by legislating longer prison sentences and making it much more difficult for those individuals returning to the community to receive the assistance necessary to make a successful transition and rejoin the outside world. However, these are concerns motivated by political opportunism and perpetuated by a culture of fear, which manufactures slogans that seek to dehumanize these men and women who must find a way to cobble together some semblance of meaning and self-respect from what remains of their shattered lives.

In a recent publication reviewing the Canadian criminal justice system, Griffiths and Cunningham (2000) suggest that it is important that we do not lose sight of the simple fact that the criminal justice system is, "first and foremost a human enterprise" (p. 4). However, if corrections and offender treatment are to be seen as a human enterprise, our approach to those individuals who we are attempting to reach must be one that is predicated upon respect, honesty, and the importance of the personal meaning of one's existence. This is a goal all too often left unrecognized and unfulfilled by current practices in corrections generally and offender treatment and rehabilitation specifically. Said more simply, the practice of corrections in all of its manifestations must first and foremost be an enterprise between human beings.

Rollo May (1958, p. 3) writes, "In recent years there has been a growing awareness on the part of some psychiatrists and psychologists that serious gaps exist in our way of understanding human beings." May (1958, p. 3) continues by stating that the crucial question that must always be asked of clinicians is: "Can we be certain that our system, admirable and beautifully wrought as it may be in principle, has anything whatever to do with this specific Mr. Jones, a living immediate reality sitting opposite us in the consulting room." Though May wrote these words nearly 50 years ago for a different audience, their importance has not diminished with age, and they evoke profound implications for the practice of corrections and offender treatment.

Current attitudes in corrections and offender treatment and the policy initiatives these evoke, reveal an underlying set of negatively defined socially constructed meanings about offenders that effectively contradict and undercut any superficial discussion about the benefits of rehabilitation, re-entry, or restorative justice practices. It is very difficult to envision what successful work in corrections, offender psychotherapy, or rehabilitation would actually look like in such an environment. Successful work with offender populations will be difficult to achieve without first thoroughly addressing the way in which these socially-generated definitions, concerning who or what the offender is, both restrict and actually prevent the type of successes the criminal justice system appears willing to pursue.

Corrections and Offender Treatment: An Alternative Voice

If it is correct to maintain that the overriding failure of contemporary corrections and offender treatment has been its unwillingness to recognize the fundamental human nature of those individuals under its control, how then do we correct this problem? As the title of this text suggests, a transformative solution for corrections and offender treatment may be found through the way in which this problem is first constructed and addressed. Is it really all that surprising that legitimate and lasting change has not been realized by many of these individuals given the context of these interactions? If, as a new employee of a correctional institution, regardless of my actual job title, I am constantly instructed to be suspicious (i.e., on guard), how can any meaningful rehabilitative relationship be formed? How can I institute any positive transformative effect? If indeed the place to begin this process of transforming corrections is within the context of the correctional relationship, then the experiential tradition of modern psychology is the necessary theoretical guide by which to undertake this task (Braswell, 2000; Polizzi, 1994).

Humanistic Psychology and Phenomenology: A Reformulation of the Problem

Though the tradition of experientially-focused theoretical perspectives in psychology represents a wide variation on the same human theme, humanistic psychology and existential-phenomenological psychology are viewed as two of its most articulate voices. Unlike more traditionally based psychological perspectives, which place a totalizing emphasis upon biological structures, externally conditioned behaviors or rational processes of thought, the traditions of humanistic psychology and existential-phenomenology seek to re-discover what it *means* to be human. It should be remembered that the humanistic psychological approach emerged as an attempt to provide a psychology of the whole person, which represented a drastic contrast to existing theoretical approaches of the day (Goble, 1970; Maslow, 1968; Moss, 2001; Rogers, 1947, 1967). Prior to the inception of this more holistic view of human existence, American psychology was dominated by the reductive theoretical formulations of Freud's classical psychoanalysis and the operant conditioning model of B.F. Skinner. For both Freud and Skinner, human experience was seen to fall outside the range and control of human agency and was viewed as epiphenomenal to these more fundamental psychological processes.

The advent of humanistic psychology sought to provide an alternative and opposing perspective to these more reductive formulations of human experience. By placing a greater emphasis on actual lived experience, humanistic psychology was able to liberate the possibility of human knowledge from pre-existing concepts or categories which sought to limit the scope of that meaning (Maslow, 1968). Humanistic psychology found an important ally within the theoretical tradition of existential-phenomenology, which also sought to privilege the meaning of subjective experience over a priori beliefs (Brazier, 1993). Although phenomenology as a philosophical tradition appeared approximately fifty years prior to the introduction of humanistic psychology, it shares many of the same foundational beliefs concerning human experience (Giorgi, 1970; May, 1983; Schneider & May, 1995).

Much like humanistic psychology, existential-phenomenology is concerned with the interrelated meaning of human experience:

> Phenomenology takes as one of its assumptions that we bring our own individual biases to our experience of the world, and experience the world through the filter of those biases. It recognizes, therefore, the inviolable subjectivity of individual experience: two people will bring different filters to the same phenomena and therefore experience them differently. (Tudor & Worrall, 2006, pp. 27–28)

From this perspective, lived experience is always situated within a social context and becomes meaningful from a specific and unique perspective (Cerbone, 2006; Heidegger, 1952/1996; Husserl, 1913/1962; Gurwitsch, 1962; Merleau-Ponty, 1945/1964; Spinelli, 2005). Rather than be concerned with the objective facts of existence, or in other words, facts that are somehow viewed as separate from that existence, phenomenology's focus is concerned with the way in which things become meaningful for a particular individual. For example, how a person's lived experience is defined will be predicated upon a variety of factors that will be more or less unique to that individual. My place in the social world, though shared with others, is never exactly the same as another's (Heidegger, 1952/1996). The above example is not meant to evoke a type of relativism, but instead it is mentioned to help elucidate the perspectival nature of human experience. Though a group of siblings are raised in the same family environment, this should not imply that the experience of their family is in any way the same, and in fact, may likely contradict similar accounts of the same familial experiences. By refusing to privilege any specific take on reality, by refusing to assume that one perspective is any more legitimate than another, the lived possibilities for human knowledge and change remain dynamic and fluid. Such is the case when we apply these ideas to the topics of corrections and offender rehabilitation or treatment.

A humanistic or existential-phenomenological theoretical approach to corrections or offender treatment is predicated upon the belief that no type of restorative or rehabilitative success can be achieved within a social context that continues to refuse to recognize the basic humanity of those individuals who find themselves in the criminal justice system. The inability to see the offender as a human being raises not only a variety of ethical concerns related to the project of criminal justice but also threatens any practical attempt to rehabilitate or restore these individuals to normal society, if, of course, the underlying purpose of incarceration is not simply to warehouse a specific segment of the population. It is difficult to understand within the current formulation of this issue how any rehabilitative success can be achieved when the target of that practice is viewed from such a negative perspective. The possibility for a successful treatment outcome, regardless of the treatment setting, is always predicated upon the strength of the relationship between client and therapist (Bozarth, 1993; Rogers, 1946, 1989). Stated another way, no rehabilitative or restorative relationship worthy of the name can exist in the absence of human respect.

The possibility for achieving any type of rehabilitative success within the criminal justice system is therefore fundamentally threatened when the experience of respect is absent from the therapeutic process. Humanistic psychology, existential-phenomenology, and a variety of related theoretical perspectives provide an answer to this dilemma insofar as they refuse to reduce human possibility to a history of past behavior. Such a perspective does not seek to deny the behavior of the offender, but instead, it seeks to place that behavior within a larger social context that is able to recognize the humanity of both sides of this equation. It seems simplistic and overly convenient to selectively focus on those behaviors which tend to reinforce the continued belief in the ontological difference of the offender without taking any serious account of those experiences which helped to create the offender in the prison yard, parole office, or community mental health consulting office.

What is Transforming Corrections?

Transforming corrections, which is more than simply a play on words, implies the need for a redirection of focus and attitude within the daily practice of criminal justice and offender treatment. Perhaps most important to this idea is the need to remember that individuals who find themselves within the criminal justice system, regardless of their actions or behavior, do indeed remain human and should be treated with both dignity and respect. Such a perspective does not seek to ignore the cold reality of those individuals who have caused great harm to others; only that the criminal action is not synonymous with existence and cannot be the sole measure by which the potentiality for human experience is judged.

To transform corrections is to transform the way in which we not only understand the reality of criminal behavior, but the lived experience of those caught up in the act of crime. To do so demands that we expand our focus and move beyond retributive-based strategies of crime control that masquerade as rehabilitative practices. Such an approach also demands that we as educators, penitentiary administrators, correctional officers, and psychotherapists examine the way in which our policies, theories, and ideological proclivities have helped to perpetuate the status quo and insure a consistent record of failure. Criminal justice is indeed, first and foremost, a human enterprise.

Rationale

The field of rehabilitative corrections continues to struggle with how to define the offender. Given that treatment success and the goal of decreasing rates of recidivism seem in some way related to the resolution of this idea, we must find an answer to this question. Unfortunately, current discourse on this subject is often influenced by an underlying political subtext, which has constructed the offender in such a way as to almost place the very nature of their humanity into question. The practical result of such thinking can be easily witnessed in any number of correctional settings across the country whereby true human respect is denied based solely on the fact of the individual's criminal behavior. More often than not, once an offender is incarcerated, their need for human respect is no longer recognized.

In their book, *The Psychology of Criminal Conduct*, Andrews and Bonta (1994) identify risk, needs, and responsivity as major aspects of effective offender treatment. Motivational interviewing, in part due to its humanist and existential-phenomenological roots and influences, recognizes the important role played by the therapeutic relationship relative to client responsivity and ties an aspect of treatment success to this interaction. The way in which the offender responds to the process of rehabilitative corrections is directly related to the quality of those relationships experienced by the individual (Braswell, 2000). If we are to expect a positive and authentic engagement in the process of rehabilitative corrections, we must first construct a therapeutic frame that refuses to objectify the offender-client. Though such a theoretical move will not guarantee clinical success, it will certainly move us closer to that goal (Bozarth, 1993).

Taken as a whole, theoretical considerations, humanistic perspectives, and applications in correctional programs, along with humanistic themes in offender treatment, offer a qualitative alternative to the correctional status quo. While empirical-based assessment and program evaluation is important, *Transforming Corrections* provides the often neglected experiential and existential aspect that can contribute dimension and definition to the "dry bones" of the quantitative skeleton of empirical outcomes with little or no understanding of therapeutic intention. The empirical needs the experiential to animate the humanity which it attempts to measure. It is our hope that this volume will encourage such an understanding—a vision that acknowledges that the whole is greater than the sum of its parts.

Layout of the Book

This edited book provides both theoretical and practical alternatives to the practice of corrections and offender treatment by introducing a different voice into this conversation. The broad scope of these articles is intended to address this fundamental gap from a variety of thematic perspectives, while, at the same time, providing a much-needed alternative theoretical understanding to who the offender is and who they can become. The book is divided into three sections: Section one is concerned with providing a general theoretical overview of the various philosophical approaches normally identified within the humanistic movement; section two will focus on a variety of non-clinical themes important to the practice of corrections; and section three will address concerns to the clinical practice of forensic psychotherapy.

Section one, "Theoretical Reflections," is made up of five theoretical chapters, all of which explore the relationship between theory and practice. In chapter two, Christopher Aanstoos calls for social science researchers to remember their philosophical roots and to be more explicit in the way in which philosophy influences research methodology. He includes a thorough discussion concerning the way in which phenomenology provides a methodological approach most consistent with the study of human experience.

Kenneth Adams and Hayden Smith explore the notion of criminal responsibility from the perspective of phenomenology in chapter three. They discuss responsibility-based themes as provided by the work of Albert Camus in his classic work, *The Stranger*.

Chapter five, written by John Ryals, Jr., explores the relationship between offender objectification and the possibilities for social change. The author contextualizes his discussion within a social constructionist frame of reference.

Following Ryals, Matthew Draper, Mark Green, and Ginger Faulkner in chapter six discuss the way in which the dialogic theory of Mikhail Bakhtin may provide therapists and counselors with a valuable theoretical tool by which to overcome many of the implicit moral assumptions often witnessed in forensic psychotherapeutic practice. The authors propose a model by which these ethical concerns may be included to expand the more traditional understanding of therapeutic theory related to forensic clients.

Chapter six begins by exploring what Bruce Arrigo defines as "critical psychological jurisprudence" and its relationship to the practice of corrections. He then applies his reconceptualization of this concept to the other theoretical perspectives provided in section one.

Section two, "Humanistic Perspectives in Corrections," will focus on non-clinical issues related to corrections and restorative justice. Terry Kupers uses chapter seven to explore the way in which humanistic and existential-phe-nomenological approaches to psychology help to bring a much-needed focus to the notion of inmate respect. Kupers rejects more traditionally punitive in-teractive discourses that tend to construct the inmate in very negative ways and offers an alternative strategy to this practice.

Chapter eight, written by Catherine Jenks and John Fuller, explores the ways in which training practices within the penitentiary help to perpetuate nega-tive attitudes between staff and inmate, which often result in the continuation of very destructive adversarial relationships that fundamentally thwart the re-habilitative process.

In chapter nine, Lana McDowell and John Whitehead discuss the practice of restorative justice relative to its therapeutic effectiveness in healing the trauma evoked by crime. The authors explore the way in which restorative therapeu-tic inventions may help offenders to heal the rupture of social relationships di-rectly caused by the act of criminality.

Section three, "Humanistic Themes in Offender Treatment," investigates a variety of psychotherapeutic themes concerning the clinical practice of forensic psychotherapy. Beginning in chapter ten, Michael Braswell and Kristin Wells explore the importance of relationships within the context of correctional treat-ment and offer their PACTS model as an alternative method to help build suc-cessful therapeutic relationships with individuals in the criminal justice system. Drake Spaeth (chapter eleven) then explores the psychological importance of ritual in the lives of adolescents. Spaeth expands the understanding of adoles-cent violence by including a discussion of the spiritual implications of this phe-nomenon. In chapter twelve, David Polizzi provides a model for building therapeutic trust with court-ordered clients. Polizzi identifies how certain as-pects of the forensic referral process help to strengthen client resistance and pro-vides strategies by which this therapeutic barrier can be successfully addressed.

References

Andrews, D. A., & Bonta, J. (1994). *The psychology of criminal conduct.* Cincinnati: Anderson.

Bozarth, J. D. (1993). Not necessarily necessary but always sufficient. In D. Brazier (Ed.), *Beyond Carl R. Rogers: Towards a psychotherapy for the 21st century* (pp. 92–105). London: Constable.

Braswell, M. (2000). Correctional treatment and the human spirit. In P. Van Voorhis, M. Braswell, & D. Lester (Eds.), *Correctional counseling & re-habilitation* (4th ed., pp. 3–22). Cincinnati: Anderson.

Brazier, D. (1993). Introduction. In D. Brazier (Ed.), *Beyond Carl Rogers*. London: Constable.

Cerbone, D. (2006). *Understanding phenomenology*. Chesham: Acumen.

Giorgi, A. (1970). *Psychology as a human science*. New York: Harper & Row.

Goble, F. (1970). *The third force: The psychology of Abraham Maslow*. New York: Washington Square Press.

Griffiths, C. T., & Cunningham, A. (2000). *Canadian criminal justice: A primer* (2nd ed.) Toronto: ITP Nelson.

Gurwitsch, A. (1962). *The field of consciousness*. Pittsburgh: Duquesne University Press.

Heidegger, M. (1996). *Being and time* (Joan Stambaugh, Trans.). Albany: SUNY. (Original work published 1952)

Husserl, E. (1962). *Ideas: General introduction to pure phenomenology* (W. Gibson, Trans.). London: Collier. (Original work published 1913)

Maslow, A. (1968). *Toward a psychology of being*. New York: Van Nostrand Reinhold.

May, R. (1958). The origins and significance of the existential movement in psychology. In R. May, E. Angel, & H. F. Ellenberger (Eds.), *Existence: A new dimension in psychiatry and psychology* (pp. 3–36). New York: Simon & Schuster.

May, R. (1983). *The discovery of being: Writings in existential psychology*. New York: W.W. Norton.

Merleau-Ponty, M. (1964). *Phenomenology of perception* (Colin Smith, Trans.). New York: Routledge. (Original work published 1945)

Moss, D. (2001). The roots and genealogy of humanistic psychology. In K. Schneider, J. Bugental, & J. F. Pierson (Eds.), *The handbook of humanistic psychology: Leading edges in theory, research, and practice* (pp. 5–20). Thousand Oaks, CA: Sage.

Polizzi, D. (1994). Facing the criminal. *The Humanistic Psychologist, 22*(1), 28–38.

Rogers, C. (1946). Significant aspects of client-centered therapy. *American Psychologist, 1*, 415–422.

Rogers, C. (1947). Some observations on the organization of personality. *American Psychologist, 2*, 358–368.

Rogers, C. (1967). *On becoming a person: A therapist's view of psychotherapy*. London: Constable.

Rogers, C. (1989). A client-centered/person-centered approach to therapy. In H. Kirschenbaum & V. L. Henderson (Eds.), *The Carl Rogers reader* (pp. 135–156). New York: Houghton Mifflin.

Schneider, K., & May, R. (1995). *The psychology of existence: An integrative, clinical perspective*. New York: McGraw-Hill.

Spinelli, E. (2005). *The interpreted world: An introduction to phenomenological psychology*. Thousand Oaks, CA: Sage.

Toch, H. (1997). *Corrections: A humanistic approach*. Albany: Harrow and Hester.

Tudor, K., & Worrall, M. (2006). *Person-centered therapy*. London: Routledge.

SECTION I

THEORETICAL REFLECTIONS

CHAPTER TWO

A Phenomenological Approach to Criminology

Christopher M. Aanstoos, University of West Georgia

A Phenomenological Philosophy for the Human Sciences

Beginning with a phenomenological philosophy must seem strange to those steeped in the common assumption that the social sciences progressed only after their loud self-conscious divorce from philosophy. However, the radical questioning of assumptions is basic to the social sciences, as it is to all science. And when scholars closely question this presupposed separation between social science and philosophy, they discover that the vaunted eschewal of philosophy did not and cannot eliminate philosophical foundations (see, e.g., Toulmin & Leary, 1985). On the contrary, the conceptual base of the social sciences remains necessarily tied to a philosophy of science, at least implicitly. Because the social sciences refused to acknowledge this tacit philosophical base, they repressed reflection on their own philosophical foundation and thus drove underground this philosophical significance where it has remained beyond the reach of critical examination. Like any repressed content, this implicit philosophy of science festered outside of time and grew increasingly inappropriate for having been left outside the pale of discourse. One might even say it has remained essentially frozen since that nineteenth century divorce, much as the rituals of a compulsive neurotic calcify. Indeed, one could argue, as Burtt (1932) and Husserl (1954/1970) have, even the natural sciences have not sufficiently reflected upon their own use of this philosophical foundation. The unfortunate result being that it has served as a kind of uncritical "metaphysics" even for these sciences themselves.

During their late nineteenth century founding, the implicit, yet guiding, philosophy of the various social sciences was that of empiricism or, more generically, positivism borrowed from the natural sciences extant. Indeed, that positivistic philosophy of the natural sciences had been the guiding vision for the human studies for centuries prior to the proclamation of their independent scientific status. For example, Hobbes, after visiting Galileo, "became fascinated with the concept of motion as a powerful explanatory principle not only of the workings of the physical world but also of the mind" (Mandler & Mandler, 1964, p. 14). "What excited Hobbes was the possibility of deducing new consequences from the laws of inertia to spheres in which it had not yet been applied" (Brett, 1962, pp. 380–381). Subsequently, Hume was also influenced by the new Newtonian physics of his time. He compared the association of ideas to natural laws, declaring that, "here is a kind of attraction which in the mental world will be found to have as extraordinary effects as in the natural" (Hume, 1739/1978, p. 12). Next, in his establishment of associationism, David Hartley self-consciously borrowed foundational concepts from Newtonian physics, in which he summarized the work of associationistic psychology to be "analogous to ... resolving the color of the sun's light or natural bodies, into their primary constituent ones" (Hartley, 1749/1964, p. 83). This foundational significance becomes even clearer with James Mill, who in 1829 identified psychological life as a "mental mechanics" in which the contents of mind are ultimately elemental and simple, united according to the laws of mechanics.

Thus, one should understand the two hundred year development of the human studies *prior to* their divorce from philosophy "as an attempt to construct a 'science of mind' modeled on the physical sciences" (Mischel, 1966, p. 133). In other words, it was not merely when they became self-consciously scientific that the social sciences began borrowing from the natural sciences; rather, for centuries prior to their emergence as disciplines independent of philosophy, scholars in the human studies looked to the natural sciences for their own conceptual foundations. Therefore, one cannot argue as, for example, Skinner (1972) has attempted, that psychology's own development was retarded by its lack of a scientific foundation. Instead, we must recognize that the particular scientific foundations it followed for two hundred years are responsible for that retarded development.

It was not, therefore, the presence of a philosophical basis that hampered progress in the social sciences, nor a separation from philosophy that spurred progress. Rather, a lack of progress has more to do with the *type* of philosophical foundations upon which they have relied: the social sciences borrowed from another domain—the sciences of nature. Upon suspending the assumption that this is their only proper foundation, a genuine questioning and revisioning of the philosophical foundations of the human sciences can therefore be developed.

We must first ask, on what basis ought the social sciences choose a philosophical foundation? Positivism was uncritically selected on the basis of a presupposed conception of psychological reality; namely, that the human order was essentially no different than, or reducible to, the reality of the natural universe, which is the physio-chemical, quantifiable manifold articulated by Galileo, Newton, and Descartes. Put another way, van Gogh's *Starry, Starry Night* is ultimately either an astronomical feature or a brain disorder. Despite their differences, the various major approaches in contemporary social science still hold to this premise. Freudian psychoanalysis was founded on the assumption that the psychic apparatus derives its energy from biological roots and that desire is ultimately instinct (Freud, 1895/1966). Skinnerian behaviorism asserts that the science of behavior is a "part of biology … [and that] the behaving organism will eventually be described and explained by the anatomist and physiologist" (Skinner, 1975, p. 42). Information processing psychology began with the conviction that "the mechanisms producing the behavior are ultimately reducible to physiological mechanisms" (Newell & Simon, 1961, p. 2012), and therefore views its own models as "the reflections of [these] physiological mechanisms" yet to be discovered (Newell, 1969, p. 207). In other words, the foundations of psychoanalysis, behaviorism, and cognitivism, uncritically adhere to the constancy hypothesis of positivism: the hypothesis that there is an underlying, constant, physical reality operating as a causal, mechanical basis beneath the human order.

Is there an alternative? Rather than argue as to whether this belief about reality is correct or incorrect, the human sciences could instead begin by suspending the belief in this hypothesis of a constant, causal, objective reality. Such a suspension of belief does not require the invocation of some sort of Berkeleyian idealism or Humean skepticism. It is not necessary to deny the existence of reality; instead, simply suspend the presupposition that it provides a causal basis for human action. By suspending this hypothesis, the human studies are freed to take reality as it presents itself within human experience and strictly and only as it so presents itself, without the baggage of any conceptualization of its objective existence apart from or beyond that appearance.

This suspension of belief is the starting point for phenomenology. Known by its Greek term *epoche*, this bracketing sets aside that level of supposition in order to become fully interested instead in another level of existence. Rather than remaining concerned with reality as a hypostatized object "over there somewhere," the phenomenologist is interested instead in reality as it appears, as it shows itself, as it manifests itself; hence, the key term *phenomenon*—which refers to appearances. One should not mistake appearances as "mere appearances," that is as merely subjective deformations of some objective reality. Phenomenology begins by suspending precisely that belief in such an underlying reality behind or beyond such appearances. By taking that which appears to be the fundamental givens, the assumption of an objectified reality is then seen to be an abstraction *from them*. What is given in actual lived experience is most real and primary. For example, when waiting on someone who is late, time passes much more slowly than when hurrying to meet someone who is waiting. One could argue that the same number of minutes elapsed, but such "clock time" is never as real as the time that is experienced. In comparison, clock time is an abstraction, an impersonal generalization, not rooted in the actual personal experience of the moment. It may be helpful as a baseline with which to contrast experience, but it should not be taken to be prior to, or the cause of, experience.

Thus, to suspend belief is the phenomenologist's way of becoming truly available to whatever shows itself, to whatever appears, taken precisely as it appears. In other words, phenomenology offers a way of beginning with an attitude of awe, of respect, of wonder. To be more precise, phenomenology begins by suspending the taken-for-grantedness that precludes this sense of wonder. And when a researcher begins so, what does appear? When one brackets all presuppositions based on a belief in reality and becomes intensely interested strictly in whatever appears, what can one notice? The first discovery is that whatever gives itself within experience does so in terms of a relationship with the experiencer. That is to say, whatever presents itself does so in terms of its relational signification. So the fundamental discovery of phenomenology is the relational, or *intentional*, character of the phenomenal field of consciousness. That is, consciousness and its objects form a correlational whole, such that whatever one experiences always presents itself primordially in terms of one's involvement with it. It is this basic relation that Husserl (1913/1962) named the "intentionality" of consciousness, and that, in the hands of the existential phenomenologists (see, e.g., Merleau-Ponty, 1945/1962; Sartre, 1942/1956) comes to be seen as the situated character of embodied consciousness in an intersubjective life world. Consciousness is fundamentally there, in the world, open to a world. The experiencer and the experienced form a whole, just as the toucher and the touched, the grasper and the grasped, the dancer and the dance.

So, by taking the phenomenological turn, researchers find themselves in the midst of this intentive relation of appearances and consciousness. They can then discover, as Heidegger (1927/1962) did, that this basic relationship is characterized by care. That is to say the objects of consciousness matter and present themselves as meaningful. The aim, then, becomes the explication of these meaningful structures of consciousness. By explicitation, phenomenology means a process of making explicit the implicit meanings by which the field of lived experience presents itself to consciousness. (In a basic way, this goal is analogous to the work of a creative artist, though it aims at a different standard of finding—intellectual rather than aesthetic.)

A Phenomenological Basis for Research in the Human Sciences

The systematic explication of such lived meaning is not a mechanical or statistical operation. Therefore, a research tradition with such an aim would not seek reductionistic, or causal, explanations or probability statements of hypothetical error variance. Rather, this analysis aims at understanding. This analysis is based upon *empathy* and proceeds *intuitively*, aided by *imagination*.

Before the specific methodological processes underlying these very general terms can be specified, it would be helpful to identify some important meta-methodological concerns. First, it is crucial to distinguish *meanings* (as phenomenology uses the term) from *facts*. Most mainstream research traditions within the social sciences study *facts*—for example, the measurement of a stimulus, or the frequency of a response. Phenomenology, in contrast, is interested in objects as they are intended by an experiencing consciousness. It is important to avoid the psychologist's fallacy of assuming that what is a structure for the researcher is necessarily a structure for the subject. (Ricoeur and Merleau-Ponty have often noted this turn from *fact* to *meaning* aligns phenomenology and psychoanalysis as both aim at a similar "latency" of meaning within experience.) For example, in an experiment, a researcher may use a word such as "penis" as a stimulus to elicit a response of a certain galvanic skin response (GSR). But it is quite clear that its value as a stimulus rests upon its signification for the subject—a signification which, in this case, is all the more striking because it seems so out of place to the subject participating in a scientific experiment (or, indeed, reading a scientific publication, for that matter). But in the real world beyond the laboratory, neither speaker nor listener intend the word as a stimulus to elicit a response of a certain GSR, but as a meaningful signifier, contextually embedded within an experiential sphere of relevancy, a situation whose meaningful structure can be explicated by a phenomenological researcher. For example, in the movie *ET*, a boy calls his brother "penis head" with an unmistakable sense of derision. That derision cannot be explicated if we take the word simply as *fact*, but only when we comprehend it as *meant*, by the experiencing person.

This point is likewise true for any area of human experience. For instance, psychology can only truly understand schizophrenia (in contrast to merely manipulating its most evident symptoms) when it comprehends the concrete experience of the schizophrenic, as, for example, Laing (1962) has done. Likewise, the significance of the perinatal can be understood only when we comprehend the neonate's concrete experience of being born, as, for example, Leboyer (1975) has done. Or, mourning can only be understood when the concrete experience of the bereaved person is comprehended, as, for example, Brice (1987) has done. Otherwise, we are left only with explanations, inferences, concepts, or dogma, which constitute a negation and denial of the person's experienced reality. Indeed, for too long psychology has excused its lack of understanding by asserting that the schizophrenic or the newborn had no experience. It is time to cease such intellectual violence, and instead turn to the actual experience of people with respect, empathy, and intuition.

It is neither necessary nor possible to attain objectivity in the social sciences by this distortive objectification of their subject matter. Rather than achieving the laudatory goal of freeing the scientist from bias, such an approach actually locks in an even deeper, presupposed bias about the nature of human existence. But it is possible to devise a methodology of openness to the fullness of the phenomenon: that is, maximum presence rather than maximum absence by the researcher. By encountering the phenomenon as openly as possible, the results would defy or overturn the confining limitations of any given researcher's bias since such biases are concerned with the objective world, which has been set aside in the epoche in order to attend to the meanings as lived by the subject. To such a claim there is the ready question: "That's fine in theory, but in actuality is it impossible to be completely open to the phenomenon that one always and necessarily brings something to that encounter?" And that is right: shedding one's bias before the phenomenon is an infinite task, but it is not a fruitless one. These limitations are as surpassable as they are inevitable. Each insight gained along the way brings the researcher closer to the phenomenon in its fullness, on its terms. That is the final goal and criterion of evidence.

Developments of Human Science Methodology

Beginning in the 1960s, phenomenology was appropriated in psychology as a basis for a specifically human science methodology by several individuals and groups. Most notable in this development was the "Duquesne group"— the psychology faculty at Duquesne University where a doctoral program in phenomenological psychology had begun. Van Kaam (1966) and Giorgi (1970,

1976) led the way in that project, but were joined by many collaborators (see, e.g., Giorgi, Fischer, & Murray, 1983).

Other human sciences soon developed research methodologies based on phenomenology, including education, nursing, political science, sociology, counseling, anthropology, geography, architecture, marketing, law, and criminology. Of course, various ways of designing a phenomenological methodology emerged from these different efforts. In addition, other post-positivistic methodologies were also being developed during the 1960s and 1970s. As an emerging trend, this new development lacked coherence in either methodology or even in terminology. The most generic name for this range of methodologies came to be "qualitative research"—since that name provided a ready contrast to the quantitative base of traditional social science research. By the late 1970s, they were prominent enough as to provoke a strong reaction from the mainstream quantitative tradition which judged qualitative data to be scientifically questionable. Nisbett and Wilson's (1977) dismissal of the validity of verbal reports from research subjects epitomizes this general skepticism. But their critique was based on an experiment in which they asked subjects to determine whether or not they would have reacted differently, if the strength of the independent variable (electric shock) had been stronger than it was. Subjects asserted that it would have been, but a control group of subjects who received the higher level shock demonstrated that it made no difference to their responses. They took the failure of the subjects to correctly identify the action in the alternative situation to indicate that subjects "say more than they know" and therefore are not reliable witnesses to their own experiences. But Nisbett and Wilson did not ask their subjects to describe their own experiences. Rather, they were asked to make a judgment about how they would have reacted in a hypothetical situation that they did not experience. Subjects' failure to be able to predict hypothetical behavior should not be conflated with a failure to be able to describe actual lived experience. Nisbett and Wilson's inability to make this very basic distinction indicates that mainstream psychology's rejection of qualitative research has come from outside it, without any "hands on" sense of what it was about. They saw description as fundamentally alien to its project to conceptualize psychological life in the same terms with which the natural sciences had come by the nineteenth century to conceptualize nature, that is, as a quantifiable manifold.

While Nisbett and Wilson's critique may have hampered the reception of qualitative research within the mainstream of the social sciences, it did not hold back developments within the field. In the three decades since then, qualitative research methods continued to be developed from within a post-positivist approach, by an expanding array of social scientists working with descriptions by means of a variety of qualitative analyses. Many of their questions are similar to those asked by mainstream psychology, though what is discovered through them is vastly more discerning. Many other questions, unimagined or taken-for-granted by quantitatively-based researchers are also being raised originally by contemporary qualitative research.

Qualitative research can be laid along a continuum with three points of critical mass: one within the core of the mainstream, a second at the edge of mainstream social science, and a third beyond the edge. Considering first the use of qualitative research within the core, a longstanding example is the methodology of subjecting descriptions to quantitative "content analysis." While this use has been around for some time, it has recently emerged much more prominently, due to the new, sophisticated computer programs that enable such content analyses to encompass much greater data bases than hitherto possible. An example of this trend is Shneidman's (1989) study of men in their seventies. He conducted open-ended interviews over several years with his subjects. Unfortunately, his methodology consisted only of obtaining "word counts" from these interviews. He found, for example, that his subjects used a total of 241,985 words, and 11,659 different words; that the most common categories of words were in the areas of health, occupation, and family; and that the most common words used were: I, the, and, that, a, to, of, it, in, and was. Such methodological trivialization spoiled a promising conceptual approach to human development as elliptical rather than linear.

Another development of qualitative research within the core of mainstream psychology — indeed, the most eminent such trend — is that established by Newell and Simon (1972), whose use of verbal reports as comparisons with information processing models has become incredibly important to contemporary cognitive psychology. Their work with verbal protocols has recently been codified methodologically by Ericsson and Simon (1980). It could even be said that the most valuable contribution of information processing theory to psychology has not been its pathetically misguided models, but its having made it methodologically acceptable to use verbal protocols. Unfortunately, their own use of such descriptive data is fatally flawed by the preconceptions with which they approach it. By understanding description from the start to be sequences of "verbal information processing," their analyses never escape the constrictions of their own prejudgment (Aanstoos, 1983, 1985).

The second context for the continuum of qualitative research methods is the "edge" rather than the "mainstream" of the social sciences. Much work on a variety of methods has been done there, for example, Berg's (1989) compilation. But the various social sciences have not been equally open to this task. The edge of mainstream sociology is further along than psychology in the development of qualitative research procedures, probably owing to its receptivity to such early qualitative methods as grounded theory and ethnographic research. That can be seen from older texts, such as Filstead's (1970), as well as more recent series of volumes on qualitative research available by Sage Publications beginning in the 1980s and 1990s (see, e.g., Heron, 1996; Kirk & Miller, 1986; Miles & Huberman, 1984; Reason, 1988). The same is true for the field of nursing (see, e.g., Morse, 1994), and for education, as exemplified by the inauguration of the *International Journal of Qualitative Studies in Education* in 1988, and the work of Max van Manen (1990, 2002). Within psychology, a variety of qualitative methods have now also been developed. Good surveys of various groupings of these have been compiled by Cairns, Bergman, and Kagan (1998), Camic, Rhodes, and Yardley (2003), and Tesch (1990), for example.

In addition to the "mainstream" and the "edge" another context for the development of qualitative methodology has come from those who have made a more decisive departure, who have gone "beyond the edge" to situate a radically new starting point for methodology. Owing likely to psychology's resistance to qualitative methodology, it is in particular in psychology that such "outer" developments have taken place. Among many representative examples are the two volumes of selected papers from the 1983 and 1985 Symposia on Qualitative Research in Psychology (Ashworth, Giorgi, & deKoning, 1986; van Zuuren, Wertz, & Mook, 1987), which contain a wide array of qualitative research studies, not only from the United States, but from several European countries as well. Indeed, the 1970s and 1980s saw many developments in this regard, so that a typology done in the late 1980s (Aanstoos, 1987) compared hermeneutics, phenomenology, phenomenography, descriptive, Kierkegaardian, experiential, perceptual, genealogical, imaginal, dialectical, and critical methodologies. Other off-shoots worthy of note here include de Rivera's (1981) method of "conceptual encounter" and Shapiro's (1985) analysis of the methodological value of our "bodily reflective modes." Since then, others have joined them as well, particularly those emphasizing hermeneutic and narrative methods, such as "heuristic inquiry" (Moustakas, 1994) and "alchemical hermeneutics" (Romanyshyn, 2007), and constructivism more generally. Works by Messer, Sass, and Woolfolk (1988), by Sarbin (1986), and by Polkinghorne (1988) are particularly meritorious for their development of the hermeneutics of narrativity in psychology. Kenneth Gergen's many contributions speckle these collections. Polkinghorne (1983) has previously also summarized current developments in existential-phenomenology and hermeneutics. Collections edited by Darroch and Silvers (1982) and Giorgi (1985) provide fruitful examples of phenomenological methodology. The *Journal of Phenomenological*

Psychology has twice devoted special issues to methodological concerns (Fall 1983 and Fall 1986), addressing the issues of reliability and verification. Kvale (1989) edited a volume on validity in qualitative research. In psychology, these efforts have resulted even in volumes that provide a properly human science introduction to the standard table of contents of general psychology (see, e.g., Barrell, 1986; Pollio, 1982; Pollio, Henley, & Thompson, 1997; Valle, 1998; Valle & Halling, 1989; Valle & King, 1978).

All of these methodological innovations are post-Cartesian, and specifically post-positivist. All see descriptive data as not merely ancillary or propaedeutic to quantification, but as a fundamental alternative way of approaching and comprehending their subject matter. All have made the shift from a study of *facts* to a study of *meanings*. All recognize the intrinsically holistic and situational, and hence, contextual nature of psychological life. So there are many to choose from. This chapter will elaborate a specifically phenomenological methodology as an exemplary qualitative approach for the human sciences in general and for the study of criminality in particular.

Phenomenological methodology has been developed especially in response to the awareness that a true paradigm shift in the social sciences from positivism to a genuine appreciation of human experience on its own terms requires not merely a new conceptual foundation, but most of all a rigorous and systematic means of accessing the deep meaningfulness of human experience. The sustained development by many researchers over the past generation has resulted in a considerable body of work on methodology (see, e.g., Ashworth, 1987; Colaizzi, 1973; Fischer, 2005; Karlsson, 1993). The contributions of Giorgi and Wertz have been particularly informative. While both continue to add to their already considerable body of writing, their early pieces have come to virtually define the field of phenomenological methodology (see, e.g., Giorgi, 1975, 1983, 2009; Wertz, 1983a, 1983b, 1985). It is their work that especially underlies the following summary of phenomenological methodology.

A Sketch of a Phenomenological Methodology

Data Collection

Data collection in phenomenological methodology is oriented to concrete situations in which the phenomenon under investigation was actually lived, thereby insuring the most rigorous standard of external validity. The raw data of phenomenological research consists of descriptions provided by subjects of their actual experiences with the phenomenon under investigation, in response to open-ended, nondirective questions posed by the researcher. Subjects are asked to describe a particular concrete situation, rather than to generalize or hypothesize abstractly. These descriptions may be related to the experience either simultaneously or retrospectively, and may be given orally or in writing, whichever is more appropriate to the investigation of the particular research question. Often, researchers will employ a mixed method, whereby subjects may first prepare a written description, which the researcher then becomes familiar with. Then a follow-up interview is arranged, at which time the subject reads the written description aloud while the researcher breaks in with questions that ask the subject to elaborate more fully wherever there seems a need to do so. (For more reflection on the intricacies of qualitative interviewing, see Kvale, 1983, 1996.) Across these variations, what is necessary is that the subjects provide an account of their experience that is as concrete and complete as possible. The researcher, meanwhile, is challenged with the task of being with the subject in such a way as to facilitate that open inquiry.

Data Analysis

The next step—the process of data analysis—shows most clearly how phenomenological research diverges from other uses of descriptive data in psychology (for instance, Newell and Simon's). Phenomenology does not leave the descriptive realm for a hypothetical one at a subsequent step; it eschews hypothesis as a premature break from description. But neither does it sanctify the ordinary description as a phenomenalism would. Rather, phenomenology recognizes the importance of the work of analysis, of explicating the essential structure of the lived experience from the naive description of the subject. This is why novels, though psychologically rich, are not by themselves an explicit psychology. Their potential still remains to be mined, just as does that of the naive description. That is properly the work of the researcher through data analysis. This work entails two parts: the attitude of the researcher and the procedures. Of course these are concurrent in actual practice; it is only discourse that requires their consecutive presentation.

The Researcher's Attitude

The researcher's attitude must begin in wonder, awe, respect, appreciation, and empathy. Wertz (1983a, 1983b) describes this initial attitude as one of empathic immersement in the world of the subject. His examples include van den Berg's analysis of the experience of being hospitalized. He empathically relates to the recession of the patient's ordinary pragmatic concerns by attending to the new significance assumed by such "little things" as cracks in the ceiling or patterns on the wall paper. To fully empathize, the researcher must not presume familiarity in advance with the subject's world, but must linger in it, dwelling patiently and slowly, magnifying and amplifying each detail involved. For example, Wertz (1985) cites Siroky's study of the experience of the other while engaged in a common task, and notes the significance of such a seemingly small detail as the timing of the shift in the subject's perception from "I" and "he" (or "she") to "we."

This empathic initiation into the subject's world does not mean, however, that the researcher loses sight of his or her own project and interest. Rather, this empathy is in the service of illuminating the experience of the subject, in order to grasp it *as* experience. The technically precise term to identify the phenomenological researcher's attitude in confronting his or her subject's experience is to say that he or she proceeds within the phenomenological epoche, or suspension of belief. What is suspended, set aside, or placed within brackets is our natural attitude or belief in the existence of an objective reality. This belief indeed forms the very foundations of the subject's own experience: that his or her world *is* what he or she takes it to be. This belief is not refuted, but merely put out of play. In other words, the researcher suspends any judgment about the objective reality of the subject's description in order to become present to it *as* it is lived by the subject. That is the deliberate phenomenological turn, noted earlier, from objects to meanings. What will matter to the researcher is not the way an outside observer may have grasped the described situation, but rather the way it was lived by the subject, with the precise interest of illuminating what it is that is given in this situation for this subject. For example, the anorexic that experiences his or her body as still too heavy is living a meaning, which can only be explicated when we understand the body not as an objective fact, but as a meaning; in this case, a still dense earthliness that continues to defy transcendence. The chess player who thinks his or her situation hopeless when it could still be won, or won when it is already lost, is another example. As Giorgi (1975) noted, psychological reality is between the physical and the rational, reducible to neither. The researcher's attitude must be to seek it there, as it presents itself to experience.

The Analysis of the Particular Experience

Standing within this phenomenological attitude, the researcher's task is to now comprehend the implicit structures of the subject's experience. Especially when confronted by a lengthy protocol, researchers may be overwhelmed by the task. So the first step is usually to delineate the description into its constituent moments or scenes. These are found by noting the shifts in meaning between one statement and the next. The protocol is thus demarcated into its natural meaning units. This demarcation is not a technical operation, requiring the protocol to be broken up in one correct way. Rather, it is for the sake of aiding the researcher's subsequent reflection, and therefore may be adapted to the particular style of the researcher. Some prefer to work with smaller scale scenes, some with larger. The point is that this operation allows an entry in depth into the protocol that may otherwise be virtually impossible. But each scene is comprehended as a constituent of the larger whole, and in relation to the research phenomenon, of which it is a scene.

Next, the researcher takes up each constituent, reflecting upon what it reveals about how this subject lived this phenomenon in this situation. To do so, the researcher must reflect upon and make explicit his or her judgment involved in the demarcation of each scene. That is, the researcher must now formulate the central theme of the scene, in order to specify what it is about that scene that lends it its coherence as a scene revelatory of the meaning of the phenomenon under investigation. It is here that one's fore-understanding must be rendered explicit, in immediate dialogue with the data. For example, in Wertz's (1983b) study of being criminally victimized, one of the meaning units in a protocol concerned calling for help, but not having anyone come. Wertz noted that in thinking about the relevance of such an expression to the phenomenon, we can discover the victim's sense of impotence and isolation from a supportive community.

Reflecting upon what is implicit is not an easy task. Its fulfillment requires that the researcher intuit, or perceive, the essential psychological significance therein. This process of eidetic intuition goes beyond mere speculation or inference. It is the researcher's responsibility to actually explicate this implicit sense. The researcher is aided by a variety of specific "reflection guiding" procedures. Wertz (1983a, 1983b) catalogued and illustrated many of these procedures. For example, the researcher may utilize an existential baseline, with which to delineate the phenomenon more clearly. This baseline is a background against which the phenomenon is *not* present. For instance, in his study of learning, Colaizzi (1973) contrasts the learning experience with the learner's previous incompetence with the learned material.

Another procedure involves penetrating the implicit horizons of any figural thematic meaning. For instance, the presence of night monsters to four-year-old Joey is what is figural. But every figure refers to and implicates a horizon, and by staying with the referential arc of this figure we may come to see that its implicit horizon includes the absence of loss of the loved caretakers who are not there in the context of the night monster.

Making distinctions is another technique to differentiate the relevant aspects of psychological life under study. For example, in Fischer's (1978) study of anxiety, one of his protocols was given by a college senior who was anxious during the week of his final exams. One might be tempted to superficially read his protocol as revealing that the student was anxious about his exams. However, Fischer (following a clue about anxiety from Martin Heidegger) notes the crucial distinction that it is not the exams that the subject is anxious about; it is failure. That is, he is anxious *in the face of* the exam, but he is anxious *about* being a failure.

Establishing essential relations between the particular scene and another one elsewhere in the protocol is another approach. Thematization of recurrences within a protocol can also be utilized. Another procedure involves the use of imaginative variation, in which an aspect of the protocol is imaginatively varied in order to intuit its significance by seeing how that significance would change were the detail otherwise. For example, when thinking about a young child changing his or her mind, a therapist can consider how the child would react at other ages, both younger and older. Such an analysis could provide insight regarding the child's ability to consider or not consider other person's points of view.

Following the rigorous exercise of these procedures with regard to each of the scenes of the individual protocol, the researcher then systematically relates these findings to each other in order to specify the overall coherence or structure of the phenomenon, as it was lived in this situation, by this individual. In doing so, the researcher must carefully verify, by going back to the raw data, that each of the insights obtained are implicated by the original description, and that nothing of relevance in the original description has been omitted from the psychological structure developed.

Analysis of the Phenomenon in General

A situated psychological structure thereby constitutes an original intuition of psychological life, as it was lived. However, it also has its limitations. It reflects only one individual occurrence of the phenomenon, of which there may be other types. For example, the experience of an attempted rape may not completely coincide with the experience of being burglarized. And what about the larger question of the experience of being criminally victimized in general? In other words, the researcher's next task is often to see her individual structural findings as instances of something more general, and to articulate that higher level of generality, without losing touch with its concrete foundations.

It is possible to discern generality within each of the individual structural descriptions. Each can be interrogated with a project of discerning general features within them. The psycho-logic of a single person's lived experience may also occur in other situations by other subjects since, as Wertz (1983a) notes, the psychological is not a private reality locked up inside one person. Even though each moment is unique, its psychological structure may re-emerge again elsewhere. On the other hand, not every aspect of every individual structure is necessarily general. Therefore, it is the researcher's task to discern the general in any individual case. For example, in an unpublished study of envy, Giorgi noted that a woman's discomfort with another remained unexpressed and judged that such reticence was true of envy in general. These judgments can become quite complex and difficult. Fortunately, the actual carrying out of this search for the general can be aided by a couple of methodological procedures.

The researcher's project to discern generality can be immensely aided by a comparison of insights about different individual cases (for which purpose, most research involves gathering descriptions from more than one subject). This "cross-checking" is achieved by reflecting on each individual psychological structure in the light of the other ones, in order to discover their invariants. As Merleau-Ponty (1945/1962) has demonstrated, however, this process is no mere factor analysis. It is not a probabilistic induction from facts that happen to be present, but rather an essential one, based on an analysis of what must be so in each case. For example, Laing (1962) never found a schizophrenic who felt loved, leading him to generalize that the absence of this experience was essential to being schizophrenic. Sometimes such insights are highly implicit in some of the individual cases, and often the researcher must go all the way back to the raw description to be sure of them. In that way, new sense can emerge about an individual case in the light of another individual structure.

Another methodological process that can assist this search for the invariant involves the use of imaginative variation. Such a means is required since no number of empirical cases can ever exhaust the realm of all possibilities. They must therefore be complemented, and completed, by imagining other variations or deformations of the individual structures. With each imagined variation, the question is asked as to whether the essence is preserved or lost with that change. For example, Wertz (1983b) found that the presence of a detrimental other is essential to the experience of criminal victimization. Even though each one of his 50 empirical cases had involved a detrimental other, Wertz completed that generalization by imagining a variation without a detrimental other, in order to consider whether it would still be experienced as criminal victimization. He varied the case in which a person returned home to find that his house had been vandalized. He saw clothes and furniture strewn about throughout his house and felt violated by another. What if he had returned home after an earthquake, thought Wertz, and seen the same scene of disarray? If he then did not feel violated by another, in that case, he would not have experienced criminal victimization.

A second, more extensive, example of the use of imaginative variation is provided by Wertz's (1982) study of perceptual thematization. One of his subjects went to a supermarket, looked for orange soda, scanned the shelves for it, and found it. In order to explicate the essence, the researcher would still have to delineate the general by imaginatively varying each constituent to discern whether or not it is essential. The least general aspect of course is what is sought: orange soda. Could it be grape soda? Could it be fish? Through such questions, the researcher can establish that what is sought is not essential to the experience of perceptual thematization. Is it then the process of "looking for, scanning, finding"? Is that what is essentially general about the phenomenon? No, because the experience of "looking for" can also be varied by imagining the possibility of instead listening for and hearing (your baby's cry), or sniffing for and smelling (the desired perfume). So, is the essence of perceptual thematization then a process of "prospecting—fulfilling." But is that true for all perception? What about varying that by imagining cases in which one is suddenly struck by something "out of the blue" without any foresense (much less prospecting) of it? That variation also involves perceptual thematization. Wertz (1982) then concluded that all perceptual thematization tends toward contact with the immediately present bodily sphere, and thereby incorporates all of the imaginative as well as empirical variations.

The final methodological procedure is the specifying of the structure of this discovered generality. The researcher makes explicit this general structure by formulating the structural relations among all of the essential meanings. In doing so, she asks of each two crucial questions: "is this essential, i.e., do we have the same phenomenon without it?" and "if just this, do we have a sense of the whole?" It is important to remember that, in specifying this general structure, different levels of generality are possible. For example, does the research aim at the essence of schizophrenia or the essence of psychopathology as such? Also, different varieties of specificity are possible, from a brief, condensed, tight structure, to a fully elaborated one. These choices are not dictated once and for all, but by each researcher depending on the research interest and purpose involved.

Conclusion

The final step of phenomenological research is to bring the explicit understanding back to the lived world from which it was derived. By having selected a topic of relevance to actually lived experience, and by having preserved its embeddedness in experience through a phenomenological mode of analysis, the researcher is now in a position to share the fruit of that research with society at large.

The above exemplification of phenomenological methodology was drawn primarily from the author's own field: psychology. But, as noted previously, the use of phenomenological methodology is spreading across the human sciences, including criminology. Within the broad field of criminology, there have already been notable uses of phenomenology. The most exemplary of these was the study of the experience of being criminally victimized, by Wertz (1985) cited above. The well-known study by Yochelson and Samenow (1977) on the experience of the criminal and Samenow's (1984) follow-up work stand as noteworthy representations of research that aimed to elucidate the experience of the person. Unfortunately, Yochelson and Samenow's use of phenomenology was constricted by the imposition of presupposed notions of who and what the offender is, which kept them from being able to access the richness of the meanings of the criminal's lived experience. In conclusion, then, it may be defensible to assert that the field of criminology, so oriented in both its theoretical and applied aspects to the experience of the person (be it criminal, victim, law enforcement, judicial, or correctional) is ripe for further adventures in phenomenology.

References

Aanstoos, C. M. (1983). The think aloud method in descriptive research. *Journal of Phenomenological Psychology, 14,* 243–266.

Aanstoos, C. M. (1985). Use of think aloud data in qualitative research. In E. E. Roskam (Ed.), *Measurement and personality assessment* (pp. 205–220). Amsterdam: Elsevier.

Aanstoos, C. M. (1987). A comparative survey of human science psychologies. *Methods, 1*(2), 1–36.

Ashworth, P. (1987). The descriptive adequacy of qualitative findings. *The Humanistic Psychologist, 15,* 38–49.

Ashworth, P. D., Giorgi, A., & deKoning, A. J. (Eds.). (1986). *Qualitative research in psychology.* Pittsburgh: Duquesne University Press.

Barrell, J. (1986). *A science of human experience.* Acton, MA: Copley.

Berg, B. L. (1989). *Qualitative research methods for the social sciences.* Needham Heights, MA: Allyn & Bacon.

Brett, G. S. (1962). *Brett's history of psychology* (Ed. and abridged by R. S. Peters). New York: MacMillan.

Brice, C. (1987). *What forever means: An empirical existential phenomenological investigation of the maternal mourning of a child's death.* Ann Arbor: UMI Press.

Burtt, E. A. (1932). *The metaphysical foundations of modern science* (rev. ed.). New York: Anchor.

Cairns, R. L., Bergman, L. R., & Kagan, J. (Eds.). (1998). *Methods and models for studying the individual.* Thousand Oaks, CA: Sage.

Camic, R., Rhodes, J., & Yardley, L. (Eds.). (2003). *Qualitative research in psychology: Expanding perspectives in methodology and design.* Washington, DC: American Psychological Association.

Colaizzi, P. F. (1973). *Reflection and research in psychology.* Dubuque, IA: Kendall/Hunt.

Darroch, V., & Silvers, R. J. (Eds.). (1982). *Interpretive human studies: An introduction to phenomenological research.* Washington, DC: University Press of America.

de Rivera, J. (Ed.). (1981). *Conceptual encounter: A method for the exploration of human experience.* Washington, DC: University Press of America.

Ericsson, K. A., & Simon, H. A. (1980). Verbal reports as data. *Psychological Review, 87,* 215–251.

Filstead, W. J. (Ed.). (1970). *Qualitative methodology: Firsthand involvement with the social world.* Chicago: Markham.

Fischer, C. T. (Ed.). (2005). *Qualitative research methods for psychologists.* New York: Academic Press.

Fischer, W. (1978). An existential-phenomenological investigation of being anxious. In R. Valle & M. King (Eds.), *Existential-phenomenological alternatives for psychology* (pp. 166–181). New York: Oxford.

Freud, S. (1966). Project for a scientific psychology. In J. Strachey (Ed. and Trans.), *The standard edition of the complete psychological works of Sigmund Freud* (Vol. 1, pp. 295–397). London: Hogarth Press. (Original work published 1895).

Giorgi, A. (1970). *Psychology as a human science.* New York: Harper & Row.

Giorgi, A. (1975). An application of phenomenological method in psychology. In A. Giorgi, C. Fischer, & E. Murray (Eds.), *Duquesne studies in phenomenological psychology* (Vol. 2, pp. 82–103). Pittsburgh: Duquesne University Press.

Giorgi, A. (1976). Phenomenology and the foundations of psychology. In W. Arnold (Ed.), *1975 Nebraska symposium on motivation: Conceptual foundations of psychology* (pp. 281–348). Lincoln: University of Nebraska Press.

Giorgi, A. (1983). Concerning the possibility of phenomenological psychological research. *Journal of Phenomenological Psychology, 14,* 129–169.

Giorgi, A. (Ed.). (1985). *Phenomenology and psychological research.* Pittsburgh: Duquesne University Press.

Giorgi, A. (2009). *The descriptive phenomenological method in psychology: A modified Husserlian approach.* Pittsburgh: Duquesne University Press.

Giorgi, A., Fischer, C. T., & Murray, E. L. (Eds.). (1983). *Duquesne studies in phenomenological psychology* (Vol. 4). Pittsburgh: Duquesne University Press.

Hartley, D. (1964). *Observations on man, his frame, his duty, and his expectations.* In J. Mandler & G. Mandler (Eds.), *Thinking: From association to Gestalt.* New York: Wiley. (Original work published 1749)

Heidegger, M. (1962). *Being and time* (J. Macquarrie & E. Robinson, Trans.). New York: Harper & Row. (Original work published 1927)

Heron, J. (1996). *Co-operative inquiry: Research into the human condition.* London: Sage.

Hume, D. (1978). *A treatise on human nature.* Oxford: Clarendon Press. (Original work published 1739)

Husserl, E. (1962). *Ideas: General introduction to pure phenomenology* (W. Gibson, Trans.). London: Collier. (Original work published 1913)

Husserl, E. (1970). *The crisis of European sciences and transcendental phenomenology: An introduction to phenomenological philosophy* (D. Carr, Trans.). Evanston, IL: Northwestern University Press. (Original work published 1954)

Karlsson, G. (1993). *Psychological qualitative research from a psychological perspective.* Stockholm, Sweden: Almquist & Wiksell.

Kirk, J., & Miller, M. L. (1986). *Reliability and validity in qualitative research.* Newbury Park, CA: Sage.

Kvale, S. (1983). The qualitative research interview: A phenomenological and a hermeneutic mode of understanding. *Journal of Phenomenological Psychology, 14,* 171–196.

Kvale, S. (Ed.). (1989). *Issues of validity in qualitative research.* Lund, Sweden: Studentlitteratur.

Kvale, S. (1996). *Interviews: An introduction to qualitative research interviewing.* Thousand Oaks, CA: Sage.

Laing, R. D. (1962). *The divided self: An existential study in sanity and madness.* New York: Pantheon.

Leboyer, F. (1975). *Birth without violence.* New York: Knopf.

Mandler, J., & Mandler, G. (1964). *Thinking: From association to Gestalt.* New York: Wiley.

Merleau-Ponty, M. (1962). *Phenomenology of perception* (C. Smith, Trans.). New York: Humanities. (Original work published 1945)

Messer, S. B., Sass, L. A., & Woolfolk, R. L. (Eds.). (1988). *Hermeneutics and psychological theory*. New Brunswick, NJ: Rutgers University Press.

Miles, M. B., & Huberman, A. M. (1984). *Qualitative data analysis*. Newbury Park, CA: Sage.

Mischel, T. (1966). "Emotion" and "motivation" in the development of English psychology: D. Hartley, J. Mill, A. Bain. *Journal of the History of the Behavioral Sciences, 3*, 123–144.

Morse, J. (Ed.). (1994). *Critical issues in qualitative research methods*. Thousand Oaks, CA: Sage.

Moustakas, C. (1994). *Phenomenological research methods*. Thousand Oaks, CA: Sage.

Newell, A. (1969). Discussion of Professor Bourne's paper: Thoughts on the concept of process. In J. Voss (Ed.), *Approaches to thought* (pp. 196–210). Columbus: Merrill.

Newell, A., & Simon, H. (1961). Computer simulation of human thinking. *Science, 134*, 2011–2017.

Newell, A., & Simon, H. (1972). *Human problem solving*. Englewood Cliffs, NJ: Prentice-Hall.

Nisbett, R. E., & Wilson, T. D. (1977). Telling more than we can know: Verbal reports on mental processes. *Psychological Review, 84*, 231–259.

Polkinghorne, D. (1983). *Methodology for the human sciences*. Albany: SUNY.

Polkinghorne, D. (1988). *Narrative knowing and the human sciences*. Albany: SUNY.

Pollio, H. R. (1982). *Behavior and existence: An introduction to empirical humanistic psychology*. Monterey, CA: Brooks/Cole.

Pollio, H. R., Henley, T., & Thompson, C. B. (1997). *Phenomenology of everyday life*. New York: Cambridge University Press.

Reason, J. (1988). *Human inquiry in action: Developments in new paradigm research*. London: Sage.

Romanyshyn, R. (2007). *The wounded researcher: Research with soul in mind*. New Orleans: Spring.

Samenow, S. (1984). *Inside the criminal mind: A further descriptive exploration of antisocial existence*. New York: Tunis.

Sarbin, T. R. (Ed.). (1986). *Narrative psychology: The storied nature of human conduct*. New York: Praeger.

Sartre, J. P. (1956). *Being and nothingness* (H. Barnes, Trans.). New York: Washington Square Press. (Original work published 1942)

Shapiro, K. J. (1985). *Bodily reflective modes: A phenomenological method for psychology*. Durham: Duke University Press.

Shneidman, E. (1989). The Indian summer of life. *American Psychologist*, *44*, 684–694.

Skinner, B. (1972). *Beyond freedom and dignity*. Toronto: Bantam.

Skinner, B. (1975). The steep and thorny way to a science of behavior. *American Psychologist*, *35*, 42–49.

Tesch, R. (1990). *Qualitative research: Analysis types and software tools*. Basingstoke, NH: Falmer.

Toulmin, S., & Leary, D. E. (1985). The cult of empiricism in psychology and beyond. In S. Koch & D. E. Leary (Eds.), *A century of psychology as science* (pp. 594–617). New York: McGraw-Hill.

Valle, R. (Ed.). (1998). *Phenomenological inquiry in psychology*. New York: Plenum.

Valle, R., & Halling, S. (Eds.). (1989). *Existential-phenomenological perspectives in psychology*. New York: Plenum.

Valle, R., & King, M. (Eds.). (1978). *Existential-phenomenological alternatives for psychology*. New York: Oxford.

van Kaam, A. (1966). *Existential foundations of psychology*. Pittsburgh: Duquesne University Press.

van Manen, M. (1990). *Researching lived experience: Human science for an action sensitive pedagogy*. Albany: SUNY.

van Manen, M. (Ed.). (2002). *Writing in the dark: Phenomenological studies in interpretive inquiry*. Ontario: Althouse.

van Zuuren, F. J., Wertz, F. J., & Mook, B. (Eds.). (1987). *Advances in qualitative psychology*. Berwyn, PA: Swets.

Wertz, F. J. (1982). *A dialog with the new look: An historical critique and a descriptive approach to everyday perceptual process*. Ann Arbor: UMI.

Wertz, F. J. (1983a). The constituents of descriptive psychological reflection. *Human Studies*, *8*, 35–51.

Wertz, F. J. (1983b). From everyday to psychological description: Analyzing the moments of a qualitative data analysis. *Journal of Phenomenological Psychology*, *14*(2), 197–241.

Wertz, F. J. (1985). Method and findings in a phenomenological psychological study of a complex life event: Being criminally victimized. In A. Giorgi (Ed.), *Phenomenology and psychological research* (pp. 155–216). Pittsburgh: Duquesne University Press.

Yochelson, S., & Samenow, S. (1977). *The criminal personality* (Vol. 3). Northwake, NJ: Aronson.

CHAPTER THREE

PHENOMENOLOGICAL AND EXISTENTIAL APPROACHES TO CRIME AND CORRECTIONS

Kenneth Adams, University of Central Florida
Hayden Smith, University of South Carolina

On April 19, 1995, Timothy McVeigh killed 168 people, including 16 children, in Oklahoma City with a homemade bomb. The ostensible reason for his crime was that he was angry at the federal government. In the aftermath, McVeigh made the following statement: "To these people in Oklahoma, who have lost a loved one, I'm sorry but it happens every day. You're not the first mother to lose a kid, or the first grandparent to lose a grandson or granddaughter. It happens every day, somewhere in the world. I'm not going to go into that courtroom, curl into a fetal ball, and cry just because the victims want me to do that" (cited in Michel & Herbeck, 2001, p. 121).

Criminal acts, such as those committed by Timothy McVeigh, create a "ripple effect" that can devastate the lives of victims, their families, the offender's family, and the broader community. Violent and disturbing crimes often present themselves as random, confusing events. In the face of this senselessness, people will struggle to find meaning in these acts in order to explain them and to assess if they will reoccur. When reacting to an offender's crimes, we also try to grasp motives to understand behavior and to assess culpability. If the offender demonstrates acceptance of responsibility for his or her behavior, social reactions to the crime are often mitigated. Remorse, shame, and self-directed guilt reinforce a sense of shared meaning and cohesive system of social values that can evoke feelings of sympathy and leniency. A lack of responsibility, in contrast, brings public scorn and perhaps harsher punishment. Without a doubt, an offender-based reality that centers on individual responsibility for past evils is important to our social understanding of crime and justice. Yet, there are surprisingly few criminal justice academics that have explored the philosophical basis of our need for offender responsibility. We hope to fill this gap a bit by discussing phenomenological and existential approaches to the study of criminal behavior and its rehabilitation. Responsibility-based treatment perspectives are discussed and analyzed with specific reference to the work of Albert Camus.

Phenomenology

Phenomenology is a branch of philosophy that seeks to understand human consciousness in relation to experience. The approach rejects many of the assumptions of traditional science, such as the search for an "objective" reality. Instead, phenomenology seeks to describe and interpret human emotions and experiences at an individual level in ways that define meaning for one's life. Presuppositions based on reason, rationalism, and theory are shunted in favor of approaches that can reduce experience to its "essence." Phenomenology was founded by German philosopher, Edmund Husserl (1913/1962) who thought that all human consciousness is intentional and can only be described through the first person. "Intentionality" means that human consciousness always is directed at something, and so all conscious human experience can be said to be of or about something. The "first-person" perspective is needed because each of us experiences reality in our own individual way.

Husserl (1913/1962) believed that human consciousness exhibits invariant forms or transcendental structures, which were the focus of his inquiry. Students of Husserl rejected this notion as speculative and focused their attention on actual human experiences in everyday life. Thus, the "transcendental" phenomenology of Husserl evolved into the existential phenomenology of Martin Heidegger, Jose Ortega y Gasset, Jean-Paul Sartre, and Rollo May, among others, in conjunction with the existentialist movement in philosophy. Existential phenomenology placed the emphasis on understanding consciousness through lived experience.

For example, Martin Heidegger, in *Being and Time* (1927/1962), explored the meaning of "being," arguing that existence and experience are inextricably linked for humans. People do not exist separate from or apart from the world; instead, they are immersed and caught up in the world in an intimate and indissolvable manner. Heidegger used the term "dasein" to describe this situation, which is translated as "being in the world." From this perspective, people and their experiences must be seen as an indivisible whole, and one cannot be understood in the absence of the other.

There are at least two ways in which phenomenology relates to humanistic approaches to crime. The first is through the use of phenomenological research methods that offer distinctive ways of knowing and understanding criminals and their behavior. The second is the application of phenomenological concepts and ideas, as reflected in existentialism, to guide correctional management and offender rehabilitation.

Phenomenological Research

Within the scope of research methodologies, phenomenological methods are considered non-quantitative and so they fall on the qualitative side of the divide. Qualitative approaches generally try to describe subjects and their experiences in rich and full detail, often with the research subject as the major source of information. This approach is taken in an effort to collect data that are more "real" in the sense of being closer to experienced reality and more understandable at an intuitive level. In terms of specific methodologies, qualitative methods favor observation and interviews, both of which may be structured or unstructured, as well as case studies and textual analysis of materials published in various forms.

In many respects, phenomenological research is closely allied with other forms of qualitative investigation. To begin with, qualitative approaches focus on description, usually from the subject's point of view. Quantification and objectification generally are avoided. Qualitative approaches also attempt to infer the meaning of behavior and actions from the situation, context, or environment. As research progresses, there is a tendency to group observations and explanations into homogeneous categories or types. Finally, observational and verbal data are supplemented with textual data as available.

In some respects, however, phenomenological research is a distinct form of qualitative investigation. For example, while qualitative research tends to focus on issues that deal with questions of how and why, phenomenological methods bring a strong assumption of self-determination and responsibility to these questions and thus are more strongly tied with humanism. Also, while qualitative methods recognize the subjectivity of experience, phenomenological approaches place this subjectivity squarely at the center of the inquiry. In terms of description, there is a distinct first person point of view in phenomenological research that derives from an emphasis on individual meaning in relation to personal experience.

Qualitative methods often rely on an inductive approach to investigation and thus are in line with the notion of "grounded theory" (Glaser & Strauss,

1967). As such, qualitative research typically does not start with a set of pre-conceived ideas, concepts, and hypotheses. Rather, the inductive approach allows key elements for understanding and explanation to emerge from the data. Phenomenological research takes the inductive approach a step further in that the investigator needs to immerse himself or herself completely in the phenomenon being studied. The idea is that by immersing oneself in the phenomenon, the meaning of human experiences can be found, and this meaning becomes clear and presents itself through intuition. Thus, phenomenological research shows an element of intense empiricism, with its strict focus on ways in which people behave or exist in relation to the world. In this sense, people create their own reality, and they are responsible for the reality that they create.

Existential Phenomenology

Existentialists argue that humans create their own reality on a daily basis. As social actors, we are constantly interpreting events and *applying meaning*. As such, any representation of an absolute reality is strongly denied, as it becomes incumbent on the individual to surpass deterministic social boundaries and flourish.[1] Among proponents of existentialism, which includes a wide array of philosophers, writers, clergypersons, and social activists, there is general consensus that humans are completely responsible for their actions, that there is always freedom of choice. The choices may not be pleasant, but the distinctly human characteristic of rationality provides the individual with the ability to select between alternatives. Existentialists acknowledge the presence of social conditions that oppress, harm, and destroy; indeed, leading existential philosophers like Jean-Paul Sartre and Albert Camus personally witnessed the impact of the Nazi occupation of France. Yet, such existentialists were intrigued by the decision of some French citizens to yield and collaborate with the Germans, in stark contrast to the bravery of French resistance members who were risking life and limb, the former taking a path of least resistance, while the later seeking meaning through opposition.

The notion of "responsibility through meaning" is at the core of existentialism. In a polarized American political environment, existentialism offends the left-wing with its dismissal of external forces that are thought to diminish free will, while equally offending the right-wing by suggesting that past trans-

---

1. Aristotle termed human flourishing, success, and happiness as a state of "eudemonia."

gressions become less significant once the individual assumes moral responsibility. For conservatives, there is also a concern for a tradition of existentialists who criticized formal religion as the basis of meaning.[2] In short, existentialism is a difficult philosophical approach because it challenges the reader's biases and preconceptions. It requires that we develop meaning through our actions and take responsibility where appropriate. It also requires that once moral responsibility has been assumed, we move forward together as better moral beings.

It is here that we turn to one of the leading examples of existentialism, Albert Camus. Camus is a name rarely heard in criminological circles, though his work is centered on criminal justice themes. Awarded the literary Nobel Peace Prize in 1957, Camus is more writer than philosopher, though his work does a wonderful job of explicating the basic tenants of existentialism. Due to his prolific writing efforts, in the form of newspapers, novels, plays, and essays, we will restrict our discussion to *The Stranger*, [3] a story that examines how meaning is applied to crime and the lack of responsibility often expressed by criminals.

Albert Camus

Albert Camus was born November 7, 1913 in Mondovi, Algeria, to semi-proletariat parents. At that time, Algeria was administratively a part of France, which caused increasing tensions between the two countries. Camus' father died during World War I, leaving the family in a dire financial situation. Camus received an educational scholarship to the Algiers *lycée*, though symptoms of tuberculosis in 1930 limited his academic goal of becoming a philosophy professor. A deep interest in philosophy remained, and while working at assorted part-time jobs he received a *diplôme d'études supérieures* (roughly equivalent to a Master of Arts by thesis) in 1936.

Camus relocated to France and was a writer for the underground newspaper, *Combat*, and actively assisted in other ways with the resistance movement. Between 1948 and 1951, Camus was associated with the father of existential-

---

2. The vast majority of existentialists reject formal religion. This is exemplified by Søren Kierkegaard's attack on Danish Christianity and Friedrich Nietzsche's famous quote that "god is dead." However, it is important to note there are many Christian existentialists who fully support a personal communication with God.

3. In French, the title is *L'Étranger,* which can also be translated as "the outsider," "the foreigner," or "the alien."

ism, Jean-Paul Sartre, though Camus' rejection of Communism created discord and the friendship dissolved. Camus developed ideas on pacifism and devoted a great deal of time to human rights issues. He opposed the bombing of Hiroshima and capital punishment in any form.

Camus produced a remarkable number of works in a short period of time. In 1957, Camus received the Nobel Prize for Literature, which was to many literary critics a surprising choice given Camus' political activism and controversial stance on many issues. On January 4, 1960, Camus was killed instantly in an automobile accident at the age of 46. Ironically, Camus had been quoted previously as commenting that the most absurd way to die would be in a car accident.

Albert Camus denied an intellectual association with the existentialists, a discord that was accentuated by his public disputes with Jean-Paul Sartre. Camus was more comfortable with the label of "absurdist"; the standpoint that life defied logical explanation and that human existence remained fundamentally irrational.[4] Paradoxically, Camus argued that within the context of absurdity, life becomes valuable and worth defending.[5] While a society without meaning presents a challenge, Camus argued that it is social interaction that gives one the freedom to control one's destiny.

Camus' notion of the absurd occurs when two forces meet: the lack of meaning in the natural world, counteracted by the desperate need of human beings to give life meaning. Humans crave order, understanding, and meaning; yet, the natural world offers chaos, flux, and randomness. For Camus, once an individual accepts this painful truth, he or she can transcend the boundaries of social constructions of meaning, and truly live a life of personal freedom and responsibility.

The Stranger: A Synopsis

The protagonist of the story, Meursault, is employed as a clerk in a shipping company. After learning that his mother has passed away, Meursault attends her funeral where he expresses no emotion. The following day he meets a woman, Marie Cardona, and they attend a movie and then engage in sexual relations. Meursault spends the week completing menial tasks at work, with lit-

---

4. More accurately, Camus preferred to be considered as a writer, philosopher, and person rather than a member of a particular school of thought.

5. The absurdist position was best expressed in Albert Camus' (1942/1955) philosophical essay, *The Myth of Sisyphus (Le Mythe de Sisyphe)*.

tle interest. His neighbor, Raymond Sintes requests that Meursault write a letter to lure a Moorish woman to the apartment. When the woman arrives, Sintes severely beats her and is arrested by the police. Meursault testifies on behalf of Sintes and is rewarded with an invitation to a beach bungalow. Meursault takes Marie Cardona to the beach weekend. While the European men are walking along the beach they are approached by the brother of the Moorish woman and his Arab friends. A confrontation occurs and Sintes is slashed on the face and taken to a nearby hospital. Meursault returns alone to the beach with a gun, and coming across the Arab, shoots and kills him.

Throughout the story, it is external circumstances that have determined the life of Meursault. Even the murder of the Arab at the end of the story is presented as an event that just "happened." There is little emotion in Meursault, and even less remorse; in fact, the shooting of the Arab is described as "the trigger gave" relegating his role to that of passive-observer (Camus, 1942/1988, p. 59). Insignificant details like walking on the beach or sleeping are experienced with equal sentiment to the murder of another man. In fact, "throughout the novel Meursault sleeps while important events are occurring. He has difficulty waking up on the murder, he naps again on the beach, and he feels drowsy after lunch. The most common interpretation is that Meursault's torpor leads to his undoing— he shoots the Arab in a moral sleep, so to speak" (Showalter, 1989, p. 36). The legal consequences facing Meursault compel him to reflect on his life. Faced with mortality, he realizes that every person is responsible for their personal destiny.

Meursault is tried for the murder, and he disinterestedly recalls the event to his lawyer and the examining magistrate. Quickly adapting to life as a prisoner, he is visited by Marie Cardona—to whom he is now engaged. Meursault's diffidence is so chronic that he tells Marie that he would have married *any* women who asked him. He notes, "That evening Marie came by to see me and asked me if I wanted to marry her. I said it didn't make any difference to me and that we could if she wanted to" (Camus, 1942/1988, p. 41).

During the trial, his friends prove largely ineffectual in his defense and soon he becomes even more disinterested in the proceedings. Meursault becomes equally detached from the presentations made by the prosecutor and his lawyer. Asked to express remorse over the murder, he informs the magistrate, "More than sorry I felt kind of annoyed" (Camus, 1942/1988, p. 70). During the prosecutor's summative, Meursault thinks, "Of course, I couldn't help admitting he was right. I didn't feel much remorse for what I'd done" (Camus, 1942/1988, p. 100). The failure to express grief at his mother's funeral is also used as evidence of his callousness, and the jury condemns Meursault to be guillotined.

The sole emotional outburst comes when an official informs Meursault that if he rejects atheism and pretends to be religious, he will be spared. Here, a prison chaplain meets with Meursault and receives a furious rebuttal. In true existentialist fashion, Meursault accepts responsibility for his crime and accepts the punishment—refusing to defer to dishonesty. The story culminates with Meursault finding a sense of internal peace, awaiting the execution, contemplating on the value of freedom.

Meursault has been described as the "anti-hero" because his behaviors are simultaneously reprehensible and totally honest. Like our assessment of modern-day criminals, we are torn between contempt and compassion. Also like most offenders, Meursault is both criminal and victim—seemingly unable to grasp the emotional consequences of his actions. The motivation of the criminal act has a familiarity to criminologists, being impulsive, instinctual, and unconscious. Indeed, these are the motives of the mentally ill, the "rabble,"[6] the oppressed, the abused, the youth, and the deranged. Yet, Meursault is none of these things; he is able to maintain relations with women, hold a steady job, go on vacations, pay the rent, and feed and clothe himself. Meursault is a functioning outsider, an intelligent and likeable fellow who has difficulties empathizing with others. Meursault has no cause; his life has no meaning, and society is viewed as essentially meaningless. Because of this perspective, he is astonished at the level of contempt held for his murderous act, with a harsh look from the prosecutor making him realize for the first time, "how much all these people hated me" (Camus, 1942/1988, p. 90).

It is the disproportionate and viscous actions of the everyday-offender, and the absence of any apparent relevant motive, that society seems to have the greatest struggle explaining. Here, we turn to contemporary corrections and discuss different correctional management strategies that promote offender-based responsibility.

Existential Phenomenology and Correctional Management

As we have seen, Meursault's lack of emotion and alienation from others were countered by his ability to "act" like a normal human. Several literary critics have pointed out that the major breakthrough into the thought processes of Meursault did not occur until his incarceration. According to Showalter (1989, p. 75), "Camus was always more concerned with the ways in which the murderer assumed responsibility for the crime, than in the self-evident moral

---

6. See John Irwin's (1985) *Jails: Managing the Underclass in American Society.*

prohibition against it. Meursault discovers his ultimate truth, not in regret, but in an affirmative of what he has done."

Interestingly, Meursault soon exhibits the traits of prisonization: "For me it was one and the same unending day that was unfolding in my cell and the same thing I was trying to do" (Camus, 1942/1988, p. 80). Meursault is taken aback to find that the voice he hears, is actually his own, and that he has been talking to himself. It is only after Meursault has spent six months in prison thinking about his offense, coupled with a challenge from the prison chaplain, that he actually expresses himself. Here, the deepest feelings of Meursault emerge as he directs a passionate diatribe towards the chaplain. Meursault and the chaplain both believe that earthly life is meaningless, though the chaplain believes that meaning will be found in repentance towards God, whereas Meursault believes that his imprisonment and death is the appropriate debt to pay for his actions. It appears that the root word of penitentiary (i.e., penance) is more germane to the priest, yet a cost-benefit analysis is central to the phenomenology of Meursault.

Either way, it is interesting that Meursault's disconnected and alienated life only takes relevance in the prison setting, and one wonders if this is commonplace in today's correctional milieu. If this is the case, how can modern-day prison administrators foster an environment that will enable contemporary Meursaults the opportunity to reflect, find meaning in past actions, and seek moral responsibility? Moreover, what is the role of correctional management in this process?

We know that correctional literature has long focused on the reluctance of the imprisoned to accept responsibility for their actions. More than four decades ago, Matza (1964) highlighted the denial of responsibility as one of the major techniques of neutralization that offenders use to justify their behavior. Many rehabilitation programs, especially those for sex offenders, emphasize that offenders must take responsibility for their actions if treatment is to be effective (Langton et al., 2008). Restorative justice programs, which focus on the relation between the offender and the community, also emphasize that offenders must take responsibility for their actions and both offenders and society must take responsibility for constructive solutions to crime offending (Braithwaite, 1989). Policies and programs are now directed with increasing consideration for offender-responsibility. For example, courts may provide victims and their families the opportunity to present Victim Impact Statements (VIS), in which they articulate the financial, physical, psychological, and emotional harm the offender brought into their lives. Victim Offender Mediation (VOM) programs also encourage accountability, requiring the offender to assume responsibility and attempt to repair the harm to the victim and their loved ones (Sullivan &

Table 3.1 DiIulio's Typology of Correctional Management

	Texas System	California System	Michigan System
Correctional Philosophy	Control Model	Consensus Model	Responsibility Model
Responsibility Focus	Compliance	Identification	Internalization
Operating Factors	Depends on rewards and punishments	Depends on satisfying relationship with others	Depends on the desire to be right
Duration of Change	While rewards/ threats last	While relationships are satisfying	Most deeply rooted, most permanent

Tifft, 2001). Yet, such interactions are restricted to suitable offenders and victims; an offender who does not accept responsibility or express remorse becomes ineligible for VOM.

At this point we turn to macro-level management approaches utilized by corrections in the context of facility operations and offender rehabilitation. A widely known typology is the one developed by John DiIulio (1987). The scheme that DiIulio presents is based on three case studies of correctional systems (Texas, California, and Michigan), and each system has distinct management approaches respectively labeled as control, consensus, and responsibility. Clearly, the responsibility model in the Michigan system comes closest to embracing principles of existential philosophy. A brief description of DiIulio's typology is presented in Table 3.1. The responsibility focus categories are taken from Kelman's (1958) classic article on attitude change.

As DiIulio details, the control model in Texas emphasizes inmate compliance with rules and regulations supported by a system of rewards and punishments. The consensus model in California is described as a system that incorporates elements of the control and responsibility models, which "presents us with no coherent pattern of correctional principles and practices" (DiIulio, 1987, p. 137). Given this operational ambiguity, Kelman's concept of identification may not be the best description of the responsibility focus in this system. The responsibility model in Michigan seeks to maximize inmate responsibility for their own behavior, and to that end, inmates are placed in the least restrictive setting and given the greatest amount of choice possible. The strategy is that by emphasizing personal responsibility and by providing opportunities for inmates to choose responsibly, they will internalize pro-social norms and attitudes.

While a detailed critique of DiIulio's scheme is beyond the scope of this chapter, suffice it to say that DiIulio's ideas have their fair share of ardent supporters (see, e.g., Muir, 1988) and strident critics (see, e.g., Irwin, Austin, & Baird, 1998). Nonetheless, a few comments about DiIulio's perspective are in order. DiIulio argues that the Texas control model stands above the other models in terms of providing better levels of order, amenity, and service. This conclusion is based on observations across three prison systems, and subsequent research calls into question the generalizability of this claim (Reisig, 1998). DiIulio criticizes the Michigan responsibility model for offering too much freedom, too many treatment opportunities, creating low staff morale, and fostering an unwieldy bureaucracy. However, this is only one implementation of the responsibility model, and the specific features that DiIulio criticizes are not necessary parts of a responsibility-based model. Finally, looking at the source of attitude change from Kelman's model, we see that change through internalization is much longer lasting than change through compliance because when the reward and punishment system is not operating, the compliant change is likely to reverse itself. DiIulio argues that compliance may bring about change through habituation, and while that may be the case, the question becomes the nature of the habits (e.g., answering "Yes, Sir" when addressed, walking to the right of a painted line, etc.) and the degree to which the habits have become automatic and operate apart from a system of rewards and punishments. Finally, we note that Kelman (1958) observes that compliance-oriented strategies can effectively limit the amount of change that takes place through internalization.

Let us examine some key principles and concepts of existential phenomenology to see how they might be applied in corrections. The first principle of existentialism, as put forth by Jean-Paul Sartre, is that "existence precedes essence." Sartre applied this concept which he characterized as "being for itself" (*le pour soi*), to human beings and not to other creatures. The argument is that people do not enter the world with a pre-determined nature given to them by a creator or otherwise obtained; instead, they enter the world undefined and undetermined. People have complete freedom to define themselves, for example, in terms of how they relate to themselves, interact with other people, and interrelate with society. With this uncompromising freedom comes uncompromising responsibility. In some respects, existential philosophy is the ultimate "no excuses" stance. It's not possible to argue "it's just the way that I'm made" or "it's in my nature." There is no one to blame but one's self. The strong emphasis on responsibility is consistent with many therapeutic approaches to treatment and with many human relations approaches to management.

A related aspect to the "existence precedes essence" concept is that there are no absolute standards or principles offered with regard to moral judgments and values. This is not to say that the perspective is totally lacking in morality or that all moral choices are the same. Rather, existential philosophy shifts the focus of morality from questions of right and wrong to questions of how do I want to live my life, highlighting concomitant notions of freedom, choice, and responsibility. Deciding how to define or live one's life and then making choices consistent with those decisions is described as authentic behavior. Notice that the focus is on the principal actor's behavior and not on his or her feelings and thoughts, nor on the behaviors of others. In terms of the existential notions of responsibility, each person is responsible completely for what he or she does. Again, this focus on behavior is consistent with many therapeutic and managerial approaches.

One of the more difficult aspects of existential philosophy as a guide for living is the lack of firm standards and criteria by which to judge different choices for living. Indeed, it would seem that the issue of congruence between one's actions and one's chosen values or philosophical positions, as reflected in authentic behavior, is the only yardstick by which to judge. Existential philosophers such as Camus and Sartre recognized this situation, and they struggled to find a way to view morality in a less highly individualized way that is less akin to a posture of moral relativism.

Along these lines, existential philosophers argued that while man may not have a common nature, there is a common condition in that all of us are struggling to find and create meaning in life. This common condition brings us into relation with each other and one person's decisions necessarily affect another's through social relations. Thus, man has some responsibility towards others and the focus should be on the values that operate in those relations. Existentialism does not provide any clear-cut answers to these issues; rather, the responsibility to take up these issues is emphasized.

Conclusion

Phenomenology and existentialism stand as two of the most significant movements in modern philosophy. Both movements are closely allied with the humanistic perspective because they focus on distinctive human qualities in an attempt to understand man's situation in the world. Phenomenology as applied to the social sciences led to development of a set of qualitative research methods that emphasize an "understanding" of people in the context of individually created reality. Existentialism, which finds its roots in phenomenology, represents a variety of strains of philosophical thought that focus on "existence" in terms of concrete, immediate, and particular experience. In terms of orientations that can be used as guides for inquiry and for action, both phenomenology and existentialism have something to offer criminology and corrections.

Several existential and phenomenological themes have particularly useful application in criminal justice. The first theme is responsibility. Given that man is born into a chaotic world in which a person's "existence proceeds essence," each person, then, has the responsibility to determine how they will live their life. The emphasis on responsibility not only is consistent with the major goals of the criminal justice system, but the emphasis on behavior, rather than on thoughts and feelings, also is consistent with many modern treatment programs. For example, psychologists in a Texas program that deals with the most violent and dangerous juvenile felons emphasize development of moral responsibility as one of the highest a high priorities. As one senior counselor states:

> Listening to their stories, I saw a lack of empathy in these kids ... they were full of anger, hostility, aggression, resentment, and they refused to accept responsibility. The more stories I heard, the more that empathy seemed to be the critical thing. Empathy keeps you from doing something that might harm someone. We had to find a way to build empathy. (Huber, 2005, p. 14)

A good example of the benefits of a responsibility-based focus can be found in the Scottish prison system. After a decade of inmate disruption and violence, the Scottish prison system rethought entirely their approach to inmate management, most especially for disruptive inmates (Cooke, Wozniak, & Johnstone, 2008). After much thinking and soul-searching, the system abandoned its traditional isolation and punishment strategy for disruptive inmates in favor of a broader system-wide perspective that sought to increase the participation, involvement, and engagement of inmates in the prison regime. The strategy was described in a policy document entitled *Opportunity and Responsibility* (Scottish Prison Service, 1990). The central theme of the new strategy was stated as follows:

> We should regard the offender as a person who is responsible, despite the fact that he or she may have acted irresponsibly many times over in the past, and that we should try to relate to the prisoner in ways which would encourage him or her to accept responsibility for their actions, by providing him or her with opportunities for responsible

choice, personal development and self-improvement. (Scottish Prison System, 1990, p. 30)

Subsequent to this change in philosophy and corresponding shifts in management practices, levels of violence in the Scottish prison system fell dramatically such that prisons now primarily deal with "low-level" types of violence (Cooke et al., 2008).

In pursuing a responsibility-based correctional system, one, of course, has to be realistic. Being realistic includes the possibility that some people will not be sincere in terms of accepting responsibility and may try to manipulate the system. Such "inauthentic" behavior needs to be recognized and confronted for what it is. Also, it is unrealistic to think that all violence and misconduct can be eliminated from prisons and different strategies may be needed to deal with some offenders (Cooke et al., 2008).

Another useful theme is freedom, which implies choice which brings us back to responsibility. In existentialist philosophy, man is not a victim of his circumstances or environment, and there always is an element of freedom in every choice and in every action. A responsibility-based correctional system would encourage offenders to improve themselves with each and every choice that is made freely and for which responsibility needs to be accepted throughout the day.

Finally, we notice that prison was a catalyst for change for Meursault, in part owing to the anxiety he felt about his situation and his recognition of limits, most notably death in one's experiences. Although the concepts of existential anxiety, limit situations, and time were not discussed here, it should be easy to see how these experiences bring a sense of immediacy and urgency to decisions that define our lives. In this context, Camus' advice offered in *The Fall* (1956/1957, p. 111) might serve as a good maxim for a correctional rehabilitation program: "Don't wait for the Last Judgment. It takes place every day."

References

Braithwaite, J. (1989). *Crime, shame, and reintegration.* New York: Cambridge University Press.

Camus, A. (1955). *The myth of Sisyphus (Le mythe de Sisyphe)* (J. O'Brien, Trans.). New York: Random House. (Original work published 1942)

Camus, A. (1957). *The fall (La chute)* (J. O'Brien, Trans.). New York: Random House. (Original work published 1956).

Camus, A. (1988). *The stranger (L'Étranger)* (M. Ward, Trans.). New York: Random House. (Original work published 1942)

Cooke, D. J., Wozniak, E., & Johnstone, L. (2008). Casting light on prison violence in Scotland: Evaluating the impact of situational risk factors. *Criminal Justice and Behavior, 35*(8), 1065–1078.

DiIulio, J. J. (1987). *Governing prisons: A comparative study of correctional management*. New York: Free Press.

Glaser, B., & Strauss, A. (1967). *The discovery of grounded theory: Strategies for qualitative research*. New York: Aldine.

Heidegger, M. (1962). *Being and time* (J. Macquarrie & E. Robinson, Trans.). New York: Harper & Row. (Original work published 1927)

Huber, J. (2005). *Last chance in Texas: The redemption of criminal youth*. New York: Random House.

Husserl, E. (1962). *Ideas: General introduction to pure phenomenology* (W. Gibson, Trans.). London: Collier. (Original work published 1913)

Irwin, J. (1985). *Jails: Managing the underclass in American society*. Los Angeles: University of California Press.

Irwin, J., Austin, J., & Baird, C. (1998). Fanning the flames of fear. *Crime & Delinquency, 44*(1), 32–48.

Kelman, H. C. (1958). Compliance, identification, and internalization: Three processes of attitude change. Journal of Conflict Resolution, 2(1), 51–60.

Langton, C. M., Barbaree, H. E., Harkins, L., Arenovich, T., McNamee, J., Peacock, E. J., Dalton, A., Hansen, K. T., Luong, D., & Marcon, H. (2008). Denial and minimization among sexual offenders: Posttreatment presentation and association with sexual recidivism. *Criminal Justice and Behavior, 35*(1), 69–98.

Matza, D. (1964). *Delinquency and drift*. New York: Wiley.

Michel, L., & Herbeck, D. (2001). *American terrorist: Timothy McVeigh and the Oklahoma City bombing*. New York: Regan.

Muir, W. K. (1988). Review of governing prisons: A comparative study of correctional management. *The American Political Science Review, 82*(4), 1374–1376.

Reisig, M. D. (1998). Rates of disorder in higher custody state prisons: A comparative analysis of managerial practices. *Crime & Delinquency, 44*(2), 229–244.

Scottish Prison Service (1990). *Opportunity and responsibility: Developing new approaches to the management of the long-term prison system in Scotland*. Edinburgh: Scottish Home and Health Department.

Showalter, E. (1989). *The Stranger: Humanity and the absurd*. Boston: Twayne.

Sullivan, D., & Tifft, L. (2001). *Restorative justice: Healing the foundations of our everyday lives*. Monsey, NY: Willow Tree Press.

CHAPTER FOUR

OFFENDER OBJECTIFICATION: IMPLICATIONS FOR SOCIAL CHANGE

John S. Ryals, Jr., Jefferson Parish
Department of Juvenile Services

Introduction

The concept of offenders as a social phenomenon has been studied from two predominant approaches that reflect the genesis of criminal behavior. Internal approaches emphasize intrapersonal qualities that cause individuals to commit criminal acts. Criminal profiling, among other methods, correlates intelligence, gender, race, educational attainment, learning disabilities, and mental disorders with criminal behavior. External theories, known as social reaction theories, include social conflict theory and labeling theory; these approaches emphasize society's reactions to criminal behavior rather than deviant intrapersonal determinants. Social conflict theory is based upon the relationship between the dominant class and the processes that define and control deviance. Labeling theory focuses on consequences of stigmatization by agents of social control, including official and unofficial institutions (Siegel & Senna, 2000).

While social reaction theories account for social influences that directly affect the commission of criminal behaviors, they do not account for the overarching institutions that cast offenders into a social class removed from compassion and unconditional social acceptance. Current offender theories also do not account for the socio-historical foundations on which current offender viewpoints are built. This chapter endeavors to apply a postmodern, social constructionist approach to criminal behaviors in general and specifically to the actors of criminal behaviors—offenders. In order to bridge the gap between social reaction theories and social construction, the proceeding discussion will utilize several key aspects of both schools of thought. However, social construction concepts will be utilized to broaden the scope of understanding the impact of social institutions on offenders and their behaviors.

Social construction branches from postmodern thought and seeks to challenge modern positivistic approaches. Social construction as a hermeneutic approach was initially introduced by Berger and Luckmann (1966) in *The Social Construction of Reality: A Treatise in the Sociology of Knowledge*. The social constructivist movement was furthered by Kenneth Gergen, who applied postmodern concepts, including social constructionism, to a broader scope of social issues. Gergen's philosophy is described in the following statement: "Social constructionism is a means of bracketing or suspending any pronouncement of the real, the reasonable, or the right. In its generative movement, constructionism offers an orientation toward creating new futures, an impetus to societal transformation" (Gergen, 1999, p. 2).

Berger and Luckmann established the theoretical foundations of social constructivist thought, which will be discussed here as an introductory framework, and applied to offenders as an objectified class. This chapter provides an overview of the history of the criminal justice system, followed by current perspectives of offenders. Offenders will also be discussed as a functional part of dysfunctional social systems. This chapter will also provide a discussion of offenders' self-perception as reinforcement for criminal behaviors, and, finally, recommendations are presented to shift from current offender objectification to accepting offenders as members of society.

For Berger and Luckmann and the social constructionists that followed, social construction theory was the result of exploring the impact of society on oppressed, marginalized groups. A key assumption for their framework is man's intrinsic need for socialization and the undeniable impact of social influences on human growth and development. The meaning we associate to life's events is the result of society's interpretation of those events, and this meaning becomes part of the learning process via socialization. Social order exists, according to Berger and Luckmann, only as a product of human activity. Social order exists as the result of humans' inherent instability when acting in absence of others. Humans surround themselves with others creating a social order for the purpose of establishing stable meanings and standards for conduct. It is through such meanings and standards for conduct that social contexts exert their influence. Thus, all human actions are influenced by social interactions.

Berger and Luckmann (1966) asserted that social order develops and is maintained and transmitted through the process of institutionalization. Two key concepts within the process of institutionalization are habituation and typification. Habituation refers to a non-social, individual activity that precedes institutionalization whereby repetitive human behaviors become habitualized (Baumer & Tomlinson, 2006). Most human activities are repetitive and often require exhaustive effort to discern from a multitude of choices which option is the most efficient, most successful, or least uncomfortable. Humans have developed an internal mechanism that efficiently reduces the amount of effort required for repetitive actions by reducing decisions into habits requiring little to no decisive effort. Decisions are made quickly based on prior experience and social context without exhaustive decision-making effort. As a simplistic example, there are multiple permutations of the order in which one performs morning hygiene activities. To re-evaluate the efficiency, expediency, and energy needed to perform one task before or after another would be overwhelming. Should I shave before I wash my face? When is the best time to dry my hair? Should I put on my undershirt before I put on deodorant? These questions, however banal, are not part of our everyday morning routines. To free ourselves from the burden of making multiple decisions, these activities have more or less become habituated, thus freeing our minds to think about the events of the day.

More relevant to social context, throughout medieval Europe and into the American colonial period, offenders, like other perceived threats to social order, were excluded from towns and colonies. Over time, exclusion led to the development of statutes and laws enacted to protect the public order. Instead of utilizing the social resources to understand the reasons fellow citizens commit criminal behaviors, society developed a classification of offenders. Citizens and those charged with ensuring public liberty and the pursuit of happiness no longer considered offenders as having contributive qualities. They were lumped into a class of individuals considered dangerous and threatening. In effect, determining what to do with citizens who committed acts contrary to public order was habitualized into the process of classifying citizens as threats to social order.

The second component of Berger and Luckmann's (1966) institutionalization process is typification. Typification occurs when individuals observe the behaviors of others and determine what types of actions are typical of which types of individuals (Baumer & Tomlinson, 2006). Institutionalization occurs whenever two agents typify each other's actions and, when combined with habitualization, becomes what Berger and Luckmann call reciprocal typification. Two examples from the criminal justice system highlight these concepts. First, the term "rehabilitation" implies that those who have offended were at some point "habilitated" and, somewhere along their misfortunate lives, somehow lost their ability to be productive citizens. "Rehabilitation" is a socially constructed concept that typifies offenders as broken and fixable given the appropriate mix of programming. It also compels the criminal justice system to act on behalf of society to repair them. The social construct of "rehabilitation" belies the fact that most offenders were never habilitated and, therefore by extension, cannot be rehabilitated.

In another example, the institution of law enforcement can be viewed through the social constructivist lens by applying the concepts of habituation and typification. Habitualized actions by offenders are oppositional behaviors and distrust of authority. Habitualized responses by law enforcement are immediate removal of threats and exertion of authority. The institutionalization of law enforcement was created by the reciprocal typification of behaviors by each set of actors. The criminal justice system expects offenders to act and respond with specific behaviors and offenders expect the criminal justice system to act and respond in specific ways. Each typifies the behaviors of the other through repetitive iterations of cause and effect responses, thus creating the institution of the current criminal justice system.

Institutions, according to Berger and Luckmann, are created over time and thus contain a shared history among agents. These institutions control human conduct by establishing pre-determined patterns of behaviors to familiar events, things, and people. As such, these patterns contribute to social control in that they reduce humans' ability to engage in a thoughtful decision-making process while responding to familiar events and people. Another aspect of institutions was initially introduced by Michel Foucault, and reinforces the temporal qualities of institutions (cited in Koch, 2005). Foucault noted that institutions contribute to the definition of truth for societies over time. The progression of thought from Berger and Luckmann to Foucault shows the impact social construction has on human conduct and its contribution to society's definition of reality over time.

Institutions are transmitted from one generation to the next by interaction with family members and members of one's social group. Institutions become regarded as the way things are done, rarely questioned, and accepted without hesitation. In terms of offenders, through the process of learning the social context of offenders (ascribed their marginalized status by institutionalization) parents and children regard offenders as people to be avoided rather than people who have made one or several undesirable choices. Offenders' capacity to become part of society is forever limited by their criminal behavior. Institutionalization causes offenders to be viewed as objects, rejected by society due to imminent threat to the welfare of others, and in need of eradication to protect the social order. The process is continuously rejuvenated when non-offenders internalize existing institutions as their own beliefs and perceptions. The social construction of dangerous offenders as objects rather than persons is perpetuated.

Institutions exert their influences through a combination of control mechanisms designed to maintain the institution and operate continuously as part of the institutionalization process. Additional control mechanisms are only needed when the process of institutionalization is not successful (Berger & Luckmann, 1966). When this principle is applied to the institutionalization of offenders, additional control mechanisms, such as changing how offenders are perceived, are not needed because the general perception of offenders as objects is an acceptable institution. Accordingly, for change to occur in the institution of objectified offenders, society needs to acknowledge that this institution is failing. The implication of control mechanisms is that they make change difficult to achieve without recognition that the current institution is deteriorating.

In order to understand current social processes surrounding the institution of offenders, it is important to review precursors of the current criminal justice system. Seminal events contributing to objectification of offenders will be discussed below as antecedents to progressively restrictive social perspectives on those considered threats to social order. The progressive restrictions exist today and are known as the institution of criminal justice.

Historical Perspectives of Objectification of Offenders

Conceptual origins of offender social constructs are entrenched in medieval England dating back into the thirteenth through sixteenth centuries. During this period, English aristocrats enacted laws to control "masterless men" and to preserve the societal culture (Rennie, 1978). With English aristocratic underpinnings, the American criminal justice institution has gone through three distinct developmental periods—the colonial era, 1820–1920, and 1920–present (Walker, 1998). The colonial period was characterized by geographically isolated communities that protected their societal values. English settlers brought with them to the American colonies basic vagrancy laws that were carried into the New World (Friedman, 1993). Colonies consisted of small homogeneous groups of settlers who shared similar values, culture, and religion. To preserve the homogeneity and social order, the process of "warning out" was conducted (Dershowitz, 1974). Through this process, colonial communities provided support to those who had fallen into poverty or sickness and sanctioned or banished citizens who had broken laws. Among those who threatened social order were criminals, the poor, and the mentally ill. In addition to "warning out," colonial communities sanctioned such threats with fines, branding irons, and the stocks. Confinement was utilized to preserve peace within communities by removing impoverished citizens and separating the mentally ill from the mentally healthy (Dershowitz, 1974). During this period, central precepts behind the enactment of laws were closely aligned with religious beliefs, rather than danger toward persons or property.

As colonies progressed toward the American Revolution, crime became increasingly viewed as any act that threatened property or economic development (Friedman, 1979). When community momentum for the possession of property and economic development increased, there was an increasing awareness of potential threats from outsiders, particularly those who entered the communities without social ties. Communities inoculated themselves from danger by enacting laws to protect themselves against harm from outsiders and insiders who threatened social prosperity. From a social construction viewpoint, these practices and laws reflected communities' responses to social misfits and deviants by engaging in habitualized behaviors. That is, practices targeting the reduction or elimination of social threats were automated through the enactment of laws, which removed the need for understanding causes of the deviant behavior and made law-breaking an objective decision—either the law was broken or it was not.

From 1820–1920, colonial laws grew into the modern criminal justice system including expansion of law enforcement agencies, court systems, confinement facilities, and probation and parole agencies. During this period, the criminal justice system grew exponentially with the growth of capitalism and industrial society. The diversity created by larger heterogeneous communities encouraged citizens to distance themselves from those around them (Kammerman, 1998). Lack of familiarity and the need to protect one's property brought about dehumanization of others setting the stage for depersonalization of deviant members of society.

The third period, 1920 until the present, is considered a reform period. Focus shifted from building larger and more facilities to determining the purpose and utilization of these facilities. Demographic and social changes disrupted social solidarity, which, in turn, disrupted social order. During this period, crime became an important political issue and is now an essential election-year strategy for many candidates who are running for office (Marion, 1994). Growth of crime since the 1960s was due in large part to an increased post-WWII population and concerns over threats to material affluence (Simon, 2007). As the complexity of society increased, the criminal justice system also grew. This growth was largely the result of typification of offenders necessitated by having to manage an increasingly complex society with limited resources.

From concern for the mentally ill and religious offenders to concern for the protection of property and social economy, processes meant to ensure public tranquility have evolved into the criminal justice institution. Such automatic responses toward those perceived to threaten the social order are habitualized reactions. For each person who exhibits threatening behaviors, the criminal justice institution has an equal and sometimes overly abundant prescribed typified response. As we shall see in the following section, offenders are viewed through several possible lenses that shape society's view of this marginalized group.

Current Perspectives of Offenders

The basic building block of the criminal justice system is the dichotomy of "us" and "them." From its inception, the criminal justice system is rooted in maintenance of the status quo of those in power by maintaining control over the disenfranchised. Compliance to mainstream values and will is forced on the segment of society that, for whatever reasons, is considered "them." Included in this group are those identified as being somewhat different by poverty, immorality, or inappropriate social character (Major & Eccleston, 2005). Minority group members are also stigmatized due to cultural and economic differences (Friedman, 1993). These individuals, through the process of typification, become key antagonists in a society built upon imposing regulations to maintain public order and interests.

From an evolutionary perspective, groups tend to exclude deviant members and non-socialized fringe members to maintain reproductive fitness of group members (Kurzban & Leary, 2001; Major & Eccleston, 2005). By excluding deviants and other threats to the group, in-group members reduce threats to the group's continued existence. In-group members make value judgments about the extent to which members belong to the group based on the social structure of the group. For example, members of the dominant in-group are characterized as possessing individualism, independence, and autonomy whereas deviants or fringe members do not possess these traits (Lorenzi-Cioldi & Chatard, 2006). Group identity is maintained through rejection of members who challenge group identity (Marques, Abrams, & Serôdio, 2001). Further, group members invest their own will in the maintenance of central identities that contain power (Simon, 2007).

More relevant to this discussion, the tendency for mainstream society to support politicians and other leaders who emphatically claim to "get tough" on crime, and by extension, remove deviant criminals from society, creates social tension between in-group members and offenders. In order to alleviate the tension, society simply removes the source. Rather than removing politicians who embody the stereotypical image of the in-group, in-group members exclude deviant members. Deviant members, whose voice is discounted, do not fit the group's stereotypical image and, therefore, are easily excluded.

From a social psychology perspective, deviants are excluded from the normal group because they are different from the majority (Hogg, Fielding, & Darley, 2005). These so-called "out-groups," through their diverse norms, culture, and characteristics, weaken the bond of the in-group or mainstream society. As a result, this group is determined to be a risk to the social order and thereby excluded through, among other means, laws and practices designed to maintain their separation from the powerful group. Hogg and colleagues (2005) reviewed several studies regarding in-group behavior toward deviants. In each of the studies, in-group behaviors reinforced the solidarity of the in-group and reinforced the superiority of the in-group's standards by rejecting those who did not fit the in-group's criteria for membership. For marginalized group members, groups tended to place pressure on members on the fringe of the group to conform to group standards. However, it is important to note that the in-group only excludes fringe members from the group membership when repeated attempts at socialization into the group fail.

Drawing a parallel with the criminal justice system, society will make some attempts to bring fringe members into society's norms, but once these attempts are thwarted, the member is cast into out-group membership by becoming labeled as a deviant and subsequently typified by society. This trait explains half-hearted attempts to "rehabilitate" offenders with programs proven to be ineffective. To the extent that a community is homogeneous, deviance and rates of crime can be expected to be lower. Homogeneous communities share a common value system and, therefore, tend to have higher levels of attachment and commitment (Miethe, 1994).

Utilizing a social construction viewpoint, the formation of the offender concept can be understood in terms of socialization. Social construction is based on groups' mental representations of others' actions. These mental representations become habituated through observing repetitive occurrences by certain types of actors as they interact with each other. Group members begin to act and react with each other based on these habituated mental representations. Habituated mental representations by specific actors become typical actions for that group. The result is the development of institutionalized responses based on typified actions. Through this process, meanings are embedded in the action/reactions, which govern social interactions. Knowledge and reality become an integral part of society (Berger & Luckmann, 1966).

From early childhood, the social construction of reality is initiated and reinforced through reacculturation into increasingly complex levels of knowledge (Warmouth, 2000). Children are taught acceptable stereotypes of socially accepted behaviors, appearances, and interactions. Strikingly similar to the concept of habituation, acculturation teaches them to discern from a number of factors who is safe and who is dangerous. They also learn that those who commit crimes must be dangerous and, therefore, comprise an undesirable segment of society.

When looking at socialization of children through social development theory (Vygotsky, 1962, 1978), social interactions in early childhood establish social learning including formation of concepts such as who is "good" and who is "bad." Interestingly, Gergen, Hoffman, and Anderson (1996) acknowledge that part of human nature is to categorize deficits in others. This tendency is fueled by the media's increasing use of language that reinforces classifications of deficits. In a parallel process, offenders are likewise classified deviants as society continues to grapple with the ever-present question regarding offenders' capacity to offend. As society's natural tendency to exclude threats to the social order continues, children are continuously indoctrinated into the same cultural morays and, as a result, perpetuate social exclusion of those who are different—including offenders, the mentally ill, and the poor.

In addition to the media, there is constant acculturation through political rhetoric, treatment advertisements, and law enforcement marketing that establishes systematic parameters for excluding offenders from society. Political advertisements frequently discuss the need to get tough on crime. Powerful and influential law enforcement public awareness campaigns highlight that criminals are threats to social safety and security. Programs targeted towards prevention focus on identifying social deviants at early ages. These efforts, while ostensibly protecting society, sublimate the process of separating deviants from mainstream culture.

Under the auspices of protecting society from dangerous people, ordinary citizens are bombarded with messages that establish norms for who should be identified as social outcasts and, as a result, excluded from society. Embedded within these norms is the socially formed meaning of offenders. The context ascribed to the offenders through a variety of social interactions, is that they are objects rather than people.

Social Construction of Offender Characteristics

Consistent with the evolution of typification, society has endeavored to empirically characterize behaviors exhibited by offenders. The first known effort to correlate precursory deviant characteristics with future criminal activity was criminal profiling, which began with Cesare Lombroso in the nineteenth century. More recently, criminal profiling has established a methodology to predict criminal behaviors from a set of precursory traits and behaviors (Fintzy, 2000; Kocsis, 2006). Research has indicated historical characteristics can predict types of offending and can explain types of offending throughout criminal careers (Armstrong & Britt, 2004). However, when questioning forensic psychologists and psychiatrists regarding their opinions about criminal profiling, fewer than 25 percent believed criminal profiling was scientifically reliable or valid (Torres, Boccaccini, & Miller, 2006).

With heightened public awareness through various forms of media, society has become increasingly aware of associations between a variety of characteristics and criminal behavior. As such, the meaning of offenders has been socially constructed through the association between behaviors and future criminal activities. In addition to individual characteristics, correlates of criminal behavior have been broadened to include other socially unfit qualities. The first description of criminal behavior was published in France in 1827 in a document that depicted an association between crime and poverty by comparing crime with socioeconomic indicators (Rennie, 1978). The association between crime and low socioeconomic status continues today. Other factors associated with criminal behaviors were high levels of mobility (Miethe, 1994), childhood physical abuse (Emler & Reicher, 2005), and poor parental relationships (Palmer & Gough, 2007).

Such characterizations contribute to the associations society makes between the propensity toward illegal behavior and other out-group characteristics. For example, a meta-analysis conducted to study the effect of physical attraction, race, socioeconomic status, and gender showed defendants who were physically attractive, female, and from high socioeconomic status were found to be less culpable by members of mock juries (Mazzella & Feingold, 1994). A study on the effects of race on attributions of guilt and consequences showed members of minority groups received more severe penalties than white majority criminals in a simulated sentencing paradigm (Gordon, 1990). Further, a study by Gleason and Harris (1976) showed that higher socioeconomic defendants were viewed as less culpable in group discussions.

Society's construction of offenders is reinforced largely by mass media. Often creating a misrepresentation of the occurrence of violent crimes, media reporting consistently depicts violent crimes while excluding other types of crimes (Graber, 1980). Offenders are shown on television being chased until they surrender or meet an unfortunate demise. Video narratives poignantly highlight offenders' carelessness, blatant disregard for the law, and lack of remorse for crime victims. An almost imperceptible and perfunctory statement regarding offenders' innocence until proven guilty in a court of law precedes videos. The reminder is soon forgotten in the "cops and robber" portrayal of alleged criminal acts.

Newspapers frequently place front-page news stories that highlight particularly gruesome crimes that threaten moral order. The adage, "if it bleeds, it leads" holds true across the media spectrum. Society is bombarded with messages that offenders threaten our safety and therefore require our constant vigilance, attention, and desire to eradicate this social scourge. By public exposure to the incidence of violent crimes, media coverage has established a norm for greater punishments for lesser level crimes (Roberts & Edwards, 1989). Media reinforces society's typification of offenders' behaviors.

The impact of society's perception of offenders has far-reaching implications for the manners in which society as a whole develops institutions based on offender objectification. The institution of governing members of lower socio-economic classes through crime is commonplace (Simon, 2007). Through reinforcing the association between crime and poverty, society increases power and control of the higher socio-economic strata at the expense of the lower socio-economic strata. The effect caused by the expansive bureaucratic criminal justice system looms largely on the establishment and perpetuation of a criminal element that must ostensibly be brought under control.

In contrast, a study using the National Youth Survey demonstrated that the criminal justice system has a high degree of discrepancy in their portrayal of crimes committed. The Center for the Study and Prevention of Violence presented survey respondents with copies of their arrest histories. Respondents reported a large degree of variance between the respondents' accounting of their arrests and their arrest history with 27 percent of the arrests being disputed by respondents for various reasons (Elliot, 1995). Through typification, socially constructed offender traits would lead less cognizant members of society to assume the offenders in this study are less than truthful. However, this typification and the presupposition that those who have offended are always offending is part of a socially constructed meaning.

In recording a review of arrest records by offenders themselves, Elliot (1995) demonstrated that those entering the criminal justice system are not a representative sample of offenders. These individuals, through inconsistencies stemming from law enforcement to the judicial process, represent the proportion of offenders who possess fewer internal, financial, and educational resources. Precursory reviews of characteristics of incarcerated offenders will show high levels of disproportionate minority confinement, educational failure, low socio-economic status, and histories of mental illness. It would appear by looking at incarcerated offenders that these are the traits of all offenders; however, careful attention must be given to offenders who, through various mechanisms, either do not face criminal proceedings or who face such proceedings with processes that are not prejudicial to the offenders' race, socio-economic status, educational level, or mental health background. These concepts raise the question that if society and the justice system are inherently influenced by cultural norms that marginalize citizens who threaten social order, then how can the criminal justice system truly render objective decisions based solely on providing consequences commensurate with criminal acts?

Functional Criminality

For those relegated to marginalized groups such as offenders, the poor, and the mentally ill, group membership includes a number of socially constructed qualities that are ascribed through such membership. These qualities demonstrate the social nature of humans and gives evidence to the indomitable need to feel included. Membership also includes engaging in behaviors that, to members of the in-group, appear to be undesirable. These behaviors, while seemingly self-destructive to members of the in-group, are far more functional to those who perform them.

For juveniles, delinquent behaviors are functional in a two ways. First, they demonstrate that offenders are part of a group of people who share similar attributes as others who are marginalized by society creating a sense of universality. Second, offending serves as a dysfunctional form of protection against potential predators by demonstrating the offender is not opposed to non-conventional responses (Emler & Reicher, 2005).

From an intrapersonal point of view, those categorized as offenders possess shared internal reinforcements of their categorization (Emler & Reicher, 2005). Constant attention placed on failure, diminishing options for equitable solutions to conflicts or grievances, and decreasing opportunities for advancement in social stature all contribute to further exclusion by the dominant cultural group. Feelings of exclusion and alienation justify aggressive and noncompliant behaviors, further reinforce offenders' self-perceptions, and perpetuate the very actions that induce their inclusion into the marginalized offender group. When children are raised with no sense of belonging, self-esteem, or sense of accomplishment, they are categorized into a marginal class of difficult-to-habilitate people resulting in frustration and aggressive behaviors. This process occurs in neighborhoods and in schools (Williams & Govan, 2005). The continuous cycle of stigmatization, reactive behaviors, and reinforced marginalization continue as institutionalized processes.

Once included into a marginalized group there are expectations that one will maintain status in that group. This dynamic makes movement from marginalized to dominant groups difficult for even members with the most resources and nearly impossible for those with no resources. In contrast, dynamics within dominant groups tend to diminish personal identity. The price of inclusion into the dominant group is the risk of losing one's personal identity (Pickett & Brewer, 2005). This tendency highlights the importance of exclusion in that it recognizes that marginalized members experience a difficult process of changing one's identity from the inculcated "deviant" identity to an unfamiliar identity that aligns with the dominant group. Even more daunting is separating from family members, friends, and a culture that provided a sense of belonging.

Associations between offenders and social class have been established for decades. Precursors to illegal behaviors have been identified by their association to criminal behaviors. Precursors, such as low-socioeconomic status, race, poverty-endemic neighborhoods, and mental illness, are simultaneously traits common among visible racial/ethnic groups. These associations, while helpful to law enforcement personnel for identifying potential for criminal activities, are not predictors of future offending. These associations have reinforced the misrepresentation of visible racial/ethnic groups' propensity towards criminal behaviors. Jarvis (2007) similarly illustrated that patients from visible racial/ethnic groups are often misdiagnosed due to a lack of understanding regarding the problems associated with racial discrimination, poverty, and residential transitions.

Regarding social interactions, persons labeled as offenders are surreptitiously segregated from non-delinquent peers. This separation, based on a combination of social exclusion, low-socioeconomic neighborhoods, and poor interpersonal skills, results in increased interactions with homogeneous peers who share similar distrust of affluence (Emler & Reicher, 2005). The resulting combination is the development of a sub-culture that shares exclusionary experiences, similar intra-personal attributes, and rejection from non-offenders.

Separate and Not Equal

One of the most influential developments differentiating offenders from non-offenders began with criminal profiling, which compared criminals to non-criminals. The subsequent generalization of factors associated with offending contributed greatly to typification of offender qualities. Burgeoning criminology theories began to focus their attention on the interpersonal attributes of offenders rather than on the criminal act itself (Miethe, 1994). Based on these theories, offenders became targets of social anxieties fueled by those in power.

Legal precursors that guide society's typification of offenders as segments of society that are separate from the majority culture have roots in political culture. From the beginning of our nation, the government's constitutional responsibility has been to ensure domestic tranquility (Cronin, Cronin, & Milakovich, 1981). The government assumes this responsibility by imposing laws to protect its citizens. Laws are enacted by politicians who create "get tough" strategies in order to mobilize citizens concerned for their safety and security. By typifying offenders' characteristics to the public, concerned citizens support reciprocal typifications that include dehumanizing offenders into a societal menace. Reciprocal typifications also include removing offenders from society through incarceration and the need to "re-habilitate" offenders. Each of these reciprocal typifications is a socially constructed objectification of offenders.

As recently as the period between the 1960s through the 1980s, public opinion has followed political rhetoric. In a review of political speeches and public opinion surveys, Beckett (1997) showed that public opinion was determined largely by political zeitgeist, which demonstrated the critical impact politicians have on society's perceptions. In effect, dramatization of criminal offending coupled with impassioned political platforms highlighting the impact of criminals on the social order generated a society intolerant of members of society labeled as offenders. Politicians then built upon public sentiment to emphasize personal responsibility, which further segregated members of society who demonstrated a lack of personal responsibility (Scheingold, 1991). Politicians knowingly appeal to the insecurities of society by creating anxieties about social chaos and carving out a segment of the population that can potentially exacerbate social disorder.

For many politicians, it is critical to create a sense of imbalance and conflict that needs to be brought into balance by the election of the politician in question that will make things right. One of the essential elements of this mobilization is creating a common identity that prospective voters can relate with—the potential of becoming a crime victim. The mere threat of victimization, spurred by political rhetoric, creates a simultaneous sense of anxiety and unity within society. Creation of societal tension based on perceived competition for money, power, security, and safety is an instrument of politicians hoping for election or re-election. In order for reform to take place, there needs to be crisis. Where there is crisis, there is the opportunity for change that can only be brought about by governmental intervention.

Throughout the nineteenth and twentieth centuries, there were a series of groups of idealized victims of criminal behavior. The prototypical victim identity is predominantly white, suburban, and middle-class (Simon, 2007), which is strikingly similar to members of the dominant culture. From a social construction viewpoint, the victimization of these groups and the identified threats have resulted from institutionalization. These groups represented society's ideals of industry, honesty, and personal responsibility, and included farmers, industrial workers, and consumers (Simon, 2007). Interestingly, threats to these groups over the years were, among other innocuous groups, Native Americans, organized labor movements, war protesters, gun owners, and offenders. These threats were targeted with the goal of mobilizing public sentiment against well-defined groups that threatened social order for the purpose of political gain. For example, history bears the burden of illuminating that the national threat Native Americans posed for the infant American nation were positively erroneous. A glance at today's once proud indigenous peoples provides a glaring example of how political will affected society's view towards "outsiders."

With regard to legal processes, there is a paradoxical process that occurs within the criminal justice system that creates a measure of unfairness. While there is a predominant cultural value that maintains people should be held responsible for the consequences of their actions, there is another cultural value held individually that the justice system should be lenient on those who have simply had an error in judgment (Kammerman, 1998). Judicial records show disparate sentencing between poor, minority defendants and wealthy, prominent defendants. Poor, minority defendants lack both the means to obtain adequate legal defense and qualities that make them contributors to the social network. On the other hand, wealthy, prominent defendants can afford a capable legal defense and ostensibly possess qualities that, if they were to be incarcerated, would be detrimental to society. This effect highlights differential expectations of both objectified offenders and idolized wealthy people. Typical behaviors of offenders are that they will reoffend, while typical behaviors of mainstream people are that criminal acts are merely mistakes. The resulting institution stacks the deck against offenders and brings suspicion on the fairness of the judicial process.

Another mechanism that reinforces the objectification of offenders is the capitalistic practices of the incarceration industry. In the twentieth century, the prison system has grown into an industry that contributes economic advantages to rural locations that lack other means of prosperity. Colvin (1997) noted that prison construction and operation have become mechanisms for economic development for poor, rural geographic locations. In spite of the increase in prisons, there has been little to no effect on recidivism or crime

(Livingston, 1996; Zimring & Hawkins, 1995). These facilities are the agents of the criminal justice institution that provide convenient storage for society's unwanted poor, minorities, and mentally ill. They are black holes where objectified offenders and society's responsibility toward fellow citizens are forgotten.

Social Importance of Offenders

The social importance of offenders is illustrated by paying careful attention to the role anxiety plays in microcosms of larger society. In a similar manner that hydrologists study scale models of tributaries and ocean currents, we can explore the dynamics of social anxieties through a representative model, such as family systems. Although the dynamics and complexities of families are much less intensive than an entire society, the manners in which they handle anxiety are similar. Family systems contain interacting and inter-related members who maintain a homeostatic balance and have various levels of attraction and aversion between members. Societies, like family systems, contain multiple subsystems each containing shared experiences, norms, and attraction.

A prominent theory of family therapy is embodied in Systemic Family Therapy (Bowen, 1978). A central component of Systemic Family Therapy is the effect anxiety has on family systems. Bowen's theory has been applied to a variety of clinical issues (Knudson-Martin, 1994; Titleman, 1998) as it postulates inter-relations between components of family systems. Bowen asserted that family systems maintain a homeostatic balance of emotions, interactions, and anxiety. When this homeostatic balance is changed, there is a subsequent adaptation between family members. One such adaptation is triangulation. Triangulation occurs in families that are enmeshed by their emotional ties and occurs typically between two people whose relationship is inherently unstable and highly anxious due to any number of internal and external influences.

To diffuse the anxiety and instability, the dyad will triangulate a third person into their interactions to act as a buffer and stabilizing agent. This third person tends to be a child or similarly fragile individual (Hurst, Sawatzky, & Pare, 1996). This third agent becomes the central focus of the tension within the dyad and, as a result, becomes the focus of the attention rather than the initial issues between the dyad. For example, a family whose clinical presentation centers on a difficult and unruly child typically identifies the child as the source of the dysfunction; however, delving deeper into the family subsystems reveals tension between the parents. Interestingly, in family systems with triangulated children, the dyad is the parents. According to Minuchin (1974) parents reinforce deviant behavior in a triangulated child to mask their own problems behind the problems of the child. These triangles serve to stabilize family systems for both nuclear families and across multiple generations (Nichols & Everett, 1986).

Family systems are similar to systems found in various organizations that are comprised of inter-related, interacting components. In his book, *Generation to Generation: Family Process in Church and Synagogue*, Edwin Friedman (1985) built upon the concept that organizations are similar to family systems and, based on this premise, exhibit similar characteristics as family systems. Friedman applies Bowen's theory to a nursery school, a law firm, a medical partnership, and a nursing staff. Based on Bowen's conceptualization of a system and the application of Systemic Family Therapy to systems larger than families, Bowen's theory can be applied to society at large. Society has many inter-related, interacting components with a shared history, culture, and norms. Many of these norms are institutionalized norms, such as offender objectification. Rather than individual components consisting of single persons, components consist of groups of people. These groups maintain a homeostasis through multigenerational interactions, emotions, and behaviors. Applying this line of reasoning to the discussion of offenders' role in society, the dynamics affecting offenders' position in the social strata become clearer.

Two likely triangles can be explored in this application. In the first triangle, one dyad is composed of the non-offending group and the influential group. Tension between ordinary society and the rich and powerful class has existed for centuries. Since before the class conflict of the French Revolution and continuing throughout the twentieth century with organized labor conflicts, the tension that exists is a strong but obscured dynamic in our society. The triangulated strata is the mentally, socially, and financially weaker component constructed to be known as offenders. Offenders lack the financial and social resources to muster adequate defenses and are the primary group to triangulate into the dyad. Little attention is given to non-offenders' cries for fair representation and equality because attention is diverted toward the ostensibly massive criminal justice crisis by the dominant group.

The second triangle is the result of racial tensions. The dyad is composed of the affluent, white, dominant majority and the disadvantaged, poor minority where significant tensions exist due to concerns for sharing power and economic opportunities between the groups. Recent events have magnified tensions between these two groups and have de-stabilized the homeostatic balance between them. In order to exert its influence over the less affluent minority group, the dominant majority triangulates the tension onto offenders. By magnifying the impact of offenders on society, the dominant group is able to increase pressure on the less affluent, minority group to comply. Also, the criminal justice system is one mechanism dominant society uses to exert influence on less affluent minorities. Offenders are triangulated because, once again, they possess few opportunities for adequate defense and, as a result, are weaker than other segments of society. In both triangles, offenders are triangulated into the tensions between two groups in order to reduce tension between them.

Offenders' Self-Definition as Reinforcement for Illegal Behaviors

As previously discussed, classification into the offender class has significant impact on the self-identity of group members. Not only do members of the offender group often maintain membership in both impoverished and minority groups, they have the added burden of being labeled as offenders as a result of committing crimes. Some are considered offenders based solely on their association with criminal phenotypes generated by dominant society.

Social development for members of both dominant and marginal groups is based on interactions with others that teach concepts of right and wrong, acceptable and unacceptable behaviors (Berger & Luckmann, 1966). These concepts develop through a process of negotiation and interpretation. Klein and Weinstein (1997) asserted that young individuals base their estimation of the level of risk assigned to a particular behavior by comparing the behavior with others. For those who are classified as offenders this social comparison has greater impact on the commission of future criminal behaviors. Implications for exclusion by the dominant group for members of the ostracized offender group are lower self-esteem, further identification with offender characteristics, and increased criminal behaviors. Further, in order for members of ostracized or marginal groups to maintain group identity, they tend to engage in behaviors characteristic of their newly formed identity. In effect, there is a downward spiral of response and reinforcement that initiates and maintains offenders' status in a marginalized group, which, in turn, provides fodder for politicians and law enforcement to mobilize non-offender society against those labeled as offenders.

Another by-product of ostracism is increased frustration and resentment that lead toward antisocial behaviors (Leary, Kowalski, Smith, & Phillips, 2003). Members of ostracized groups feel oppression brought on by laws and barriers that prevent them from advancing. In response to the level of oppression, they become increasingly determined through their behaviors to combat the oppression, often in ways that invariably lead to contact with law enforcement.

Inclusion into the marginalized group of offenders often induces responses from members who feel ostracized (Williams, 1997, 2001). These responses, according to Williams, are to attempt to regain inclusion and to try to reduce negative feelings created by rejection by attempting to belong to another group.

From a humanistic viewpoint, people generally compare themselves to others in their abilities, opinions, and social identity (Lorenzi-Cioldi & Chatard, 2006). The inception of low self-esteem occurs when members are repeatedly exposed to prejudice and discrimination, which negatively impacts their self-concept. As a result of the dissonant identity, excluded members respond by building associations with similarly ostracized individuals. Through these associations, individuals fulfill their inherent needs for belonging and self-esteem (Williams & Govan, 2005). Rennie (1978) acknowledged that people do not commit criminal acts because they lack monetary means, but because they quickly move from a state of comfort to one of misery.

Indeed, the challenges created for objectified offenders are daunting. They face social obstacles that include institutionalized assumptions that significantly limit their advancement. They also face substantial personal identification issues that limit their ability to know there is an identity separate from the one to which they have come accustomed. However, there is an opportunity for society to contribute to the redemption of objectified offenders.

From Objectification to Inclusion

Societal views of offenders are rooted in centuries of socially established norms. Society established the contextual foundation for the identification and disposition of offenders. In terms of social change, there is a considerable challenge facing society as we attempt to diminish the effects of social construction of the offender class. As noted by Hogg and colleagues (2005), social change is difficult because it threatens the identity and cohesion of the group. Further, Pickett and Brewer (2005) observed that change is difficult due to the high level of cultural identity that is ascribed to dominant majority groups. Through self-regulation that is achieved through group-wide agreed-upon communication signals, social groups tend to rebound from attempts to change group norms making any appreciable changes in social norms difficult (Wallat & Green, 1982).

In order to erase the distinction between offenders and the dominant in-group, Jean Piaget offered a poignant observation. He observed that unless individuals are equal to each other, there cannot be any reciprocity and reversibility of normative gestures (cited in Kitchener, 2004). There is a current sociological perspective that offers respite from offender classification and societal triangulation known as restorative justice. The principles of restorative justice are rooted in the philosophies of indigenous tribes of New Zealand and North America. Indigenous peoples viewed those who committed offenses as part of their communities. Crimes against the people were not grounds for exclusion, but rather indicated the offender was in need of additional community support. In addition, offenders were held accountable for their crimes by having to repair the harm caused by their offensive acts. As such, an essential three-part approach containing the offender, the community, and the victim evolved.

More recently, a seminal work by Howard Zehr (1990) entitled *Changing Lenses* began the movement that is currently utilized by the criminal justice system of many states. The restorative justice movement has expanded with the help of Central Mennonite University and the University of Minnesota. Restorative justice conceptualizes offenders as members of society in need of assistance. Their crimes, while threatening to public safety, are indicators of a deficiency causing a respectable, capable community member to act against their neighbors and community. Philosophically, restorative justice seeks to build upon the strengths of the offender rather than to mandate sanctions for their transgressions.

The current criminal justice system seeks to magnify the impact of the crime and minimize contact with the victim of the crime. Restorative justice is a victim-driven process that is agreed upon by the victim, the offender, and the community and is aligned with many approaches that foster inclusion (Ryals, 2004). Contrary to the current retributive criminal justice system, restorative justice enables victims to engage in conversations with offenders. Conversations are healing for both the offender and the victim. Victims have the opportunity to speak to the offender and to offer assistance if they are able. Through these conversations, the victim expresses the impact of the crime on their lives and seeks reparation for the damages. Often, crime reparation is simply an opportunity for the offender to apologize to the victim or can be as complex as the offender providing assistance to the victim to repair physical damages to property.

Through this process the offender sees firsthand the impact of his or her crime on the victim in terms of the emotional, physical, and psychological damage. Offenders are not ostracized by victims because offenders are not viewed as objects of hate, rejection, or retribution, but rather as human beings and fellow community members. Offenders likewise see their victims as fellow community members and feel the primary impact of their crime on the victim and the secondary impact on the community.

The third component of restorative justice is the community. As a whole, when crimes are committed they impact community cohesion. Through media and community communication networks, crime impacts public perceptions about safety and security. Offenders rely on community members to provide supportive services and ongoing resources. An overarching element of this support is that the offender is not ostracized by the community, and instead of feeling rejected, feels accepted by the community, which fosters a sense of responsibility and ownership of community welfare. The result is a greater attachment to the community and fewer incidents of criminal behaviors.

The underlying concepts of restorative justice challenge current perspectives on offender objectification in that they radically transform society's construction of offenders from "one of them" to "one of us." Through this recognition, we are more likely to offer assistance to those in need.

Conclusion

The current societal construction of offenders has evolved over several centuries of social development. Beginning in microcosms of small homogeneous communities, members of societies have historically been concerned with those who did not fit into mainstream society. Pre-colonial and colonial societal practices singled out religious heretics as objects of rejection. As communities grew into larger heterogeneous societies and economic resources became scarce, laws were enacted to protect property and social welfare. The twentieth century witnessed an explosion of the criminal justice system as classes conflicted over power, authority, and economic advantage.

Through this history, society became increasingly aware of the imminent threat of victimization and, as a result, enacted laws to control the social stigma known as offenders. Underlying the identification and eradication efforts, individuals lost their personal traits and were categorized as offenders. In this category, they were afforded few opportunities for advancement and self-defense, and they lost their ability to be considered fellow humans. They became objectified.

This chapter endeavors to present the development and maintenance of the offender class from a social construction perspective. Society has simplified the process of determining who is a threat and who is not by typifying offenders' behaviors. The resultant process is a habitualized response to offending.

By applying a family systems approach, the concept of triangulation highlights unrecognized dynamics operating against offenders. These dynamics hold offenders in their marginalized group and make acceptance by the majority virtually impossible. Society's utilization of the offender class as a convenient mechanism to diminish or divert anxiety perpetuates triangulation. The recognition of the existence of social triangles brings the responsibility of implementing social changes.

In order to initiate social change, members of society need to acknowledge that the current mechanisms are ineffective. In truth, if we are to recognize that our society incarcerates millions of potentially productive citizens and brings many more into the criminal justice system unwittingly, there will be no recognition that the control mechanism known as the criminal justice system is broken. Until society becomes cognizant of the exorbitant social, monetary, personal, and bureaucratic costs created by the criminal justice system, society will continue to support objectification of offenders.

However, a valid case can be made for the adoption of a new philosophy that brings equality to everyone, including those who offend. Philosophies, such as restorative justice, give examples of how citizens can recognize the shortcomings of others and provide mechanisms for redemption and competency development. By recognizing inherent needs for inclusion and self-esteem, society can build stronger citizens by becoming more tolerant of others and by providing assistance to those in need.

References

Armstrong, T. A., & Britt, C. L. (2004). The effect of offender characteristics on offense specialization. *Justice Quarterly*, *21*(4), 843–876.

Baumer, E., & Tomlinson, B. (2006). Institutionalization through reciprocal habitualization and typification. *Lecture Notes in Computer Science*, *3825*, 122–134.

Beckett, K. (1997). *Making crime pay: Law and order in contemporary American politics*. New York: Oxford.

Berger, P. L., & Luckmann, T. (1966). *The social construction of reality: A treatise in the sociology of knowledge*. Garden City, NY: Anchor.

Bowen, M. (1978). *Family therapy in clinical practice*. New York: Jason Aronson.

Colvin, M. (1997). *Penitentiaries, reformatories, and chain gangs: Social theory and the history of punishment in nineteenth century America*. New York: St. Martin's.

Cronin, T., Cronin, T., & Milakovich, M. (1981). *U.S. v. crime in the streets*. Bloomington: Indiana University Press.

Dershowitz, A. (1974). The origins of preventive confinement in Anglo-American law, part II: The American experience. *Cincinnati Law Review*, *43*, 781–846.

Elliot, D. (1995). Lies, damn lies, and arrest statistics. Paper presented at the Annual Meeting of the American Society of Criminology, Boston, MA.

Emler, N., & Reicher, S. (2005). Delinquency: Cause or consequence of social exclusion. In D. Abrams, M. A. Hogg, & J. M. Marques (Eds.), *The social psychology of inclusion and exclusion* (pp. 211–241). New York: Psychology Press.

Fintzy, R. T. (2000). Criminal profiling: An introduction to behavioral evidence analysis. *The American Journal of Psychiatry, 157*(9), 1532–1535.

Friedman, E. H. (1985). Generation to generation: Family process in church and synagogue. *New York: Guilford.*

Friedman, L. M. (1979). The development of American criminal law. In J. M. Hawes (Ed.), *Law and order in American history* (pp. 6–24). Port Washington, NY: Kennikat.

Friedman, L. M. (1993). *Crime and punishment in American history.* New York: Basic Books.

Gergen, K. J. (1999). Social construction and the transformation of identity politics. In F. Newman & L. Holzman (Eds.), *The end of knowing: A new developmental way of learning.* New York: Routledge.

Gergen, K. J., Hoffman, L., & Anderson, H. (1996). Is diagnosis a disaster? A constructionist trialogue. In F. Kaslow (Ed.), *Handbook of relational diagnosis and dysfunctional family patterns* (pp. 102–118). Hoboken, NJ: Wiley.

Gleason, J. M., & Harris, V. A. (1976). Group discussion and defendant's socio-economic status as determinants of judgments by simulated jurors. *Journal of Applied Social Psychology, 6*(2), 186–191.

Gordon, R. A. (1990). Attributions for blue-collar and white-collar crime: The effects of subject and defendant race on simulated juror decisions. *Journal of Applied Social Psychology, 20*(12), 971–983.

Graber, D. A. (1980). *Crime news and the public.* New York: Praeger.

Hogg, M. A., Fielding, K. S., & Darley, J. (2005). Fringe dwellers: Processes of deviance and marginalization in groups. In D. Abrams, M. A. Hogg, & J. M. Marques (Eds.), *The social psychology of inclusion and exclusion* (pp. 191–210). New York: Psychology Press.

Hurst, N. C., Sawatzky, D. D., & Pare, D. P. (1996). Families with multiple problems through a Bowenian lens. *Child Welfare, 75*(6), 693–709.

Jarvis, G. E. (2007). The social causes of psychosis in North American psychiatry: A review of a disappearing literature. *Canadian Journal of Psychiatry, 52*(5), 287–295.

Kammerman, J. B. (1998). The social construction of responsibility. In J. B. Kammerman (Ed.), *Negotiating responsibility in the criminal justice system* (pp. 3–14). Carbondale, IL: Southern Illinois University Press.

Kitchener, R. F. (2004). Piaget's social epistemology. In J. I. M. Carpendale & U. Müller (Eds.), *Social interaction and the development of knowledge* (pp. 45–66). Hillsdale, NJ: Erlbaum.

Klein, W. M., & Weinstein, N. D. (1997). Social comparison and unrealistic optimism about personal risk. In B. P. Buunk & F. X. Gibbins (Eds.), *Health, coping, and well-being: Perspectives from social comparison theory* (pp. 25–61). Hillsdale, NJ: Erlbaum.

Knudson-Martin, C. (1994). The female voice: Applications to Bowen's family systems theory. *Journal of Marital and Family Therapy, 20*(1), 35–49.

Koch, A. M. (2005). *Knowledge and social construction.* Lanham, MD: Lexington.

Kocsis, R. N. (2006). *Criminal profiling: Principles and practice.* Totowa, NJ: Humana.

Kurzban, R., & Leary, M. R. (2001). Evolutionary origins of stigmatizations: The functions of social exclusion. *Psychology Bulletin, 127*(2), 187–208.

Leary, M. R., Kowalski, R. M., Smith, L., & Phillips, S. (2003). Teasing, rejection, and violence: Case studies of the school shootings. *Aggressive Behavior, 29,* 204–214.

Livingston, J. (1996). *Crime and criminology* (2nd ed.). Upper Saddle River, NJ: Prentice-Hall.

Lorenzi-Cioldi, F., & Chatard, A. (2006). The cultural norm of individualism and group status: Implications for social comparisons. In S. Guimond (Ed.), *Social comparison and social psychology: Understanding cognitions, intergroup relations, and culture* (pp. 264–282). New York: Cambridge.

Major, B., & Eccleston, C. P. (2005). Stigma and social exclusion. In D. Abrams, M. A. Hogg, & J. M. Marques (Eds.), *The social psychology of inclusion and exclusion* (pp. 63–87). New York: Psychology Press.

Marion, N. E. (1994). *A history of federal crime control initiatives, 1960–1993.* Westport, CT: Praeger.

Marques, J. M., Abrams, D., & Serôdio, R. (2001). Being better by being right: Subjective group dynamics and derogation of in-group deviants when generic norms are undermined. *Journal of Personality and Social Psychology, 81,* 436–447.

Mazzella, R., & Feingold, A. (1994). The effects of physical attractiveness, race, socioeconomic status, and gender of defendants and victims on judgments of mock jurors: A meta-analysis. *Journal of Applied Social Psychology, 24*(15), 1315–1338.

Miethe, T. D. (1994). *Crime and its social context: Toward an integrated theory of offenders, victims, and situations.* Albany: SUNY.

Minuchin, S. (1974). *Families and family therapy*. Cambridge, MA: Harvard University Press.

Nichols, W. C., & Everett, C. A. (1986). *Systemic family therapy: An integrative approach*. New York: Guilford.

Palmer, E. J., & Gough, K. (2007). Childhood experiences of parenting and causal attributions for criminal behavior among young offenders and non-offenders. *Journal of Applied Social Psychology, 37*(4), 790–806.

Pickett, C. L., & Brewer, M. B. (2005). The role of exclusion in maintaining ingroup inclusion. In D. Abrams, M. A. Hogg, & J. M. Marques (Eds.), *The social psychology of inclusion and exclusion* (pp. 89–109). New York: Psychology Press.

Rennie, Y. F. (1978). *The search for criminal man: A conceptual history of the dangerous offender*. Lexington, MA: Lexington Books.

Roberts, J. V., & Edwards, D. (1989). Contextual effects in judgments of crimes, criminals, and the purposes of sentencing. *Journal of Applied Social Psychology, 19*(11), 902–917.

Ryals, J. S., Jr. (2004). Restorative justice: New horizons in juvenile offender counseling. *Journal of Addictions & Offender Counseling, 25*(1), 18–25.

Scheingold, S. (1991). *The politics of street crime: Criminal process and cultural obsession*. Philadelphia: Temple University Press.

Siegel, L. J., & Senna, J. J. (2000). *Juvenile delinquency: Theory practice and law* (7th ed.). Belmont, CA: Wadsworth.

Simon, J. (2007). *Governing through crime: How the War on Crime transformed American democracy and created a culture of fear*. New York: Oxford.

Titleman, P. (Ed.). (1998). *Clinical applications of Bowen family systems theory*. New York: Haworth.

Torres, A. N., Boccaccini, M. T., & Miller, H. A. (2006). Perceptions of the validity and utility of criminal profiling among forensic psychologists and psychiatrists. *Professional Psychology, Research and Practice, 37*(1), 51–59.

Vygotsky, L. S. (1962). *Thought and language*. Cambridge, MA: MIT Press.

Vygotsky, L. S. (1978). *Mind in society*. Cambridge, MA: Harvard University Press.

Walker, S. (1998). *Popular justice: A history of American criminal justice* (2nd ed.). New York: Oxford.

Wallat, C., & Green, J. (1982). Construction of social norms by teachers and children: The first year of school. In K. M. Borman (Ed.), *Social life of children in a changing society* (pp. 97–121). Hillsdale, NJ: Erlbaum.

Warmouth, A. (2000). *Social constructionist epistemology.* Retrieved August 8, 2007, from Sonoma State University Web site: http://www.sonoma.edu/users/w/warmotha/epistemology.html

Williams, K. D. (1997). Social ostracism. In R. Kowalski (Ed.), *Aversive interpersonal behaviors* (pp. 133–170). New York: Plenum.

Williams, K. D. (2001). *Ostracism: The power of silence.* New York: Guilford.

Williams, K. D., & Govan, C. L. (2005). Reacting to ostracism: Retaliation or reconciliation? In D. Abrams, M. A. Hogg, & J. M. Marques (Eds.), *The social psychology of inclusion and exclusion* (pp. 47–62). New York: Psychology Press.

Zehr, H. (1990). *Changing lenses.* Scottsdale, PA: Herald.

Zimring, F. E., & Hawkins, G. (1995). *Incapacitation: Penal confinement and restraint of crime.* New York: Oxford University Press.

CHAPTER FIVE

DIALOGUE: A UNIQUE PERSPECTIVE FOR CORRECTIONAL COUNSELING

Matthew R. Draper, Utah Valley State University
Mark S. Green, Indiana State University
Ginger Faulkner, Indiana State University

Mikhail Bakhtin, historically unacknowledged in the West, is now becoming recognized as one of the leading thinkers of the twentieth century. Bakhtin dedicated his life to philosophy and literary theory, and much of what he had to say is clearly relevant to psychology. He particularly took issue with Freudian and psychoanalytic thought, and questioned whether such conceptualizations accurately described human life and the human condition. By engaging with prevalent ideas in psychology, Bakhtin developed a model for understanding what it means to be human. In other words, through his criticisms of psychology, he developed a model for psychology himself. Rather than abstracting life in the theoretical realm, he chose instead to describe life as he actually lived it, and thus developed his own prosaic explanation. In Bakhtin's writing, "prosaic" denotes a commonplace, straightforward, or matter-of-fact explanation or understanding.

Bakhtin's largest concerns with psychology regarded ethical questions. In his view, psychology managed to take human thought and behavior and wring the meaning out of it entirely through the often-unexplored implicit assumptions of reductionism and determinism (Slife & Williams, 1995). If, for example, a man who has lived his life in gangs and has essentially been raised by gang members commits a murder and is sentenced to prison, many mainstream psychological theories would rely on a reductionistic explanation of his behavior, such as biological neurochemistry, or a deterministic explanation based on unconscious libidinal energies or behavioral shaping. Theories that wish to understand the man's engagement with fear and uncertainty, or with loyalty to his family of gang members, are less accepted, and are often dismissed as unempirical. It is important to note here that much of mainstream psychology, by relying on reductionistic or deterministic explanations, fails to conceptualize the man's lived experience, and instead focuses on unconscious forces and biological reactions. Bakhtin had a distinct ethical problem with such explanations because they wring the meaning out of our thoughts, behaviors, and emotions. By giving our feelings and the meaningful events in our lives such "scientific" explanations, psychologists reduce poignant events to mere scientific trivialities or absurdities. Bakhtin proposed an explanation of human thought and experience that put meaning (i.e., prosaic meaning) back into our explanations.

Despite the richness and potential for diverse application of this important philosopher's ideas in psychology, there are still relatively few examining his important and ground-breaking ideas in our field. That is what this chapter seeks to do. First, we will outline some of the major points and concepts of Bakhtin's theory and contrast those with traditional psychological thought. Then we will build a brief model of personality from this perspective and follow this with its implications for therapy in a correctional setting. While we offer some criticism of mainstream psychology throughout this chapter, we do wish to acknowledge that many therapists are highly sympathetic to the same critiques offered by Bakhtin, and that many have attempted to incorporate similar ideas into therapeutic models. Our primary goal is to provide an explicit application, namely therapy in a counseling setting, of one philosophy to demonstrate specifically how therapists can bridge the gap between theories that at times seem to have an inadequate framework for envisaging true human experience.

Review of the Theoretical Perspective

Different theorists have defined the "self" in myriad different ways (Cushman, 1995). For example, Freud (1940/1964) argued that the core of the self was a dark pit of lustful and aggressive urges ruling the life of the self, demanding subservience at all costs. This primitive core of the self is the id, that which underlies all of human behavior and interaction. The id is driven by the primitive need for pleasure (the energy of the libido), and the urge to destroy or kill (the "thanatos," or death energy). As the self develops, the id comes in contact with a world that does not tolerate unrestrained lustful and aggressive behavior, so an ego develops, conscious and aware of time and limitations, best able to deal with the world, with the id remaining unconscious but still motivating all behavior. Through the interaction with parents and overcom-

ing competition with the same sex parent and letting go of the desire to possess the opposite sex parent (the Oedipal complex), the self develops an additional component when it internalizes the rules of parents and society. This is
called the superego, and it becomes (at best) semiconscious. The ego's difficult
task then, is to best meet the needs of the id while satisfying the demands of
the superego. The self, in this light, is an ongoing effort to meet primitive
needs; all behavior is in service to the id (Rychlak, 1981). According to this
definition of the self, the id's interaction with the ego and superego causes all
behavior. In fact, Freud defined the self in such a way that creative change is
not possible; all behavior is in service to the id, and psychologists explain it
away as caused by unconscious processes and forces (Morson & Emerson,
1990). In this model of personality, the self is inherently separated and distinct from the world. The world is in essence "out there" to meet the needs of
the id, while the self remains "in here," or within the mind, which in turn is
located in the body. Many other theories of psychology assume a similar spilt
between the self and world.

Bakhtin's view of self, however, does not involve such a separation of the self
from its surroundings. His view of the self seems to suggest a way in which
the self and the world become one. This view is similar to that of another
prominent philosopher, Martin Heidegger (1927/1962). Both argue that selves
have different "modes of engagement" (Slife & Williams, 1995, p. 83). One
mode of engagement does not entail a distinction between the self and the
world around it. Instead, the self is partially dissolved in the world, completely
engaged with it. This mode of engagement is the "occurrent" mode (Dreyfus,
1991, p. 70), and is so engaged with the world that there can be no meaningful distinction between the self and the world. The world could not exist as it
is without the selves who partly compose it, and selves conversely derive a significant part of their meaning from their context.

Bakhtin became very interested in describing the self as it actually engaged
in the world. He described how one might

> get back to the naked immediacy of experience as it is felt from within
> the utmost particularity of a specific life, the molten lava of events as
> they happen. He seeks the sheer quality of happening in life before
> the magma of such experience cools, hardening into igneous theo-
> ries, or accounts of what happened ... meditating the originary dif-
> ference between acts (physical and mental) we feel to be uniquely ours
> in their performance ... the "once occurrent event of Being" and the
> consequences of such events. (Bakhtin, 1995, p. 10)

Bakhtin sought to describe the self in the occurrent mode, the self that is always in process, flowing like lava, rather than sitting, crystallized like a rock. This engaged self, so part of the world, is incredibly difficult to define because it is always shifting and changing. Whereas Freud postulated a definition for a self that attributed all personality to the unconscious forces that rule it, Bakhtin argued for a self that even he could never succinctly or easily define. He called this "unfinalizeability" (cited in Morson & Emerson, 1990, p. 36). Unfinalizeability became a central thesis to Bakhtin. He believed that it is through the recognition of the inherently unfinalizeable nature of the self that such things as creativity, openness, and continual responsibility, and hence therapeutic change, become possible in the face of challenges as great as imprisonment.

Before defining directly how unfinalizeability makes creativity, openness, and continual responsibility possible, it will help to examine how the self remains unfinalizeable. To do so, we need to develop several key ideas. The first is Bakhtin's concept of dialogue. When most people think of dialogue, they most likely imagine a conversation between two separate people. Meaning passes back and forth between them through space and time, each "self" bounded within the physical walls of the body. The two conversationalists are separate and distinct from one another, and from the meanings each other conveys. Bakhtin, however, did not view dialogue in such a separating way. Instead, he argued that in dialogue, the self is very much in the occurrent mode, unselfconscious and engaged with conversational partners in a mutual creation of meaning. This is a key distinction, because when two or more voices come together, interpreting and negotiating, true creativity can happen, a creative unity that transcends any one voice alone.

This creativity in engaged dialogue defines a key feature of Bakhtin's conception of the self. The personality or the self does not manifest without interaction. Instead, the self manifests and is constantly recreated in the boundary between self and other, in an ongoing, creative, and ultimately unfinalizeable process (Morson & Emerson, 1990). Any definitions that describe such a self by ascribing changeless and causal features to this person or self are by nature inadequate and harmful. For example, if a therapist "defines" a client, labeling him in some finalizing way (e.g., as "a sociopath" or being "incapable of following societal guidelines"), the therapist artificially forces a finalized, static definition on an unfinalizeable person. People are capable of change because they are constantly engaging with others and growing because of those dialogic engagements.

Dialogue is thus central to Bakhtin's definition of personality and the self. Bakhtin recognized, however, that he had to continue to develop his definition in order to avoid the implication that the self could not exist without dialogue with another. His explications of polyphony, spirit, and soul provide a more complete understanding of this concept.

Previously, we described the outer experience of the personality engaged in dialogue with others as creative. Bakhtin argued that inner and outer experience differ only in degree (Morson & Emerson, 1990). As we engage in a realm of meaning at birth, we begin to use the voices of others in our own thoughts. Just as dialogue can occur between two people, it can also occur when we are alone, within our own thoughts. We carry the perspectives of others with us, and these perspectives manifest themselves when we have an important decision to make. We often weigh options through the voices of others, and our private conversation is very similar to a conversation we would have with another.

If, for example, as a therapist, I am faced with an ethical decision, such as how to best treat a client convicted of murder, I consider various perspectives in examining the issue. One perspective might be very similar to my supervisor's, another similar to that of my instructor in correctional counseling, and others similar to those of clients I have worked with in the past. All alone, I sit and ponder, weighing these different perspectives, each voice holding a certain amount of authority and validity, and the decision I make will be a creative combination of these differing perspectives. As this example shows, the self still exists dialogically, carried out with the voices of others, still creatively using them in our lives, even when we are alone. As the essayist Michel de Montaigne commented, "There is as much difference between us and ourselves, as between us and others" (cited in Myers, 1999, p. 404).

This idea that we are multi-voiced selves is called polyphony (Morson & Emerson, 1990). A polyphonic engagement not only occurs intra-psychically; it occurs inter-psychically as well. One of the core features of polyphony is our openness to another's voice and perspective, while remaining in touch with our own view of the world and our own value base. If two or more people come together polyphonically, appropriate and creative understanding takes place. We can be polyphonic selves when alone or with others, dedicated to our values and ways of understanding but still open to the perspective of others. Problems arise when people cease to be open, and a monological approach becomes dominant (Morson & Emerson, 1990).

A monological approach characterizes people who listen to only one voice, and who are able to take only one perspective on an issue or a problem. One example of this might be a person who is incarcerated and hears that the rules he has grown up with are "wrong," and that the only way he can be accepted by society is to reject or betray those who have taught him to survive. Polyphonic selves can more easily engage with others to more successfully adapt to diverse environments and to find their own way to best bridge unique societies with conflicting demands. The idea of polyphonic selves does lead us to wonder how this engagement can take place and what types of perspectives of others we hold when we engage with them in dialogue.

Just as we all have different modes of engaging with the world, we also have different perspectives on others and ourselves. Types of perspectives include the I-for-myself, the I-for-another, and the other-for-me. Understanding each of these common perspectives of self and others is vital to understanding the nature of the dialogical self. The I-for-myself is our own experience of our selves in an occurrent mode, always changing and openly growing. This unfinalizeable process is characteristic of what Bakhtin called the "spirit." The spirit contains no points of absolute consummation, no outside perspective that could define it or finalize it. We all experience the spirit, but it is extremely hard to define because it is always engaged and creatively changing.

The spirit is the ultimate semantic position of the personality, the creative essence on which we base our opinion, our assertions, and our approach to life (Morson & Emerson, 1990). Spirits are always oriented toward the future, always behaving for the sake of the next goal or the completion of an ideal. One of the primary characteristics of the spirit is the loophole. This loophole defines spirits: "Spirit and inner perspective provide us with an 'intuitively experienced loophole out of time, out of everything given, everything already present and on hand'" (Morson & Emerson, 1990, p. 193). The loophole is sheer potential, always allowing us to engage responsibly in life; for it is through this loophole that we can show the central nature of our character. All of our actions and words spring forth from the spirit, from this core of our dialogic processes to which we cannot ascribe causal language nor readily finalize. Unconscious processes do not cause our behavior; rather, we behave as engaged agents, living creatively, oriented toward the future, in the present.

This presentation of the personality may appear to present an idea of the self that makes it seem not only unfinalizeable, but also unknowable. However, there is another central component to the spirit. Integrity opens a window to our unfinalized selves. We do have a certain sense of who we are, what we believe in, and where we would like to go in life. It is this sense that allows others to feel they know us as well. This core of our dialogic process allows us to have a sense of integrity, a sense of wholeness and a certain degree of predictability. Researchers and theorists in other areas have noted that trying to predict a single act based on a sense of someone's personality is similar to predicting how a gifted mathematician will perform on a specific exam question (Epstein, 1983). In general, this person is good at math, but predicting the outcome of a given question is problematic at best. Similarly, we cannot so readily define a personality or finalize a spirit.

Our spirit is the raw dialogic process of living, but within that dialogue we take a certain consistent stance, the first perspective through which we polyphonically engage with other points of view. This stance is the dominant dialogical stance, and it allows us to maintain a certain sense of knowing ourselves (Morson & Emerson, 1990). Even this dominant stance, however, can change slowly through the course of time, because it is always engaged with other perspectives, values, and life experiences. Our client may be the same person he was before committing the crime, but that act will forever change his world. Hence, his dominant dialogical stance towards life may change as well. Some prisoners may become more open to meaning and wondering about the purpose of life, while others may shift and withdraw emotionally, feeling that there could be no meaning in life.

In addition to the I-for-myself perspective, in which we engage ourselves in polyphonic dialogue, the I-for-another and the other-for-me perspectives are also very important. It is through holding and using certain perspectives of one another that we can engage and influence one another in an occurrent fashion. The I-for-another is central to Bakhtin's notion of the "soul" (cited in Morson & Emerson, 1990), but this perspective also has certain inherent risks. A soul is somewhat of a paradox in the I-for-another perspective because when someone sees us, they define and finalize who they see and communicate their perception of us. For example, someone may tell our client that their crime has defined them and that they are now a murderer, and this other person communicates this momentarily-finalized impression to the client. The outsider offers a different perspective as a gift dialogically, and the client engages with it rather than accepting it whole-heartedly or unquestioningly. When told who he or she is, the client may think, "Well, yes, I did commit a murder, but there is more to who I am." The other's offered perspective may change the client's point of view, perhaps, but not completely. We exchange these gifts of soul back and forth with one another constantly, our personalities forming and shifting in the boundary between ourselves and others, spirit to spirit through the gift of soul. We do this verbally and non-verbally in a dialogical creation of meaning (Myers, 1999).

Sometimes, however, we do not engage with the perspective of others, but instead we give ourselves over to it completely, finalizing ourselves according to their view, living our lives according to their definition. Other times we detach from our occurrent living and rigidly rule our lives according to a fixed pattern, so we know the future of the event. When we detach from our lives and live them according to the definitions of others, give ourselves over to habit, or rule out the possibility of change, we fall into a state known as "rhythm" (Morson & Emerson, 1990). Rhythm is hopeless to new meaning because we already know the future, and we have ceased creative engagement. When we live our lives according to the way others have defined us, we are hopeless to new possibility and growth, just as when we disengage from life creatively. All rhythm allows us to do is relate to others by imitating them, but this prevents us from ever knowing ourselves as we are lost in the perspective of the other, the future known. We must not lose ourselves in the rhythm completely, or our unique voice and perspective is lost, and we merely harmonize in the chorus of the other.

All lives have patches of rhythm to them, but under normal circumstances these patches of rhythm are constantly changing and in flux, so our lives are always hopeful to new meaning, creative engagement, and expression. Problems arise when we encounter someone who is given over to rhythm completely. They live their lives according to how people "should" behave, according to the rules they received from an outside source, or they have detached from engaging fully in life. This is similar to a client who, attempting to fit into a correctional setting, joins a gang. He or she uncritically dissolves himself or herself in the various tasks that the gang requires, never stopping to think or feel what he or she would like to, or even *should*, in a given situation. When we engage with life creatively, there is always the risk that uncomfortable emotions may surface in the near future. In order to avoid such discomfort, clients lose themselves in the rhythm of life, finalizing every moment by uniting past and present, thus securing the future from creative, risky, and emotional engagement, especially when that engagement may entail very difficult change.

An even more pernicious problem than rhythm is pretendership, which happens when people knowingly give themselves over fully to outside perceptions, living their lives according to the other's definition of them, becoming finalized and rhythmitized. These people try to look at themselves as if from the outside, to live their lives according to how they think others view them. They are trapped in the available mode of being, always detached from creatively and occurrently engaging with the world, watching them like they would watch a character in a novel. To engage in pretendership is to suffer a loss of self, because a true self is always "yet to be" (Morson & Emerson, 1990, p. 195). This is very telic because "the real center of gravity of … self definition lies in the future," so it motivates us to strive on, "strengthening our backs, lifting our eyes, and ever directing our gaze forward" (p. 196). A true self is always in the process of becoming; it never ceases. Pretenders lose their self, so to speak, because they allow others to concretely and absolutely define them. This loss of self is characteristic of the client who ignores or denies his own feelings about his crime, and instead lives his life according to how he thinks others view him. If someone else tells this client that he is weak, he gives himself over to the weakness fully, never escaping. If another tells him that he is strong, he is vigilant to be as strong as possible. Pretenders are never themselves; they live only according to the strict definitions of others. A therapist's goal with such clients would be to help them rediscover the creative, ever-growing self, helping them break free of stagnant rhythm or perpetual pretendership.

As mentioned initially, one of Bakhtin's greatest concerns with psychology was his realization that many psychological theories rob human nature of creativity, openness, and continual responsibility. His descriptions of unfinalizeability, polyphony, spirit, loophole, soul, and rhythm help us see how creativity, openness, and continual responsibility are necessary, and how some psychological theories seem to erase them from the human experience. Creativity, when examined under the microscope of traditional psychological science, becomes quite impossible. Psychology assigns causal labels to behaviors, believing such behaviors spring only from unconscious forces, past influences, schematic processing, or systemic dynamics (Rychlak, 1981). Once we define an action in causal terms, it is no longer a creative action, but a mechanical reaction to these forces that shape or cause it. No force of will or engagement of meaning took place to create it; the action is merely a product of some empirically explained cause (Morson & Emerson, 1990).

From a dialogic perspective, however, creativity is genuine. When we write a poem, a story, or even this chapter, we constantly wrestle over the right words to choose. The lessons in writing and the words of Bakhtin are like voices in our heads, coming together with our dominant dialogic stance to develop this chapter. When writing is truly creative, all of the voices and perspectives combine to produce something that no single perspective could offer alone. The process of the spirit brings about such signs of creativity as heartfelt discussion, writing, sculpture, painting, music, dance, and theater. It is creativity—this polyphonic nature of the spirit and the interchange of soul with others—that allows us to grow, develop, and creatively change in an ongoing and gloriously unfinalizeable fashion. It is through this possibility of creativity that change can occur in our thoughts, feelings, and behaviors, even in very difficult settings.

Openness is another key item that psychological science tends to overlook or attempt to explain away. Like creativity, if we assign causal finalization to human thought and behavior, it is never open, never creatively available for change. The very notion that biological or unconscious forces cause our behavior and that we can change those behaviors with talk therapy, is quite paradoxical at best. If defining the causes of our thoughts and behaviors finalizes them, then we cannot be open to new ideas because the cause of our behavior has already determined our perspective. From a dialogic stance, however, our spirit is always engaging polyphonically with the soul offered to us by others, and that, by definition, entails openness and engagement with new ways of thinking. Problems arise when openness is limited because we may not hear the new perspective either intra- or inter-psychically, leaving us trapped in our own misery and limited point of view. It takes great skill to engage with someone who is mostly closed, in order to provide the possibility of creative interchange.

In addition to openness, one of the most important aspects of the dialogical approach when working with clients is the idea of continual responsibility (Morson & Emerson, 1990). This responsibility towards self and others is often entirely absent in the utilization of psychological science to explain human thought and behavior. If our unconscious, environment, or physiology has already caused and finalized our behavior, then we are, in essence, trapped. We cannot go outside the cause of our behavior to fix it. Hence, we are not responsible for our behavior. If a person is raised in a household characterized by brutal violence, and this person grows up to be a rapacious serial killer, a psychological scientist might explain that the earlier environment caused the criminal behavior. In this view, the person is not responsible for their behavior because it shifts the blame to the earlier environment. By doing so, however, it does not question why others raised in brutal environments grow up to be less violent or nonviolent. From the dialogic perspective, on the other hand, we are always responsible for our actions because through the course of life we engage with many different perspectives that we use to creatively form a path for ourselves. Our past does not determine us wholly; we can grow from the bonds of our past by remaining open to the perspectives of others, creatively integrating and processing the meaning in our lives spiritually, and by accepting the responsibility for ourselves.

However, continual responsibility entails more than an individualistic need to be responsible for our own actions and change. It also means that we are intimately connected to others in the web of meaning of our world. In the ongoing interchange of soul to spirit, we find that we are co-creators of meaning in our dialogues, offering differing views about the topic at hand, as well as differing perspectives on each other. Because our gifts of soul to others play such a large role in their lives, it seems wise that we carefully choose how we treat others and what we say. If we continually tell other people disparaging things about them, they may incorporate what we say into their thoughts about themselves. In the lives of many of our clients in a correctional setting, they have entire lifetimes of disparaging perspectives echoing through their souls polyphonically. From the Bakhtinian perspective, we are not only our own keepers, so to speak, but our brothers' keepers as well.

Brief Theory Summary

Throughout this chapter, we have described a new model for understanding human thought and behavior. It is a model that entails creativity, openness, and continual responsibility as three of its core features. Bakhtin's argument that we are unfinalizeable beings, each co-constituting meaning in our shared life and world makes all of these features possible. We engage with the world both in occurrent and available modes, becoming one, then detaching and examining ourselves in our world. The core principle of Bakhtin's theory is polyphonic dialogue. Polyphonic dialogue entails occurrent engagement with others in a co-creation of meaning, a dialogue that can occur intra- as well as interpsychically. The spirit is the I-for-myself, the ultimate semantic core of the personality, the basis from which we speak and engage in meaning in our world. It is an intrapsychic, open-ended dialogue that is always creatively growing. The spirit's openness is called the loophole, the experienced moment outside of time and context that offers ground to what the ongoing dialogue creates.

We cannot know one another spirit to spirit, so we communicate with others through the soul, the momentarily finalized view of the other that we offer them. When others offer us the gift of soul dialogically, we co-create our being with them, in the space where spirit and soul intersect. There is danger, however, in offering a soul to another who has no room for unfinalizeability. If we finalize others, we rob them of their essence of self, their capacity for creative change. They may be tempted to give their lives over to a predetermined pattern, a rhythm that takes the anxiety out of risking creative change. Or, they may become pretenders, living their lives according to how they believe others see them, according to how they assume others would tell them how to think, act, and feel. This interchange of soul to spirit indicates how each individual is, in a way, responsible to the individuals around them, each sharing an ethical base of common understanding.

Implications for Therapy within a Correctional Institution

Individuals within a correctional institution have unique needs; many wonder what drives individuals to make certain choices in their lives. There are many psychological theories that seek to explain why humans hurt themselves, others, and society. Some argue that such behaviors are caused by chaotic environments of abuse or neglect. They might theorize that appropriate attachments were not developed, and the individual thus has difficulty connecting to others and having meaningful relationships. This could set the stage for a lack of empathy and regard for others, and the inability to engage in the human bonding experience. Biological compulsions are another plausible explanation. Certain genetic coding can influence an individual by providing a predisposition for crime or disregard for others. According to the diathesis stress model, stressful events such as abuse would trigger this predisposition with unfortunate consequences. Lastly, libidinal urges demanding aggressive release or an unrepressed id could cause an individual to engage in criminal activity. All of these explanations are causal, and inherently finalize human behavior. From the dialogic perspective, we can understand distress in terms that do not entail hard causal explanations and still allow for creativity and change, providing us a unique framework for working with those whom society has labeled "uncurable."

One of the authors, Mark Green, worked as a therapist with a client in a state maximum security prison who had been convicted of felony drug trafficking. The client had been diagnosed with antisocial personality disorder, yet as Green learned his story, he saw a dramatically different picture than a stereotypical antisocial drug dealer. Zeke (not his real name) had been involved in gang activity since he was seven years old. He was intensely loyal to his gang and had always followed the rules he had learned growing up in a gang. In Zeke's first session with Green, Zeke explained that he had been falsely accused. He said that he had committed crimes in the past similar to the one for which he was convicted, but that he was innocent of this conviction. He still took some responsibility because he knew that if he had not been so involved with the drug community, he would not have been in a position to be accused at all. When he was arrested, he refused to give the name of the actual person who committed the crime, so the prosecution proceeded with his case in an effort to get him to provide the real name. He was eventually convicted and sentenced to 20 years in prison. When Green met Zeke, he had served three years and was beginning to question his decision to protect his friend. While he still insisted that he could not "snitch," he was beginning to realize that if he stayed in prison for as long as he was sentenced to be, he would not see his two children until they were grown. His daughter's mother had pointed out to him that by being loyal to his friend, he was failing to be loyal to his own daughter. This perspective was one he had not seen before, and it led him to an internal crisis. He did not know how to reconcile these conflicting loyalties.

Green conceptualized his work with Zeke from a dialogical perspective, which allowed Green to avoid either finalizing or disengaging from Zeke, as others had most likely done in the past. Green immediately saw that Zeke was struggling to reconcile different voices and unique perspectives in a polyphonic engagement with his current situation. He had clearly lived a life full of crime, but rather than labeling his behavior as antisocial, Zeke was encouraged to examine the pro-social context in which much of his behavior had occurred. In most cases, the crimes he had committed were demonstrations of great loyalty and sacrifice. This perspective, of course, had to be balanced with the fact that he was causing harm to a larger society while serving his own smaller society, but witnessing this openness was liberating to Zeke.

Another sense of balance was important as Green began to engage with Zeke's attempts to explore his conflicted loyalties. Even in dialogue we must retain our outsideness, for the act of relating to another entails a reassumption and reconfirmation of ourselves and the other during an encounter. Rather than fuse emotionally with our clients, together we can creatively produce something new and valuable. As Bakhtin noted, "I experience [another's suffering] precisely as *his* suffering, in the category of the other, and my reaction to him is not a cry of pain but a word of consolation and a gesture of assistance" (cited in Morson & Emerson, 1990, p. 185, emphasis in original). We can use our outsideness to offer a perspective of the clients in a way that they may not have seen or may not have known was possible.

During their sessions, Green began to add a new voice to Zeke's polyphony, a voice offering new hope and a different perspective. Green's voice remained with Zeke each time the sessions ended and he returned to his cell, and the voice began to grow more dominant with each meeting because Zeke became more open. He appreciated Green's refusal to finalize him as "criminal" or "antisocial."

It is much more difficult to work with clients who have given themselves over to rhythm or become pretenders during their incarceration. It is through openness and dialogue that we can encourage change, soul to spirit. If a person is closed to that interaction, no such engagement can take place. This requires a greater amount of patience on the part of the therapist. With clients who have given themselves over to rhythm, slowing them down and offering consistent counter-perspectives can encourage them to return to the process of creativity, to once again find their own spirits. The therapist should prepare to engage in different discourses if the client is too resistant to creativity, bringing back a sense of rhythm to comfort against the overwhelming feelings that may loom if the future is left open-ended. Gradually, as the client broadens his own perspective, he will be better able to engage with life occurrently and participate in dialogue once more.

In addition to these suggestions for applying Bakhtin's ideas to therapy, there are two more important points which are logical outgrowths of the dialogical stance. The first is that influence goes both ways, not just from therapist to client but from client to therapist as well. This follows the relational models posited by other existential and interpersonal theorists (Bugenthal & Sterling, 1995; Teyber, 1997). Unfortunately, this approach may cause apprehension among some counselors and therapists, because it removes part of their "expert" status. In reality, only the individual in question is an expert on his or her own life. The therapist's role, after developing sufficient skill in dialogic counseling, is to openly engage in dialogue, and to know how best to communicate, empathize, and promote creative change. Such training is invaluable in our service to the client. The other ramification of this theory is a breakdown of the individualism so rampant in our society. Some critical writers talk about the growing individualism in our society, causing us to be self-focused, self-centered, and ultimately perhaps self-destructive (Richardson, Fowers, & Guignon, 1999). Unfortunately, therapy and psychology may in some cases be perpetuating the individualism and self-focus that is causing great interpersonal distance in our society (Fancher, 1995). From the dialogical perspective, personal responsibility is a constant requirement, as is responsibility to another. Such a view in counseling and throughout the mental health care system may help to reverse the trend, and help people to grow increasingly connected.

In summary, the dialogic theory Bakhtin advocated is highly consistent both in theory and in practice. It acknowledges and describes the value base from which people behave in embedded ways in their life world. Problems also arise dialogically, when people adopt meanings without remaining open to future dialogic engagement or creative change. Hence, a client can fix dialogic problems dialogically by connecting in a soul to spirit interaction with a therapist or counselor, opening up new realms of meaning greater than those possible to either therapist or client alone.

Conclusion

In this chapter we have discussed some of Bakhtin's critiques of the field of scientific psychology, beginning with his reconceptualization of what it means to be human, and describing how he argues that some theories in psychology may detract from humanity. We also described the necessity for openness, continual responsibility, and creativity in personality, and how we can broaden a psychological or therapeutic theory by those ideas. We pointed out the importance of others and embeddedness in a common ground of meaning, and how the spirit's engagement with the soul is vital for continual growth on a private and interpersonal level. Ethical problems in psychology were addressed from a Bakhtinian perspective, namely questioning the lack of moral responsibility in the field, and also the harm caused by finalizing clients.

Examining correctional counseling from this perspective makes the implications of these ideas clear. It permits us to engage with our clients in a beneficent manner, to acknowledge their humanity and their own capacity to change. By thinking dialogically ourselves, we inhabit our own space in the therapy frame with a great deal of integrity, reaching out to assist the other and to stay human with them, even when they do not behave humanely towards themselves or other people. By thinking dialogically we better understand the importance of others in our lives, not only because of what they do for us, but because of the meaning they themselves have in our lives and the lives of others. Bakhtin offers many important insights for our ever-changing field, and offers new ways to help not only clients in a correctional setting, but also a society that grows more fragmented and disconnected.

References

Bakhtin, M. M. (1995). *Toward a philosophy of the act* (V. Liapunov, Trans.; V. Liapunov & M. Holquist, Eds.). Austin: University of Texas Press.

Bugenthal, J. F. T., & Sterling, M. M. (1995). Existential-humanistic psychotherapy: New perspectives. In A. S. Gurman & S. B. Messer (Eds.), *Essential psychotherapies: Theory and practice* (pp. 226–260). New York: Guilford.

Cushman, P. (1995). *Constructing the self, constructing America: A cultural history of psychotherapy.* Reading, MA: Addison-Wesley.

Dreyfus, H. L. (1991). *Being-in-the-world: A commentary on Division 1 of Heidegger's Being and Time.* Cambridge, MA: MIT Press.

Epstein, S. (1983). The stability of behavior across time and situations. In R. Zucker, J. Aronoff, & A. I. Rabin (Eds.), *Personality and the prediction of behavior* (p. 209–268). San Diego: Academic Press.

Fancher, R. T. (1995). *Cultures of healing: Correcting the image of American mental health care.* New York: W. H. Freeman.

Freud, S. (1964). An outline of psychoanalysis. In J. Strachey (Ed. and Trans.), *The standard edition of the complete psychological works of Sig-*

mund Freud (Vol. 23, pp. 137–207). London: Hogarth. (Original work published 1940)

Heidegger, M. (1962). *Being and time* (J. Macquarrie & E. Robinson, Trans.). New York: Harper & Row. (Original work published 1927)

Morson, G. S., & Emerson, C. (1990). *Mikhail Bakhtin: Creation of a prosaics*. Palo Alto, CA: Stanford University Press.

Myers, D. G. (1999). *Exploring psychology*. New York: Worth.

Richardson, F. C., Fowers, B. J., & Guignon, C. B. (1999). *Re-envisioning psychology: Moral dimensions of theory and practice*. San Francisco: Jossey-Bass.

Rychlak, J. F. (1981). *Introduction to personality and psychotherapy: A theory-construction approach*. Boston: Houghton Mifflin.

Slife, B. D., & Williams, R. N. (1995). *What's behind the research? Discovering hidden assumptions in the behavioral sciences*. Thousand Oaks, CA: Sage.

Teyber, E. (1997). *Interpersonal processes in psychotherapy: A relational approach*. Pacific Grove, CA: Brooks/Cole.

CHAPTER SIX

Transforming Corrections through Psychological Jurisprudence: A Preliminary Review and Critique of Theory

Bruce A. Arrigo, University of North Carolina, Charlotte

Introduction

Despite sustained efforts to grow the theory-sensitive field of psychological jurisprudence (see, e.g., Arrigo, 2002, 2003a, 2003b, 2004a; Arrigo & Fox, in press; Fox, 2001; Shon & Arrigo, 2006; Williams & Arrigo, 2002), its philosophical roots remain mostly under-developed (Arrigo, 2004b). One facet of this development includes the correctional field (Maruna, 2001; Maruna & Immarigeon, 2004; Ward & Maruna, 2007) and its existential, phenomenological, and postmodern strains of analysis (Arrigo, 2007; Arrigo & Williams, in press). Central to this critique are the manifold contexts in which the mutuality of human agency and social structure is engulfed in a constitutive dialectical process whereby harms of reduction (denials to one's being) and harms of repression (denials to one's becoming) undergo cyclical and recursive reification (Arrigo, Milovanovic, & Schehr, 2005; Henry & Milovanovic, 1996). Understood as the "pains of imprisonment" phenomenon (Arrigo & Milovanovic, 2009), these harms draw attention to the systemic pathology (Fromm, 1941/1994) that permeates human social interaction and renders as "captive" all those who essentialize the logic and language of penology. This includes the kept, their keepers (correctional workers), agents of the prison industrial complex (correctional administrators, government officials, policy analysts/strategists), and the punitive general public.

This chapter examines the relevance of a critically-animated psychological jurisprudence for the purpose of furthering a much needed transformation within the domain of corrections. The proposed metamorphosis argues that panoptic power (Foucault, 1965, 1977), technologized culture (Baudrillard, 1983a, 1983b), negative freedom (Fromm, 1941/1994), the metaphysics of presence (Derrida, 1977, 1978), the desiring subject as lack (Lacan, 1977, 1981), and molar larval rigidities, especially the process of subjectification (Deleuze, 1983; Deleuze & Guattari, 1983, 1987) can be displaced wherein an "overcoming" in reflection, discourse, and action materializes (Nietzsche, 1888/1968). This is a mutating and evolving will to power that takes hold provisionally, positionally, and relationally (Arrigo et al., 2005). The discursive work of deterritorialization and reterritorialization is how the recovering subject (being) and the transforming subject (becoming) emerge in the socius (SOCIETY + I + US) (Deleuze & Guattari, 1983), such that the "criminological stranger" is mobilized and activated (Arrigo & Milovanovic, 2009). Indeed, this engaged re-authoring of the self and the social again and anew is how the sorely needed "revolution" in penology is made that much more realizable.

To address these concerns, this chapter is divided into two substantive parts. First, exposition on a critical psychological jurisprudence in the correctional realm is delineated. This theoretical work describes the constitutive features of the criminological stranger and specifies how the agency/structure duality can be reconfigured. Moreover, as a correctional practice designed to overcome the pains of imprisonment phenomenon, a radicalized desistance or "trans-desistance" strategy in penology is outlined. This strategy is juxtaposed against the two predominant modernist approaches employed in the correction field: the "deficit" and "desistance" models, respectively. Second, the contexts in which this overall radical reconceptualization is addressed in the other theoretical chapters of this book are preliminarily reviewed. To this extent, then, the examination and critique here endeavors to extend and deepen the critical theorizing needed to significantly transform the field of corrections.

Critical Psychological Jurisprudence, the Criminological Stranger, and the Trans-Desistance Model

Several protean forces emanating from the constitutive dialectics of the agency/structure duality are responsible for the pains of imprisonment phenomenon. The philosophic and psychoanalytic dimensions of these forces have been delineated as the cultural identity of modernist penology (Arrigo & Milovanovic, 2009). Interpreted as the "criminology of the shadow" (e.g., Arrigo, 2008; Arrigo & Williams, in press), both the breadth and depth of how molar (rather than molecular) dynamics reduce/repress (i.e., capture) multiplicities in nominal, static form and subsequently undergo reification have been cogently examined (Arrigo & Milovanovic, 2009). The self and the social are rendered a mere fiction; textual artifacts of simulated hyper-reality (Baudrillard, 1983a); the hermeneutics of suspicions and bio-power (Foucault, 1977); the abstract machines of the control society, including Oedipal and capital logic (Deleuze, 1995); the terror-inducing mechanisms of escape from materialist existence (Fromm, 1941/1994); the divided or de-centered subject of the "symbolic order" (Lacan, 1977); and the logo-centrism of Western thought (Derrida, 1978).

In the realm of contemporary penology, these forces reciprocally and simultaneously sustain as legitimate the co-production (human agency/social structure) of correctional reality. Indeed, the recursive activities of the criminological shadow explain how human flourishing and becoming for *all* concerned are reduced and repressed. This is how the pains of imprisonment phenomenon cultivates and perpetuates the normalization of violence (Arrigo & Milovanovic, 2009). This is violence in which, among other things, difference is pathologized, the body is territorialized, and knowledge/truth is homogenized. All that remains is docility and automaton conformity in which the State's psychology of mass governance regulates the duality of the self and the social culturally, materially, linguistically, and symbolically.

In response to the pains of imprisonment phenomenon, the criminological shadow, and the normalization of violence, a trans-desistance model steeped in the logic of the criminology of the stranger is posited. Pivotal to this conceptualization is the reconstitution of the socius such that the dynamic, mutually interdependent, co-productive relationship between human agency and social structure transcends the criminological shadow, always already in non-hierarchical and non-linear ways (e.g., Patton, 2000). However, before depicting this logic in both diagrammatic and narrative form, some review of the two prevailing modernist correctional models, as well as the radicalized model proposed to overcome the limitations of both, warrants attention.

On the Deficit and Desistance Correctional Models: A Brief Review

The prevailing paradigm in contemporary corrections is the "deficit model." It addresses the offender's failures, the need to punish transgressors, and "going straight" (e.g., Maruna, 2001; Ward & Maruna, 2007). It focuses on the singularity of the event, on unilaterally constructed plans (operative while incarcerated and in release plans), on the behavioral surface of bodies, and on creating docility (Arrigo & Milovanovic, 2009). Collectively, these activities are "geared toward recognizing and responding to failure" (Halsey, 2006, p. 167). Elsewhere, Halsey (2008) compellingly elaborates on this point:

> Young men in custody generally are not permitted, let alone expected, to show initiative or take anything approaching a meaningful degree of responsibility for their daily lives. Instead, things are done to them and for them and only very rarely with them (and with their consent). In this sense, inmates are taught to react rather than act. They are taught to respond rather than initiate. They are taught what to think rather than to consider their own thoughts and fears as natural and legitimate. (p. 1227)

In short, the deficit model fosters "learned helplessness" in which subjects are passive, anonymous, and vanquished (Arrigo & Takahashi, 2006, 2008). This logic is consistent with Deleuze and Guattari's (1987) subjectification thesis.[1] Everyday connective-disjunctive-conjunctive syntheses foster a recoiling of the individual. The subject of the statement reverts into the subject of enunciation. This reconstituted person is compatible with the noological image (the representation of/in thought) generated by conventional "law and order" de-

---

1. Following Deleuze and Guattari (1983, 1987), desire's natural state is to make connections, to expand its capacities. Similar to the Lacanian version of subjectivity, Deleuze and Guattari asserted that the self was caught in symbolic play, arising after three syntheses (connective, dealing with libidinal investments; disjunctive, dealing with recording; and conjunctive, dealing with consumption). The subject appears at a conjunctive synthesis: "So that was me!" "The subject emerges only as an after-effect of the selections made by desire among various disjunctive and connective syntheses, not as the agent of selection" (Holland, 1999, p. 33; Massumi, 1992, pp. 75–76). This is a passive synthesis. Moreover, the "I" that emerges, much like in Lacan's (1977) schematization, often finds itself captured in nominal forms; for Lacan, in the "discourse of the master" and "university"; for Deleuze and Guattari, in particular regimes of signs replete with "order words" (akin to Lacan's master signifiers) that are molar and majoritarian, rather than molecular and minoritarian.

cision-making practices and their agents who repetitively reify the control society (e.g., Banks, in press; Mauer & Chesney-Lind, 2003).

A second modernist framework in corrections is the "desistance model" (e.g., Farrall & Calverley, 2006; Maruna & Immarigeon, 2004). This framework amounts to something of a paradigmatic shift in the meaning of reintegration or community reentry for the post-custodial subject. The desistance model draws support from already existing forms of recovery. Unlike the deficit model and its focus on needs-based intervention, the desistance approach acknowledges that a dynamic—rather than a linear—process[2] best exemplifies the overall reintegrative experience. Over time, the ex-incarcerate gradually refrains from investing in harm to others or to one's self. The desistance model endeavors to strike a balance between the "good lives" philosophy of pro-social behavior (e.g., Ward & Maruna, 2007; Whitehead, Ward, & Collie, 2007) and the normative, system-sustaining strategy of reducing/avoiding risk (e.g., Arrigo, 2007; Garland, 2001).

According to proponents of desistance theory, the purpose of the strategy is to maximize one's "social capital" (Farrall, 2004). In this instance, growing social capital refers to such things as increasing one's commitment to work, establishing the presence of a stable family structure, promoting hope (American/British "dream"), and initiating re-entry based on the core values of community justice (Taxman, Young, & Byrne, 2004). This approach is consistent with restorative justice theorizing, programming, and policy (e.g., Braithwaite, 1989; Sullivan & Tifft, 2005). The reintegration strategy emanating from the desistance model improves prospects for crime abatement and "restores" the ex-offender within civil society (Strang & Braithwaite, 2005). In this model, the noological image that pervades the social consciousness is not about "going straight"; rather, it is about "going crooked" and establishing correctional treatment mechanisms that undermine or undo the likelihood of this occurrence (Arrigo & Milovanovic, 2009).

The Trans-Desistance Model: An Overview

A third framework builds on the desistance approach; however, its orientation is decidedly more radical (constitutive/postmodern) in its logic and direction. This is the "trans-desistance model." Much like the desistance strategy, the trans-desistance approach is concerned with prison and post-prison connectivity. Unlike the desistance model in corrections, the proposed radical

---

2. Indeed, it is more rhizomatic in character (Deleuze & Guattari, 1987).

framework questions the core categories endorsed by desistance theory advocates. In particular, this would include the nature of employment under capitalism, the nature of the nuclear family, and the political economic bases on which hope, dreams, and collective aspirations are generated (Arrigo & Milovanovic, 2009). These activities promote recovery in being but only under conditions that are consistent with prevailing social norms. Moreover, critical pathways to becoming remain altogether unaddressed. A trans-desistance model endeavors to overcome both of these limitations.

According to Halsey (2006), the post-released typically find themselves ensnarled in the tensions of a hope-despair dynamic. He notes that in far too many instances the family structure simply does not exist for the former incarcerate. Moreover, when it does, it is composed of social-psychological and material forces that often affirm hopelessness and despair. As such, the "pains of release," must be juxtaposed against the "pains of imprisonment" and the manner in which both are recursively sustained. Halsey's (2006, 2008) response to these conditions is a call to mobilize the body, to foster active lines of flight, and to form symmetry-breaking flows, consistent with the insights of Deleuze, Guattari, and Nietzsche.

Halsey (2006) maintains that Deleuze and Guattari's (1987) notion of desire as flow (i.e., production) can be applied to criminality. Desire is a flow, much as is recidivism.[3] Indeed, as Halsey (2006, p. 162) explains it, " ... recidivism ... has most often been dealt with as if it were an administrative event to be managed as opposed to a lived and therefore inherently unpredictable process." In the correctional realm, desire has been "captured" by administrative categories, not the realities of those entering, leaving, and returning to prison in a cyclical fashion (e.g., Maruna, 2001). In order to respond to these realities, the mobilization of the body and its dynamic capabilities must be

---

3. A "flow" of energy along a particular pathway and not another can be seen as a "line of flight." One form of this is repetition of the same, following what fixed axioms dictate. Another flow of energy consists of lines of opposition, mutation, and transformation. Recidivism is a flow; it follows the presuppositions built into the various abstract machines that are the core of its multi-level and intersecting assemblages. Becoming is a flow; it is a continuous process of change and transformation. It is not rooted in fixed axiomatics. The disjunctive synthesis organizes energy-matter flows on the body and the socius. Savagery, despotism, and capitalism each encourage a particular flow of energy-matter. For example, commodity-fetishism as an abstract machine produces exchange-value. This is the transformation of energy-matter from use-vale to an abstraction that takes a life of its own and becomes a core manufacturer in the axiomatics of capital logic. On the other hand, schizoanalysis suggests flows that are becoming in form: indeterminate, fluid, nomadic, and mutating.

thoroughly considered (Arrigo & Milovanovic, 2009).⁴ This is an effort to re-imagine and to re-ontologize the post-custodial citizen in a non-static, non-linear fashion. Indeed, following Halsey's (2006) perceptive application of Deleuze and Guattari (1983, 1987) in the correctional domain, the ex-incarcerate must be regarded as a multiplicity rather than as a subject dwelling only within the limiting constrains of the release plan and its corresponding discourse of control.

The culture of control that engulfs the post-custodial citizen resonates as well with all others subject to the pains of imprisonment phenomenon, the criminology of the shadow, and the normalization of violence (Arrigo & Milovanovic, 2009). Halsey (2006) argues further that the various correctional personnel and policy-makers of the penal system must be re-conceptualized, consistent with the insights of Deleuze and Guattari (1983, 1987); so, too, must managers and administrators of the prison edifice as well as the general public that insists on punitive, reactive interventions. They all must be noologically re-constituted. These groups (and the individuals that compose them) are "linked to processes, contexts, and events occurring beyond yet contiguous with each [and every] person" (Halsey, 2006, p. 172). "Variables" or "factors" (e.g., gender, sexual orientation, race, class) prominently essentialized in the contemporary penological canon must be deconstructed along the lines proposed by Derrida (1977, 1978). Interpreting these categories as static, fixed, and rigid affirms prevailing system-maintaining renditions of what "is" without offering any critical engagement of what "could be." Moreover, these closed categories must be seen as concepts (molar forms) rooted in assemblages representing a narrowly defined socius. In short, what is missing are the imminent forces of deterritorialization, of desires captured in one set of assemblages rather than another, of the body and its multiple forms of expression, only some aspects of which are allowed materialization (Arrigo & Milovanovic, 2009). These replacement forms of expression remain as the Lacanian lack,

---

4. The ex-offender's "release plan" is illustrative of this point. Its language reflects a fixed, closed, and rigid cataloguing of rules, responsibilities, prohibitions, and schedules. How does the plan's logic comport with the desires of the newly released custodial subject? Halsey's (2006, p. 164) response is illuminating: "Young men on conditional release desire to be young men—to be able to drink, relax, have a good time, sit around with friends, stay up late, and to choose whether they will participate in this or that programme." When ex-incarcerates are released from custody, they "continue to offend because that is what works best for them relative to the milieus they inhabit" (Halsey, 2006, p. 166). As emblematic of the deficit model of prison release, the plan itself focuses principally on monitoring potential failures or deficiencies, not on dynamics or flows that may lead to desistance (Arrigo & Milovanovic, 2009; Halsey, 2006).

the criminological stranger, awaiting mobilization and embodiment (Lacan, 1977).

What needs to be theorized, then, is a radicalized version of desistance theory, a trans-desistance model of corrections. This is a critical theory that moves beyond the (often unintended) linearity and hierarchy of entrenched system-sustaining logic. This critical theory would include energy investments (productive flows) away from the axiomatics of capital and Oedipal logic. Rehabilitating or restoring the ex-offender to some fixed, certain, or pre-determined endpoint mostly under-values process, contradiction, non-linearity, spontaneity, the nature of choice, absurdity, and the hope-despair dynamic that the post-custodial citizen confronts daily. Indeed, without something more, only the molar structure is reconstituted in desistance theory. This is a reaffirmation of and a recovery in being; however, it is not a transmutation of or a transformation in becoming. Both are needed to establish a will to power, to overcoming the criminological shadow.

The proposed trans-desistance theory advocates for an end to the recursively constructed thoughts and actions that repeatedly reify the reality of prisons. What must change are the pivotal situations themselves that define the agency/structure duality that nurtures and grows the pains of imprisonment thesis. To instigate this change, opportunities for *disruption* are needed (Halsey, 2008). The penal-assemblage must be creatively and pragmatically challenged in order that molecular lines of flight become dominant over molar, always already in provisional, positional, and relational ways (Arrigo & Milovanovic, 2009). This entails the construction of a narrative by those struggling to refrain from criminality that does not itself give ascendancy to existing regimes of signs. These are signs (order words) that are consistent with the "discourse of the master" (Lacan, 1977). A Hegelian reaction-negation dynamic here does not overcome the lack the ex-incarcerate experiences through a discourse that is a stand-in for the subject's interiorized desire.

Moreover, the strategy of deterritorialization (which tends toward the molecular) must be applied to the conception of the family; the "American" dream (e.g., hope, opportunity); the nature of employment; and the experience of identity and recovery. The logic of capital and Oedipal must be understood and situated within a historically contingent socius. Alternative configurations or mutations of the same (reterritorialization) must be articulated, enacted, and endorsed if the stranger's transformative becoming is to be more completely realizable in non-recursive ways (Arrigo & Milovanovic, 2009).

These genealogical activities, as dimensions of a trans-desistance model in corrections, help deconstruct or de-center the (mostly unreflective) capture of desire that sustains as legitimate the pains of imprisonment, the criminological shadow, and the normalization of violence. This desire—whether harnessed by/for the kept, their keepers, their managers, or their spectators (the general public)—is reduced/repressed within the nuclear family via Oedipus, and under capitalism via its various embedded abstract machines (e.g., panopticism, commodity fetishism, logocentrism). Lacan's (e.g., 1977, 1981, and especially 1991) psycho-semiotic insights specify how the subject's "lack" or *pas tout(e)* (the not-all) is manufactured such that circumscribed desire materializes. This is made most evident through the "discourse of the master" and the signifiers/signifieds that it sustains, consistent with the prevailing political-economic order. To this extent, Lacan's formulations significantly clarify the intra-psychic and interpersonal facets of the criminological shadow in penology. However, the material side of this process remains largely underdeveloped.

The seminal contributions of Deleuze and Guattari amplify the work of Lacan in that their observations represent a critically-animated basis to decode the interconnection of social and libidinal production. Moreover, through their engaged strategy of schizoanalysis (deterritorialization/reterritorialization), the development and deployment of active forces and molecular structures that overcome molar forms and reactive lines of flight are made that much more identifiable. Thus, the theorizing of Deleuze and Guattari (along with others) provides a potent transition from the silencing of the subject's being (as embodied in the criminological shadow) to the emergence of the subject's becoming (as personified in the criminological stranger) (Arrigo & Milovanovic, 2009).

Diagram 6.1 depicts that processes by which the stranger is resuscitated in non-hierarchical (i.e., contingent, relational, positional) fashion.[5] This depiction constitutes a vision of change; it is not a totalizing blueprint for reform. It implicates the ex-incarcerate, those who serve as keepers of the kept, the general public, and all others who reconstitute and legitimize the pains of imprisonment/release recursive cycle, the criminological stranger, and the normalization of violence. In short, Diagram 6.1 proposes a reconceptualization in which the subject is liberated from the agency/structure duality that repetitively fosters penal harm, essentializes prison discourse, and reifies the correctional edifice that stands above and is informed by both.

In the proposed schema, a replacement socius is envisioned. This replacement socius is akin to a "permanent revolution" (Deleuze & Guattari, 1983, 1987; Holland, 1999) where the molar is dislodged, destabilized, and replaced

---

5. See Appendix for an explanation of the symbols for Diagram 6.1.

Diagram 6.1: The Criminological Stranger and the Trans-Desistance Model

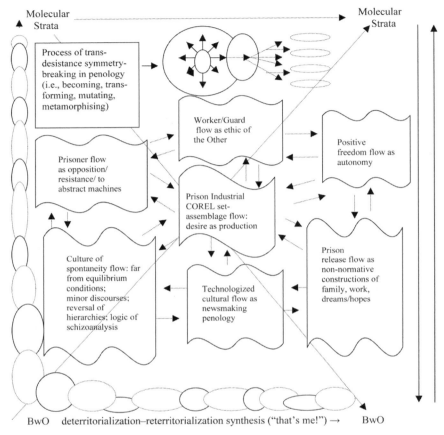

(Adapted from Arrigo & Milovanovic, 2009)

with the molecular. The molecular strata convey non-static movement, the presence of spontaneity and fluidity, openness to change, randomness, and active forces.[6] The dotted line situated from the upper left-hand to the upper right-hand of the diagram depicts this movement. At the agency level is the

---

6. Molecular forms as dissipative structures are much more prevalent in far-from-equilibrium conditions, as dynamic systems theory (chaos theory) suggests. Molar forms, such as bureaucracies, are more prevalent in static (homeostatic) conditions. In part, the logic of non-linear, dynamical systems theory informs the ensuing critique. For recent applications of this logic in criminology, see Arrigo and Barrett (2008).

Symbols for Diagram 6.1

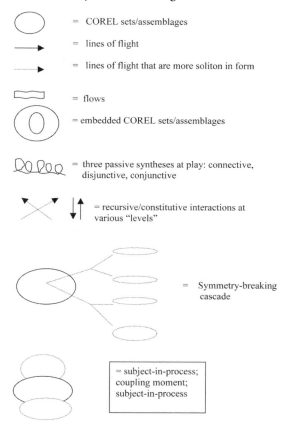

= COREL sets/assemblages

= lines of flight

= lines of flight that are more soliton in form

= flows

= embedded COREL sets/assemblages

= three passive syntheses at play: connective, disjunctive, conjunctive

= recursive/constitutive interactions at various "levels"

= Symmetry-breaking cascade

= subject-in-process; coupling moment; subject-in-process

body-without-organs (BwO).[7] In the trans-desistance formulation, the person is a subject-in-process (Kristeva, 1984): transparent, in flux, mutating, and experiencing various flows, speeds, and threshold levels. This is depicted by the dotted circles and their differing sizes.

Further, unlike a Deleuzian-Guattarian conjunctive synthesis in which the person recoils (is the subject of enunciation), the transforming subject experiences fleeting epiphanies (Giddens, 1984), a "flash of light" (Deleuze, 1988),

---

7. This concept is borrowed from Artaud (see Sontag, 1988). The body is perceived as a field of intensities, of flows, of differing speeds, of various threshold levels where perturbations (changing inputs) produce bifurcations, symmetry-breaking, and an interruption of repetition.

a "poetic spark" (Lacan, 1977), contingent universalities, (Butler, 1993), and experimental/pragmatic insights (Rorty, 1989; Unger, 1987). These awarenesses provide the basis of a temporary, though incomplete, sense of one's identity: an evolving self. These transitory, though lucid, instances entail the strategic use of deterritorialization and reterritorialization. These techniques resist and de-center molar, axiomatic categories of sense-making (the passive syntheses in which gender/race/class "variables" are constructed; i.e., the process of subjectification), while simultaneously embracing, extolling, and celebrating molecular intensities (active lines of flights, minor literatures, schizoanalysis). This engaged re-working of the self, of both continuously displacing and re-defining one's authorship, is termed a "coupling moment" (Arrigo & Milovanovic, 2009). These moments emerge from the subject-in-process in which the activities of deterritorialization and reterritorialization occur. In Diagram 6.1 they are depicted by the solid circles that further specify the conceptualization of human agency as becoming. Their differing shapes convey the variable impact each has on a person's evolution. Thus, as a dimension of a radicalized transdesistance theory, the subject's mutating identity (i.e., as correctional worker, prison administrator, the public at large, and incarcerate), depends on the activities of deconstruction/reconstruction, of disassembling and reassembling the self. This representation of human agency (as a subject-in-process in which coupling moments materialize) extends from the molecular strata to the BwO as well as from the BwO at one time versus another.

The dynamic process of symmetry-breaking is prominently featured in Diagram 6.1. As conceptualized in the schema, a COREL (constitutive-relational) set-assemblage flow begins with molar rigidities. Statistical regularities, organizational closure, order-words, and reactionary forces dominate. This is depicted by the embedded COREL set-assemblage (middle-top of diagram) in which various static lines of flight are featured where point and cyclical attractors prevail. The pains of imprisonment, the pains of release, and the normalization of violence prevail in a cyclical, crystallized fashion, reenacted and reified by all those who essentialize the prison form.

However, as the socius experiences molecular intensities contributing to human agents undergoing transformations (as subjects-in-process prone to coupling moments), a symmetry-breaking cascade begins to take form. This cascade represents a transition from what is (being) to what could be (becoming). It surfaces from the intersection of various COREL set-assemblages in which dynamic flows, varying intensities, differential speeds, and fluctuating threshold levels are both mobilized and activated. In Diagram 6.1 this is depicted by an active line of flight moving to the right that perturbs a neighboring COREL set-assemblage otherwise resting at some equilibrium state with its characteristic point or limit attractor. In penology, examples of equilibrium or status quo conditions that result in delimited outcomes are manifold (e.g., routine drills/inspections by correctional staff, standard release plans for probationers/parolees, maintenance of sentencing guidelines by judges, sustained public support for capital punishment). However, the perturbation to the "system" that the symmetry-breaking cascade represents is a function of the ever-reconstituted agency-structure, molecular-molar tensions. As conceptualized in the diagram, novel and emergent outcome basins can be discerned, characterized by distinct attractors. In the trans-desistance model, four such possibilities are depicted and each functions to resuscitate the stranger, given their sensitivity to the critical timing, frequency, intensity, and duration of an active line of flight.

How does the revitalization of the stranger as a molecular body-without-organs materialize? The four COREL set-assemblage flows presented in Diagram 6.1 help to address this concern. With further perturbations and symmetry-breaking intensities, additional lines of flight would follow. Indeed, the amplification of this trans-desistance process is more completely illustrated in the remaining portions of the schema and is summarily discussed below.

Several active COREL set-assemblage flows are depicted in Diagram 6.1. These include the prisoner flow as challenging/resisting/opposing abstract machines (molar investments such as panopticism and docility, the logic of capital, bureaucracy, and formal rationality); the correctional worker flow as facilitator/healer (generating a care ethic for the Other; embracing the Lacanian "discourse of the hysteric" and "analyst" in a dialogical fashion); the positive freedom flow (libidinal investments in autonomy rather than security; authenticity rather than anxiety, fear, terror, etc.); the prison release flow as disruption in the repetition of "going straight" (non-normative constructions of family, work, hope, and aspirations); the technologized cultural flow as the conspicuous consumption of replacement images, sound bytes, iconic symbols, and simulated themes/messages for, by, and about incarcerates and the logic/discourse of "corrections" (the activities of newsmaking penology);[8] and the culture of spontaneity (rather than control) flow (including the presence of far-from-equilibrium conditions, minor discourses, the non-hierarchical reversal of dominant values, and the logic of schizoanalysis).

Central to these COREL set-assemblage flows, their intersectionalities, and the active lines of flight that foster molecular intensities is the prison industrial

---

8. For a lucid discussion of newsmaking criminology in various crime and justice contexts, see Barak (1994). For a critical theoretical application of the same in penology, see Arrigo (2006).

assemblage flow. As depicted, this assemblage is saturated in desire as production. Desire as production is a reference to "overcoming" (Nietzsche, 1888/1968) the constraints of the shadow in criminology and, more specifically, penology proper. This is the emergence of a will to power (Nietzsche, 1888/1968; see also Deleuze, 1983): a primal and creative force that mobilizes and activates (Nietzsche, 1886/1966). This overcoming, as active movement, is not an ontological representation of the self (i.e., being); rather, it is the embodiment of those energy flows (in the trans-desistance model, intersecting and active COREL set-assemblages) that reside within the process of becoming itself.[9] This will to power—as a fundamental drive, impulse, or motivation—is what makes metamorphosis possible. This overcoming is the desire to exert one's will, one's potentiality, in transcending the social, material, linguistic, and symbolic forces that unconsciously or otherwise reduce and repress the self's actualizations and transformations.

The various and intersecting COREL set-assemblages featured in Diagram 6.1 converge on the prison industrial flow and, simultaneously and correspondingly, the latter extends to all other assemblages found in the schema. This active and ongoing movement—consisting of diverse molecular intensities, differing speeds, and various threshold levels—signifies the mobilization of lines of flight agitating for change, mutation, and transformation. These energy flows—as the nexus for becoming Other and for disassembling and reassembling the agency/structure duality that sustains penal harm, that normalizes violence, and that essentializes prison discourse—displace and transcend molar forces. These reactive forces represent nothing more than the criminology of the shadow. Incarcerates, their jailers, correctional officials, and administrators, as well as the general public are all situated and insert themselves within the circumscribed logic and grammar of its abstract machines (e.g., the "discourse of the master," the disciplinary society, status quo and equilibrium conditions, the logic of capital, the metaphysics of presence, risk-avoidance and governmentality, the iron cage of bureaucracy, simulated hyper-reality, and formal rationality).

However, in the radicalized model of trans-desistance theory, the stranger will only be resuscitated with the emergence of a new socius, a "permanent revolution" (Holland, 1999), which assures continuous transformation and

---

9. At the stage where the person begins to identify with the more complete being of the other, we arrive at "becoming Other." At the stage whereby I and other are mutually constituted, we arrive at "becoming imperceptible" (Deleuze & Guattari, 1987). This becoming Other, becoming imperceptible, sets the challenge for theorizing ethics and conceptions of justice that are compatible with it.

the benefits of active molecular forces. The stranger, as a BwO, will begin to reap the rewards of new inscriptions, of coupling moments, of new realizations ("that's me!"), through productive forms of desire. In penology, the intersecting COREL set-assemblages depicted in Diagram 6.1 provide a noological representation for the character of these emergent potentialities.[10] Consistent with Nietzsche's vision of a will to power, of overcoming through the interplay of active forces within the process of becoming, is the re-birth of the stranger as mutating, evolving, and transforming.

Transforming Corrections: A Preliminary Critique of Theory

The philosophically-animated chapters of this book address various aspects of how to meaningfully conceptualize a much needed transformation in corrections. To the extent that they appropriate insights derived from existential phenomenology, dialogical humanism, and social constructivism, these chapters collectively move the debate on this matter in the direction of citizen justice and societal change. This is a path that penology proper can ill-afford to ignore or forestall, especially given the swelling numbers of individuals confined within the prison industrial complex, the families crippled by its debilitating programs and policies, and the eroding character of a nation steeped in a language and logic that essentializes prisons. Under conditions such as these, we are all held captive; we are our own jailers; we are imprisoned by our thoughts as much as we imprison others for their presumably wayward actions.

In this section, several statements will be made about how the other theory chapters of this book are (or are not) consistent with critical psychological jurisprudence and the radicalized desistance model previously proposed in diagrammatic and narrative form. The observations that follow are clearly

---

10. Again, what is proposed is not a static or fixed blue print for the society to come. Instead, what is critically and theoretically proposed are alternative possible diagrams more akin to quantum mechanics, hodological (non-striated) spaces, and far-from-equilibrium conditions in which a plethora of "larval selves" (Deleuze & Guattari, 1987) and dissipative structures are provided space within which to emerge and take on form. These are spaces where experimentalism at all levels of the socius is valued and experienced, where the molecular is privileged over the molar, and where point and cyclical attractors become secondary to tori and strange attractors. Thus, what is advocated for is an ongoing transmutation; a "molecular revolution" in penology (Arrigo & Milovanovic, 2009).

provisional and speculative. The principal aim is to demonstrate points of congruency and consistency while, at the same time, suggesting avenues for future work in theory development. To this extent, then, the ensuing commentary represents a direction for conceptual synthesis (Arrigo, 2004c) in the realm of critical psychological jurisprudence, mindful of how this theoretical integration could further transform the correctional sphere.

Existential Phenomenology and Critical Psychological Jurisprudence

Two theory chapters emphasize the role of existential phenomenology in reconceptualizing corrections and correctional treatment. These include articles by Christopher Aanstoos, and by Kenneth Adams and Hayden Smith. The contribution of Aanstoos provides a thoughtful and vivid re-description of how phenomenological philosophy is relevant to the human sciences theoretically, methodologically, and analytically. As such, it offers significant and useful background information concerning the application of the "epoche," "intentionality," "embodied consciousness," "the intersubjective life world," the "imagination," and much more.

Interestingly, the chapter by Aanstoos is more exactingly situated within the realm of criminology and penology with the essay penned by Adams and Smith. Relying on the "absurdist" insights of Albert Camus in his work, *The Stranger*, the authors discuss the existential (more so than phenomenological) importance of such interrelated themes as responsibility, choice, freedom, meaning making, authenticity, and behavior. Through their assessment of the anti-hero, Meursault, in Camus' *The Stranger*, Adams and Smith offer a model of correctional treatment. This is a model in which those imprisoned are invited to take responsibility for their behavior, to make meaning through such responsibility, and to decide how to dwell in society such that authentic choices follow. This is the meaning making path for incarcerates, those subjected to community reentry, and for anyone else. Indeed, as the authors note, citing Camus, "freedom is nothing but a chance to be better." This is an invitation that awaits us all.

These two chapters are illuminating for what they suggest about who we all uniquely could *be* and, quite possibly, uniquely could *become*. As such, these contributions are consistent with critical psychological jurisprudence, the stranger's resuscitation, and the trans-desistance correctional approach. However, both essays appear to make several assumptions that warrant further examination and reflection.

First, the duality of human agency/social structure is "responsible" for the co-production of the subject. This rationale applies to the kept, their keepers, their managers, and their spectators. Meaning emerges from this co-constitutive dialectical process for all who undergo the pains of imprisonment, suffer reduction/repression by way of the criminological shadow, and endorse as legitimate the normalization of violence. In effect, then, the scale at which a transformation in corrections must be envisioned, entails an assessment of the macro-, meso-, and micro-level contexts in which such harm is simultaneously and reciprocally reproduced within and throughout penology. Existential phenomenology needs to reconcile itself to or otherwise address these manifold expressions of penal harm.

Second, a dimension of this harm is reliance on language that essentializes prison discourse. The signifier/signified chains of this communicative system—whether articulated in terms of retribution, incapacitation, deterrence, rehabilitation, peacemaking/restorative justice, or even penal abolition—do nothing but instantiate the correctional edifice that stands above and is informed by them all. In part, Lacan's (1977, 1981, 1991) schematizations on the desiring subject's failure to find embodiment or locate meaning through a discourse (master/university) that temporarily, though incompletely, represents a substitute for the interiorized self, specify the intra-psychic and interpersonal dimensions of this problem. The existential-phenomenological commitment to choice, freedom, responsibility, embodied subjectivity, intentionality, and the like, must be resolved with the "lack" that engulfs the self, wherein prospects for actualizing meaning, authenticity, and being for *all* concerned are thwarted.

Third, when incarcerates, correctional workers, prison administrators, policy analysts, and citizens at large witness a recovery in being liberated from a discourse that renders each of them *pas tout(e)* (not-all), then refraining from excessive investments in harms of reduction/repression may (hopefully will) emerge. However, the quality of this desistance, the nature of this reconfigured being, does not encompass possibilities for becoming, mutating, or evolving. In their critique of libidinal (the logic of Oedipus) and economic (the logic of capital) production, Deleuze and Guattari (1983, 1987) systematically comment on this concern. Specifically, they call for a will to power consistent with Nietzsche (1888/1968). This is an overcoming in which the socius is nomadically and noologically re-imagined. Various intersecting COREL set-assemblages as active, molecular lines of flight are necessary in order to alter the agency/structure mutuality that otherwise sustains the criminological shadow and renders as silent the criminological stranger awaiting embodied mobilization. The philosophy of existential-phenomenology, while ostensibly consistent with this analysis, is further informed by a targeted focus on becoming as developed throughout this chapter. This is a transpraxis (Henry & Milovanovic, 1996) in which a metamorphosis of the self and the social are always already pursued provisionally, positionally, and relationally.

Social Constructivism, Dialogical Humanism, and Critical Psychological Jurisprudence

The chapter authored by John Ryals reviews the process of objectification for offenders, whether assigned by others or self-imposed. Appropriating the philosophy of postmodernism and social construction, especially Gergen (1999, 2000) and Berger and Luckmann (1966), the manifold contexts in which the incarcerate functions as an entrenched part of a dysfunctional social-psychological system are enumerated. The socialized mental representations of offenders as diseased, deviant, and/or dangerous are habituated, resulting in institutionalized (correctional system) responses that are self-reinforced by the offender based on typified actions. Reality and knowledge about incarcerates, the prison setting, and correctional treatment are constructed through this ongoing, circumscribed, and reciprocal process. Reviewing the history of offender objectification, Ryals suggests that restorative justice theory and practice represents a protean basis for fostering social change and for engendering inclusion for victims, offenders, and the community to which both are inexorably bound.

The chapter by Matthew Draper, Mark Green, and Ginger Faulkner is guided by the conceptual insights of Mikhail Bakhtin (1995). To the extent that it acknowledges a need for offender treatment, the chapter builds on the social constructivist and postmodernist observations as developed by Ryals. The authors draw attention to such notions as fluidity and openness, creativity in personality, continual responsibility, and interpersonal integrity, maintaining that they represent a framework for ethical therapeutic intervention in the correctional setting. As a model for envisioning true human experience, both the self and the social are regarded as interwoven, consistent with Heidegger and Socrates. It is only when we recognize the "unfinalizabilty" of the self or the self as a subject-in-process (Kristeva, 1984), that dialogue can unfold imaginatively (Bakhtin, 1981). This is a condition in which the mutuality of meaning is created through interaction with others, their poly-vocal identities, and our own multi-voiced, though often unreflective, selves. Draper, Green, and Faulkner go on to describe other facets of Bakhtin's theory on the dialogical imagination including, among others, spirit, soul, and rhythm. While they do not expressly comment on restorative justice, narrative therapy, or the desistance theory literature (e.g., Maruna, 2001, Maruna & Immarigeon, 2004), the implications of their model for correctional treatment are explored. This includes the relational nature of the therapeutic process for offenders and clinicians, as well as the necessary erosion of individualism that affirms interconnectedness, intra-psychic/inter-psychic meaning, and communitarian awareness.

Both of these chapters are consistent with critical psychological jurisprudence in that they seek insight and inclusion, as well as recovery and rehabilitation for the offender. While the chapter written by Ryals relies on restorative justice as a vehicle for this change, the chapter penned by Draper, Green, and Faulkner utilizes the dialogical imagination for this same purpose. However, the shared trajectory of these works is about transcendence, about overcoming what is and embracing what could be. More specifically, how the therapeutic interactions in the correctional milieu potentially and meaningfully affect the client and clinician (Draper et al.), as well as the offender, victim, and community (Ryals) are also cogently discussed. Here, too, we see movement acknowledging much needed transformation.

Still, more attention to the molar larval forces that sustain the criminological shadow warrants interrogation. In short, the question is not simply about recovery, healing, redemption, or any other normative interpretation of the self or the social; rather, the question is about being and becoming based on a reconfiguration of the agency/structure duality that maximizes this potentiality. Certainly, restorative justice, much like desistance theory, seeks to empower incarcerates or ex-offenders so that they can rebuild their lives (Maruna, 2001). Certainly, Bakhtin's dialogical imagination, much like desistance theory, encourages the narrative re-telling, re-shaping, and re-evaluation of the drama that is one's life (Presser, 2008). But on whose terms does this rebuilding take place? Whose voice does this narrative embody? What reactive forces saturate the socius in which recovery (being) and transformation (becoming) unfold? To what extent are disruptions in repetition, coupling moments, an ethic of the Other, positive freedom flows, and the culture of spontaneity extolled? In short, how is the molecular revolution in penology nomadically and rhizomatically featured? The answers to these questions add considerable value to the social constructionist and dialogical humanist perspectives.

Conclusion

This chapter outlined the constitutive dialectical features of the trans-desistance model and the criminological stranger. In the realm of penology, both were identified as key dimensions of a critically-informed psychological jurisprudence. Sustaining this philosophical work is the proposed direction for fostering a radicalized vision of what could be for the imprisonment of us all. The other theory-animated chapters in this volume clearly move in this direction. The conceptual integration of these works within the framework articulated may very well represent a basis for transforming corrections.

References

Arrigo, B. A. (2002). The critical perspective in psychological jurisprudence: Theoretical advances and epistemological assumptions. *International Journal of Law and Psychiatry, 25*(1), 151–172.

Arrigo, B. A. (2003a). Psychology and the law: The critical agenda for citizen justice and radical social change. *Justice Quarterly, 20*(2), 399–444.

Arrigo, B. A. (2003b). Justice and the deconstruction of psychological jurisprudence: The case of competency to stand trial. *Theoretical Criminology: An International Journal, 7*(1), 55–88.

Arrigo, B. A. (2004a). The ethics of therapeutic jurisprudence: A critical and theoretical inquiry of law, psychology, and crime. *Psychiatry, Psychology, and Law: An Interdisciplinary Journal, 11*(1): 23–43.

Arrigo, B. A. (Ed.). (2004b). *Psychological jurisprudence: Critical explorations in law, crime, and society*. Albany: SUNY.

Arrigo, B. A. (2004c). Prospects for justice at the law-psychology divide: An agenda for theory, research, and practice. In B. A. Arrigo (Ed.), *Psychological jurisprudence: Critical explorations in law, crime, and society* (pp. 201–230). Albany: SUNY.

Arrigo, B. A. (2006). The ontology of crime: On the construction of the real, the image, and the hyper-real. In B. A. Arrigo & C. R. Williams (Eds.), *Philosophy, crime, and criminology* (pp. 41–73). Urbana and Chicago: University of Illinois Press.

Arrigo, B. A. (2007). Punishment, freedom, and the culture of control: The case of brain imaging and the law. *American Journal of Law and Medicine, 33*(3), 457–482.

Arrigo, B. A. (2008). Crime, justice, and the under-laborer: On the criminology of the shadow and the search for disciplinary legitimacy and identity. *Justice Quarterly, 25*(3): 439–468.

Arrigo, B. A., & Barrett, L. (2008). Philosophical criminology and complex systems science: Towards a critical theory of justice. *Critical Criminology: An International Journal, 16*(3), 165–184.

Arrigo, B. A., & Fox, D. (in press). Psychology and law: The crime of policy and the search for justice. In D. Fox, I. Prilleltensky, & S. Austin (Eds.), *Critical psychology: An introduction* (2nd ed.). London: Sage.

Arrigo, B. A., & Milovanovic, D. (2009). *Revolution in penology: On constitutive theory and practice.* New York: Rowman & Littlefield.

Arrigo, B. A., & Takahashi, Y. (2006). Recommunalization of the disenfranchised: A theoretical and critical criminological inquiry. *Theoretical Criminology: An International Journal, 10*(3), 307–336.

Arrigo, B. A., & Takahashi, Y. (2008). Theorizing community reentry for male incarcerates and confined mothers: Lessons learned from housing the homeless. *Journal of Offender Rehabilitation, 46*(1/2), 133–162.

Arrigo, B. A., & Williams, C. R. (in press). Existentialism and the criminology of the shadow. In D. Crewe & R. Lippens (Eds.), *The uses of existentialism in criminology and criminal justice.* New York: Routledge.

Arrigo, B. A., Milovanovic, D., & Schehr, R. C. (2005). *The French connection in criminology: Rediscovering crime, law, and social change.* Albany: SUNY.

Bakhtin, M. M. (1981). *The dialogic imagination* (C. Emerson & M. Holquist, Trans.; M. Holquist, Ed.). Austin: The University of Texas Press.

Bakhtin, M. M. (1995). *Toward a philosophy of the act* (V. Liapunov, Trans.; V. Liapunov & M. Holquist, Eds.). Austin: University of Texas Press.

Banks, C. (in press). *"Waiting for the outs": Power, resistance and culture in a juvenile institution.* Lewiston, NY: Mellen Press.

Barak, G. (Ed.). (1994). *Media, process, and the social construction of crime: Studies in newsmaking criminology.* New York: Garland.

Baudrillard, J. (1983a). *Simulations.* New York: Semiotext(e).

Baudrillard, J. (1983b). *In the shadow of the silent majorities.* New York: Semiotext(e).

Berger, P. L., & Luckmann, T. (1966). *The social construction of reality: A treatise on the sociology of knowledge.* Garden City, NY: Anchor.

Braithwaite, J. (1989). *Crime, shame, and reintegration.* Cambridge, UK: Cambridge University Press.

Butler, J. (1993). *Fundamental feminism.* New York: Routledge.

Deleuze, G. (1983). *Nietzsche and philosophy.* New York: Columbia University Press.

Deleuze, G. (1988). *Foucault.* Minneapolis: University of Minnesota Press.

Deleuze, G. (1995). *Negotiations.* New York: Columbia University Press.

Deleuze, G., & Guattari, F. (1983). *Anti-Oedipus.* Minneapolis: University of Minnesota Press.

Deleuze, G., & Guattari, F. (1987). *A thousand plateaus.* Minneapolis: University of Minnesota Press.

Derrida, J. (1977). *Of grammatology.* Baltimore: Johns Hopkins University Press.

Derrida, J. (1978). *Writing and difference.* Chicago: University of Chicago Press.

Farrall, S. (2004). Social capital and offender reintegration: Making probation desistance focused. In S. Maruna & R. Immarigeon (Eds.), *After crime and punishment: Pathways to offender reintegration* (pp. 57–84). Cullompton, UK: Willan.

Farrall, S., & Calverley, A. (2006). *Understanding desistance from crime.* Berkshire, UK: Open University Press.

Foucault, M. (1965). *Madness and civilization: A history of insanity in the age of reason.* New York: Pantheon.

Foucault, M. (1977). *Discipline and punish: The birth of a prison.* New York: Pantheon.

Fox, D. R. (2001). A critical-psychology approach to law's legitimacy. *Legal Studies Forum, 25*(4), 519–538.

Fromm, E. (1994). *Escape from freedom.* New York: Henry Holt. (Original work published 1941)

Garland, D. (2001). *The culture of control: Crime and social order in contemporary society.* Chicago: University of Chicago Press.

Gergen, K. (1999). *An invitation to social construction.* London: Sage.

Gergen, K. (2000). *The saturated self: Dilemmas of identity in contemporary life.* New York: Basic Books.

Giddens, A. (1984). *The constitution of society: Outline of a theory of structuration.* Stanford, CA: Stanford University Press.

Halsey, M. (2006). Negotiating conditional release. *Punishment and Society, 8*(2), 147–181.

Halsey, M. (2008). Assembling recidivism: The promise and contingencies of post-release life. *Journal of Criminal Law and Criminology, 97*(4), 1209–1260.

Henry, S. D., & Milovanovic, D. (1996). *Constitutive criminology: Beyond postmodernism.* London: Sage.

Holland, E. (1999). *Deleuze and Guattari's anti-Oedipus.* New York: Routledge.

Kristeva, J. (1984). *Revolution in poetic language.* New York: Columbia University Press.

Lacan, J. (1977). *Écrits: A selection.* New York: W. W. Norton.

Lacan, J. (1981). *The four fundamental concepts of psychoanalysis.* New York: W. W. Norton.

Lacan, J. (1991). *L'Envers de la psychanalyse.* Paris: Editions du Seuil.

Maruna, S. (2001). *Making good: How ex-convicts reform and rebuild their lives.* Washington, DC: American Psychological Association.

Maruna, S., & Immarigeon, R. (Eds.). (2004). *After crime and punishment: Pathways to offender reintegration.* Cullompton, UK: Willan.

Massumi, B. (1992). *A user's guide to capitalism and schizophrenia.* London: MIT Press.

Mauer, M., & Chesney-Lind, M. (Eds.). (2003). *Invisible punishment: The collateral consequences of mass imprisonment.* London: The New Press.

Nietzsche, F. W. (1966). *Beyond good and evil: Prelude to a philosophy of the future* (W. A. Kaufmann, Ed. and Trans.). New York: Vintage. (Original work published 1886)

Nietzsche, F. W. (1968). *The will to power* (W. A. Kaufmann, Ed. and Trans.). New York: Vintage. (Original work published 1888)

Patton, P. (2000). *Deleuze and the political.* New York: Routledge.

Presser, L. (2008). *Been a heavy life: Stories of violent men.* Urbana and Chicago: University of Illinois Press.

Rorty, R. (1989). *Contingency, irony, and solidarity.* Cambridge, UK: Cambridge University Press.

Shon, P., & Arrigo, B. A. (2006). Reality-based TV and police-citizen encounters: The intertextual construction and situated meaning of mental illness-as-punishment. *Punishment & Society: The International Journal of Penology, 8*(1), 59–85.

Sontag, S., (Ed.). (1988). *Antonin Artaud: Selected writings.* Berkeley, CA: University of California Press.

Strang, H., & Braithwaite, J. (Eds.). (2005). *Restorative justice and civil society.* Cambridge, UK: Cambridge University Press.

Sullivan, D., & Tifft, L. (2005). *Restorative justice: Healing the foundations of our everyday lives* (2nd ed.). Monsey, NY: Criminal Justice Press.

Taxman, F., Young, D., & Byrne, J. (2004). With eyes wide open: Formalizing community and social control intervention in offender reintegration programmes. In S. Maruna & R. Immarigeon (Eds.), *After crime and punishment: Pathways to offender reintegration* (pp. 233–260). Cullompton, UK: Willan.

Unger, R. (1987). *False necessity.* New York: Cambridge University Press.

Ward, T., & Maruna, S. (2007). *Rehabilitation.* London: Routledge.

Whitehead, P. R., Ward, T., & Collie, R. M. (2007). Time for a change: Applying the "good lives" model of rehabilitation to a high-risk violent offender. *International Journal of Offender Therapy and Comparative Criminology, 51*(5), 578–598.

Williams, C. R., & Arrigo, B. A. (2002). *Law, psychology, and justice: Chaos theory and the new (dis)order.* Albany: SUNY.

Section II

Humanistic Perspectives in Corrections

CHAPTER SEVEN

MUTUAL RESPECT AND EFFECTIVE PRISON MANAGEMENT

Terry A. Kupers, The Wright Institute, Berkeley, CA

The traditions of existentialism and phenomenology, supplemented by humanistic psychology in the United States in the 1960s, and then the spiritual movements (e.g., Buddhism) and some therapy movements (e.g., existential and narrative psychotherapies) in recent decades, pursue a quest for deep understanding of the essence of what it means to be human. Basic components of human-ness are identified, including self-reflexive consciousness, the capacity for empathy and various core freedoms. This chapter will focus on two aspects of being human that are included as core components on the lists of most commentators: the need to be respected and the capacity for human agency. There is something about the deprivations characterizing life inside prison that both highlight these fundamental aspects of our humanity and illustrate what happens to human beings when they experience deprivations in these two regards. The current pervasiveness of disrespect and the almost total lack of agency in correctional settings actually provide an important opportunity for effective rehabilitation: restore respect and a sense of agency in the prison systems, so prisoners will be in a better position to succeed at re-entering society-at-large and successfully "going straight." Meanwhile, prison life will become less angry and deadly. On the other hand, if the pervasive disrespect and lack of agency are permitted to continue, prison violence will rise and recidivism rates will continue to climb.

Respect and Agency

Concerns about respect are rampant on the streets of our inner cities. Young men become enraged when they feel disrespected, are willing to fight to the death to attain "a little respect," and only consider their quest successful when there are sufficient outward signs pointing to their being respected by peers and establishment figures alike. Ironically, this quest to be respected occurs in a social context where low-income youth of color, as a group, suffer disrespect at every turn. On average, the young men who fight it out on the streets and participate in drive-by shootings are the most disadvantaged in our society. They are provided a less-than-quality education (relative to what the public and private schools provide in middle-class neighborhoods), and then they are told that the reason for their academic failure is their own lack of intelligence or laziness. They are the last hired and first fired; they are forced to work for subsistence wages; they are routinely pulled over by police and frisked for no apparent reason, and if they talk back to the officers they are likely beaten or arrested. It is as if the gang members are demanding as street gladiators precisely that which they are systematically denied in the larger society. They are fighting with each other for what they think of as a modicum of respect, but meanwhile they are brutalizing others and committing crimes that send many to prison.

In prison, gladiators continue to fight for respect that is denied to them by society-at-large (Kupers, 2005). There is a familiar scenario on the prison yard: one prisoner defeats another in combat, but then yells at him, "You're not a man, you're a pussy." In too many cases, rape follows (Human Rights Watch, 1996, 2001). The author has spoken with many prisoners about rape and discover repeatedly it is not really about sex; it is about power, and expressing domination is a desperate way to attain some respect. Then, when the officers arbitrarily punish prisoners, insult them, and deprive them of the most basic human necessities, the prisoners feel disrespected anew and their resentment mounts.

Agency is about being the subject of one's own life rather than the object of designs established by others. A number of things increase one's sense of agency, including a good education, high earning capacity, financial reserves, personal attractiveness, good friends, and a quality primary relationship with healthy offspring. Personal capacities also play a big part, including the capacity to play, to create, to be deeply intimate, even the capacity to envision a better future.

Psychotherapists work hard to instill a sense of agency in their patients. Depression can be directly related to a lack of agency. The depressed wife tells her therapist she is mad at her husband because he stays too late at the office and then comes home and ignores her and their children, but she is afraid to confront him about his behavior because she is afraid he would desert the family. She has no tenable move to make, no way to alter the unfortunate family dynamic, so she sinks into depression. We analyze the messages she received from her parents about a wife's role. We look at ways she can raise the subject with her husband without making him feel criticized and attacked. We talk about some incremental gains that would make her feel she is moving toward improving her situation. She decides on a non-threatening (i.e., non-critical) tact to take with her husband involving asking him to select two evenings a week to leave work at a decent hour and be home in time to have dinner with the family. If he agrees, his staying late at the office on the other evenings would be acceptable for her. Her depression lightens. It is not necessarily the case that her dissatisfaction and unhappiness will be entirely eased; rather, her sense that there is something she can do to affect her situation is a great improvement over the helplessness she had been feeling. Finding a way to move forward is the beginning of restoring a sense of agency, and often in psychotherapy, it is the moment when the depression decreases and the patient begins to work on his or her issues in a new and more effective way.

Similarly, everyone the author has spoken with who works with "at risk" or "troubled youth," for example in a school or juvenile court program, indicates that they are successful to a great extent with their wards. They also say that what they offer the youths is respect and a path forward, a way to complete their schooling, a way to escape from an abusive home situation, a way to take care of a baby as a single mother, or a way to move away from gang influences and connections. In other words, they offer the youths respect and a greater sense of agency in determining their life trajectory.

Respect and agency fit together. The counselor or teacher must win the youth's respect, and often there is much testing. The youth challenges the counselor as if to say, "You're not really interested in my welfare; nobody is." The counselor must demonstrate, not with easy words but often with very difficult deeds, that he or she has the youth's best interest at heart and deserves his or her respect. When the counselor turns the tide and wins the youth's respect, and then provides a path toward greater agency in the larger legal society, then the youth stands a much better chance of leaving the life of crime and succeeding at "going straight." In too many cases, with the crowding of youth facilities and prisons, the population of "at risk" youth wind up behind bars, and then their entire life trajectory becomes much more problematic.

Deprivation of Respect and Agency in Prison

Anyone who is familiar with contemporary prison life is aware that respect and agency are all-important issues (Hallinan, 2001; Sabo, Kupers, & London, 2002). Think about all the fights over respect and reports by prisoners of feeling they have no control over anything that happens to them. Some loss of agency is inherent in the prison experience. Prisoners lose the unique identity they enjoyed in the community; they don prison-issued garb; they are given an identification number and are forced to follow orders (Haney, 2003b). There are rules governing almost all aspects of everyday life, and there are guards watching over the prisoners to make certain they follow every rule, always ready to issue a "ticket" for misconduct. As an expert witness in class action litigation related to unconstitutional prison conditions and programming, the author has had the opportunity to interview thousands of prisoners in over a dozen states (Kupers, 1999). Universally, they complain about feeling disrespected and feeling they have little or no agency in their lives.

A term in prison does not need to be accompanied by strong feelings of being disrespected and entirely deprived of agency. There are inevitably going to be some moments of disrespect from others as well as some loss of agency. The names one is called while being challenged to fight are an example of everyday disrespect, and a stint in "the hole" or segregation unit as punishment for an infraction illustrates the loss of agency to which prisoners are regularly subjected. The question is whether the amount of disrespect and degree to which choices are taken from prisoners are necessary. In other words, is there some "penological objective"? Consider the increasing number of prisoners consigned to some form of isolated confinement today, including administrative segregation, supermaximum security, and death rows located inside supermaximum units. Isolation is over-utilized relative to an effective disciplinary system that metes out short stints in "the hole" for rule infractions and assaults (Kupers, 2008).

Once the term in isolation surpasses a certain length of time, the prisoner stops learning from the disciplinary procedure, begins resenting the excessively harsh punishment, loses hope of ever gaining freedom from isolation, and begins to act as if he or she has nothing to lose (Rhodes, 2004; Toch & Kupers, 2007). Where a 10 day or 2 week stint in "the hole" for fighting may have a valid penological objective in maintaining institutional discipline, 10 years of extreme isolation in a supermaximum security unit is outrageously excessive and turns prisoners into broken individuals who are prone to act out of desperation rather than rationally considering their options (Toch & Adams, 2002). The proof is the recently uncovered rate of successful suicides in prison. It is much higher than the comparable rate in the community, but the stunning news is that as many as 50 percent of successful suicides that occur in prison involve the six to eight percent of prisoners who are in segregation at any given time (Correctional Association of New York, 2004; Liebling, 1999). Long stints in isolation are a clear example of excessively denying prisoners agency, and if one speaks with a prisoner who has been in isolated confinement for a substantial period of time, he or she will say that isolation fosters disrespect at every turn. For example, officers are more prone to insult prisoners confined to a cell 24 hours per day than they are to disrespect prisoners on a general population yard with whom they have to interact daily.

In this regard, a historic wrong turn occurred in American correctional practices in the mid-1980s, a development that substantially increased wanton and unnecessary disrespect and denial of agency within the prisons. With the War on Drugs and stiffer penalties at all levels, the prison population was growing by leaps and bounds (Irwin & Austin, 1994). The prison population today is 10 times what it was in the early 1970s and is still growing. After de-institutionalization of state mental hospitals, a considerable number of individuals with serious mental illnesses flooded prisons (Human Rights Watch, 2003). The prisons were massively overcrowded, the violence rate was skyrocketing, and the rate of psychiatric breakdown in the prisons had reached epidemic proportions.

Also in the 1980s, prison rehabilitation programs were being dismantled in a misguided but politically convenient effort to "get tough on crime" and halt "coddling" of prisoners. In the minds of some criminologists, there could be only one logical and effective response to the extraordinary rise in the rate of prison violence and psychiatric breakdown: decrease the prison population by placing low-level drug offenders and mentally ill offenders in community supervision and send them to treatment programs in the community. Another response was to re-instate the rehabilitation programs so that prisoners could develop the skills they would need to succeed in "going straight" after being released. It seems clear that crowding a large number of idle prisoners into small spaces would only lead to more violence and psychiatric breakdown. However, correctional authorities refused to heed offered advice, and instead turned their attention to building supermaximum security facilities for the "superpredators" and the "worst of the worst." Beginning in the late 1980s, an unprecedented number of prisoners were consigned to long-term isolation in a cell where they would eat all their meals, speak to almost no one, and perhaps only get out of their cell for an hour of recreation in a small "yard" with no athletic equipment or companionship.

Supermaximum security units are also known as control units. The name is justified because the isolated occupants of supermaximum segregation cells have no control over even the smallest and most personal aspects of their daily lives. They are totally dependent on officers to bring them their meals, give them toilet paper and cleaning materials, turn on and off the lights and water in their cells, take them to shower, bring them their mail, tell them what pictures they can have in their cell, and so forth. In other words, control units were designed to entirely eradicate any sense of agency a prisoner might have felt in his or her life. All control would be in the hands of the staff, and the prisoners would have to adjust to their total lack of agency. However, the tendency to isolate prisoners in their cells and diminish their sense of agency was not limited to actual segregation settings such as a supermaximum security unit. At all levels of security, the trend in penology since the 1980s has been for staff to maintain relatively more control of the prisoners' lives. The hours when prisoners are permitted to roam the facility have been incrementally diminished, the kinds of mail and packages prisoners can receive have been increasingly limited (e.g., families in many states cannot send packages; they must pay an approved vendor to send a uniformly packaged set of items), visits have been restricted, and so forth. Prisoners' control over their lives has been systematically reduced at all levels of security.

The author has been privy to some shocking abuses and has testified in civil litigation on behalf of women prisoners who have been sexually abused or raped by male staff. In one state, the author learned of officers "macing" prisoners (spraying them with immobilizing gas, either mace or some other gas) inside their cells for trivial misconduct, and then leaving them, unwashed, in the contaminated cell. Officers have sprayed mace through the food port of a prisoner's segregation cell, sometimes merely because the officers were annoyed with the prisoner. Since the prisoner was obviously already locked in a cell, there was no imminent danger and therefore, no justification for the officers' actions. Many of the prisoners maced in this fashion were mentally ill. In some cases, the macing occurred after a prisoner cut himself or smeared feces, and in other cases, the inmate was merely hollering and making a racket. Usually, by policy, as outlined in published minimum standards for correctional facilities, when an officer sprays a prisoner with mace, the prisoner must be allowed to wash thoroughly, the cell must be decontaminated, and there must be medical attention provided, a report written, and an investigation conducted. None of these required steps occurred in the supermaximum unit to which the author is referring. There is no explanation for this kind of excessive "use of force" except as abusive, brutal punishment arbitrarily meted out by officers in direct violation of prisoners' basic rights.

Results from the Stanford Mock Prison Experiment show that ordinary people are capable of abusing their peers whenever one group is given total control over another (Haney, 2003a). The experiment at Stanford University enlisted students as experimental subjects who were randomly assigned to act the role of guard or prisoner. The "guards" proceeded to disrespect, humiliate, and deny any agency to the "prisoners," and the abuses reached a level where the experimenters had to precipitously end the experiment out of fear that the "guards" would seriously injure the unfortunate "prisoners." The more important point is that real prisoners, who are actually under the total control of officers and cannot call off the "experiment," are regularly disrespected and denied even the most basic human agency. This should not be the case; there is no legitimate "penological objective" in denying prisoners respect and agency while they are incarcerated.

This is not to imply that correctional staff as a group are malevolent. There are bad apples, for certain, and they are the instigators of much of the abuse. The author's work as an expert witness and consultant/trainer in correctional settings has brought her into contact with very admirable staff who are involved with prisoners in some inspiring human relationships. For example, a psychologist in a maximum security prison administrative segregation unit was treating a disturbed prisoner who repeatedly wrote threatening letters to important dignitaries from his prison cell. The prisoner suffered from severe obsessive-compulsive disorder and psychosis, and the letter-writing was a symptom of his psychiatric disorder. He had never harmed anyone and was not an especially dangerous prisoner, but because he kept writing the letters, he was repeatedly convicted of threatening an official, and his prison term and his stay in administrative segregation continued to grow longer. The psychologist negotiated with security staff so that she could take over screening this disturbed prisoner's outgoing mail. She then simply destroyed his threatening letters so he would not receive additional punishments.

Restoration of Respect and Agency as Rehabilitation

What would happen if we gave prisoners a greater degree of respect and a significant amount of agency? We know that when prisoners are disrespected in various ways and denied choice and agency in most regards, on average, they become sullen. They lose the capacity to pursue their own initiatives, become angry and act out ineffectually, or become passive and numb. Then when they are released from prison, they are prone to failure at re-integration into the community (i.e., they have a high recidivism rate or likelihood of returning to prison).

In fact, evidence is accruing that shows simply increasing the respect and agency provided to prisoners leads to safer prisons and less problems for the prisoner when adjusting to life in the community after their release from prison. This is not to suggest that the evidence has the shape of rigorous empirical/statistical studies. It is extremely difficult to gain sufficient access to prisons to accomplish research, though some preliminary data does support such an argument (Lovell, Johnson, & Cain, 2007). Rather, the evidence is mostly recorded by expert witnesses in prison litigation or human rights groups looking into allegations of abuse within prisons. Instead of appearing in juried professional journals, results appear in expert reports and declarations to the courts as well as in court testimony. A few examples will be provided which illustrate how increased respect and agency help the prisoner remain peaceful while incarcerated and increase his or her potential for successful re-integration into the community after release. Some of the examples will demonstrate how difficult prisoners were managed simply by increasing the respect and agency accorded them, and the result was increased cooperation and reduced misbehavior and violence.

Example #1. The author testified in a civil lawsuit on behalf of a Montana prisoner who was suffering from serious mental illness, but instead of being provided adequate mental health treatment, he was placed in segregation and deprived of even the meager amenities most prisoners in segregation are allotted (the case is summarized in Human Rights Watch, 2003). During the trial, a sergeant testified about an incident that had occurred some weeks earlier. Deprived of all other means of expression and in a psychotic state, a prisoner had placed a piece of paper over the small window of his solid metal cell door. This created an emergency for the security staff. They could not see into the prisoner's cell, so they could not know what he was doing or maintain safety on the unit. The usual procedure would be to assemble an "extraction team" of several officers and burst in on the prisoner. By chance, the sergeant was on duty that day and was sensitive to this prisoner's precarious mental state. The sergeant looked through the food port in the door and noticed that the prisoner was on the other side of the cell. The sergeant then slid his arm through the food port, reached up, and scraped enough of the paper off the window so that officers outside the cell could see that the prisoner was not doing anything dangerous. The sergeant then turned to the other concerned officers in the area and said, "Now you don't need to do a cell extraction." The sergeant's behavior violated the Department of Corrections' policies and procedures, and he was taking a risk acting in this idiosyncratic manner, but when the prisoner saw that the sergeant went out on a limb for him, he came to the cell door and scraped the remaining paper from the window. In other words, the sergeant's caring display of respect for the prisoner caused the prisoner to act somewhat more rationally and appropriately.

Example #2. A year after the Human Rights Watch report, *Cold Storage*, was published in 1997, outlining excessively harsh conditions in Indiana's supermaximum security units and the psychiatric damage done by those conditions, Commissioner Cohn of the Indiana Department of Corrections asked the authors of the report to return to Indiana and witness the improvements that had occurred in the year since the report came out. The report was critical of harsh and depriving conditions at the Security Housing Unit (SHU) at Wabash Valley Correctional Facility and the unusually high number of incidents requiring officers to use force. In fact, when the authors of the report returned to the Wabash Valley facility, they discovered a reduced use of force. Generally, use of force incidents increase in frequency in more despairing prisons with severe conditions, so the precipitous reduction in use of force at the SHU meant that the human rights abuses which had been reported a year earlier had been ameliorated to some extent. When asked how he had effected the impressive reduction in use of force inside the SHU, the shift commander indicated that at Commissioner Cohn's behest, he had instituted two procedural changes. First, he gave all the prisoners in the SHU a television and decreed that if they broke rules or became assaultive, their television would be taken from them. The reasoning was that prisoners will behave better if they have something to lose for unacceptable behavior. Second, he instituted a policy that required officers to notify the shift commander before initiating any use of force, such as spraying a prisoner with immobilizing gas or performing a cell extraction. The shift commander then must go to the unit and talk to the recalcitrant prisoner. The facility is large and the shift commander might not be near the SHU at the time the call arrives, but the officers in the SHU must wait until the shift commander arrives. This creates a "cooling off period." The appearance of the shift commander gives the prisoner the message that his complaints matter enough for the shift commander to come and listen to him. The shift commander might do something to alleviate the prisoner's concern. For example, often a cell extraction would be initiated because a prisoner refused to return his food tray. His stated reason might be that the food was rotten or inedible, and he was not going to return the tray until someone in authority came and witnessed the rotten food. The shift commander might arrive, agree the food is rotten, and order a change in kitchen procedures. Even if the shift commander does nothing to assuage the prisoner's complaints, his arrival on the scene provides the prisoner with a degree of respect, and this might lead the prisoner to return the food tray or halt the unacceptable behavior.

Example #3. A supermaximum security unit was experiencing a startlingly high incidence of cell extractions. The procedure usually begins by spraying the prisoner with immobilizing gas and often involves slamming the prisoner against a wall. Injuries are commonplace. The number of times staff must resort to using cell extractions reflects on the quality of administration in the facility. On average, staff in better-administered facilities with better training feel a need to resort to using force less often. This supermaximum security unit was relatively small, and for a period of many months, there were dozens of cell extractions each week. The unit seemed out of control. Central Administration of the Department of Corrections intervened, removed the superintendent (i.e., the warden) of the institution, and replaced him with another. The new superintendent spoke with the staff as a group and to every prisoner in the unit. He gained agreement from all staff and prisoners to address each other only by last names, the staff calling prisoners Mr. Jones or Mr. Smith, and prisoners calling staff Officer Brown or Sergeant Green, for example. In addition, staff and prisoners agreed to cease using profanity while addressing each other. After these agreements were initiated, the incidents requiring use of force diminished impressively. From then on, the occurrence of cell extractions decreased to one or two per month. Thus, with the introduction of enhanced mutual respect between staff and prisoners, the level of violence in the supermaximum security unit diminished precipitously.

Example #4. One of the best illustrations of the rehabilitative potential of increased prisoner agency is the remarkable therapeutic community that has been in operation for 20 years at Grendon Prison, a maximum security facility in the United Kingdom (Jones, 2004; Morris, 2004). There are no segregation units in the facility, and the prisoners, as a whole, decide on punishments for members of the "community" who break rules or become assaultive. Their ultimate sanction is to evict a member from the community, meaning the evicted prisoner is transferred to another maximum security prison. Staff include trained psychotherapists who lead frequent therapy and milieu groups, but staff do not get a vote when the community decides on programmatic or disciplinary matters. Obviously, the community cannot vote to release its members from prison, but short of that, the community has a great deal of decision-making power, and this means the prisoners experience much more agency than their counterparts in other institutions. The result is that prisoners at Grendon, a significant number incarcerated for murder or armed robbery, are willing to open up with each other in groups about their feelings and their fears, even about how it felt to commit their crimes (Aitkenhead, 2007). The violence rate within the prison is low, and the recidivism rate for the therapeutic community's graduates is substantially lower than it is at other maximum security prisons.

Each of the aforementioned examples provide evidence that increasing the respect and agency accorded a prisoner increases the likelihood he or she will cooperate with the prison program, avoid violence, and prepare more effectively for post-release adjustment.

Conclusion

The tragedy of contemporary correctional policy is that our prisons too often breed disrespect and excessively deprive prisoners of agency. Of course, some loss of agency is inherent in incarceration, but the tragic constriction of human agency is excessive relative to the requirements for running a safe institution. The disrespect and excessive constriction of prisoners' agency sets up an unfortunate vicious cycle: the disrespected men and women become menacing and disruptive, further constraints are instituted to contain their unacceptable behaviors (e.g., greater isolation in a segregation setting), and the enhanced constraints further compromise the prisoners' sense of being respected and having agency. As a result, prisoners are more prone to feel there is nothing to lose and to proceed to act inappropriately, and the bad behavior serves as justification for further constraints and encroachments on prisoners' agency.

Over the past few decades, human rights organizations and civil courts have monitored the state of prisons and have established limits for correctional managers regarding disrespecting prisoners and denying them agency. For example, according to international human rights standards and court determinations of prisoners' constitutional rights, staff are not permitted to disrespect prisoners to the point of sexual abuse or arbitrary beatings; prisoners suffering from serious mental illness are entitled to adequate mental health treatment; even prisoners in extreme punitive isolation units are entitled to time out of their cells for recreation and contact with loved ones through the mail and visits. Implicitly, when prisoners are able to stand up for their rights and win class action lawsuits, and when human rights organizations step in to influence correctional managers to grant prisoners their human rights, the prisoners have reason to feel more respected and to experience a slightly greater sense of agency in their lives. This is all a very positive development, but it barely scratches the surface in terms of what is needed.

Respect and enhancement of the prisoner's sense of agency must be taken further, so that they form the core of a robust effort to rehabilitate prisoners. As this chapter has discussed, when the prisoner is afforded a greater degree of respect and agency, he or she is in a better position to sustain hope of one day being accepted back into the company of law-abiding men and women in the community. With that goal in mind, he or she is less prone to act out in prison and jeopardize the opportunity for a timely release. In fact, mutual respect is the key to healthy relationships in the community, including relationships within the family, among friends, among co-workers and in the community at large—just the kinds of relationships one hopes the ex-prisoner will resume after he or she is released. In other words, by instituting attitudes and programs within the prisons that highlight mutual respect and by increasing agency for the prisoners, the prisons could be better preparing incarcerated men and women for success at "going straight" after they complete their prison term.

References

Aitkenhead, D. (2007, July 14). Inside Grendon Prison. *The Guardian*. Retrieved January 10, 2008, from http://www.guardian.co.uk/uk/2007/jul/14/ukcrime.prisonsandprobation

Correctional Association of New York (2004). *Mental health in the house of corrections: A study of mental health care in New York state prisons*. Albany: Prison Visiting Project of the Correctional Association of New York.

Hallinan, J. (2001). *Going up the river: Travels in a prison nation*. New York: Random House.

Haney, C. (2003a). Mental health issues in long-term solitary and "supermax" confinement. *Crime & Delinquency*, 49(1), 124–156.

Haney, C. (2003b). The psychological impact of incarceration: Implications for postprison adjustment. In J. Travis & M. Waul (Eds.), *Prisoners once removed* (pp. 33–65). Washington, DC: Urban Institute.

Human Rights Watch (1996). *All too familiar: Sexual abuse of women in U.S. state prisons*. New York: Human Rights Watch.

Human Rights Watch (1997). *Cold storage: Super-maximum security confinement in Indiana*. New York: Human Rights Watch.

Human Rights Watch (2001). *No escape: Male rape in U.S. prisons*. New York: Human Rights Watch.

Human Rights Watch (2003). *Ill-prepared: U.S. prisons and offenders with mental illness*. New York: Human Rights Watch.

Irwin, J., & Austin, J. (1994). *It's about time: America's imprisonment binge*. Belmont, CA: Wadsworth.

Jones, D. (Ed.). (2004). *Working with dangerous people: The psychotherapy of violence*. Oxford: Radcliffe Medical Press.

Kupers, T. (1999). *Prison madness: The mental health crisis behind bars and what we must do about it*. San Francisco: Jossey-Bass.

Kupers, T. (2005). Toxic masculinity as a barrier to mental health treatment in prison. *Journal of Clinical Psychology*, 61(6), 713–724.

Kupers, T. (2008). Prison and the decimation of pro-social life skills. In G. Reyes & A. Ojeda (Eds.), *Psychological torture: Phenomenology, psychiatry, neurobiology and ethics* (Vol. 5). Westport, CT: Praeger.

Liebling, A. (1999). Prison suicide and prisoner coping. In M. Tonry & J. Petersilia (Eds.), *Prisons* (pp. 283–359). Chicago: University of Chicago Press.

Lovell, D., Johnson, L. C., & Cain, K. C. (2007). Recidivism of supermax prisoners in Washington State. *Crime & Delinquency, 53*(4), 633–656.

Morris, M. (2004). *Dangerous and severe: Process, programme and person: Grendon's work*. London: Jessica Kingsley.

Rhodes, L. (2004). *Total confinement: Madness and reason in maximum security*. Berkeley, CA: University of California Press.

Sabo, D., Kupers, T., & London, W. (Eds.). (2002). *Prison masculinities*. Philadelphia: Temple University Press.

Toch, H., & Adams, K. (2002). *Acting out: Maladaptive behavior in confinement*. Washington, DC: American Psychological Association.

Toch, H., & Kupers, T. (2007). Violence in prison: Revisited. *Journal of Offender Rehabilitation, 45*(3/4), 1–28.

CHAPTER EIGHT

CIVILITY IN PRISONS: A RADICAL PROPOSAL

Catherine A. Jenks, University of West Georgia
John Randolph Fuller, University of West Georgia

In 1971, a new warden arrived at the Statesville prison in Joliet, Illinois. John Twomey represented a dramatic change in the administration of the prison. Rather than coming up through the security ranks like most prison administrators, Twomey's experience was in correctional treatment. With a master's degree in psychology he fully embraced the rehabilitative ideal. His arrival at Joliet was met with great skepticism, and his initial behaviors further fueled this attitude. In addressing a high school graduation of prison inmates, he stated in front of a packed gymnasium that he was there to serve them (in Jacobs, 1977).

This statement was viewed by the security staff as a complete repudiation of current prison practices. The prison experienced several months of turmoil, and Twomey was eventually replaced. This episode would not be noteworthy if it did not illustrate the major social change in the atmosphere of prisons around the country during this time. The rehabilitative era of the prisons in the 1960s and 1970s greatly concerned the security staffs. Wardens like John Twomey initiated a new viewpoint in the prison in which inmates were treated as human beings. The philosophy behind this rehabilitative ideal is that if people are treated with civility, they will not only act with civility, but will change the social environment of the prison into one that is more positive.

Unfortunately, this new civility was not to last. Broad social forces were battering the country in the 1960s and 1970s, and this brief liberalism gave way to a new tentativeness (Irwin, 1980). Today in prison systems across the country, prison staffs are trained to keep a social and emotional distance from the inmates, in order to minimize the risk of manipulation.

The purpose of this chapter is to revisit the philosophy of treating inmates with civility. Given the failure of the contemporary prison to enact positive change in inmate behavior, it is argued that this philosophy of civility be given another try. Accomplishing this would require a visionary prison administrator who is able to effectively communicate his or her ideas to the staff, as well as structure the reward system so that those who behave in a civil manner are acknowledged and rewarded appropriately. In order to appreciate this new attitude of civility, it is useful to consider how the prison can make inmates troublesome through its brutalization effects.

The prison is the only institution that has ramped up its efforts at brutalization in the past two decades. Brutalization can be viewed as a top-down phenomenon that has trickled down from the government and law enforcement agencies and permeated the entire criminal justice system. As the government has become more stringent and brutal in its War on Drugs and anticrime tactics, it has filled prisons with minor drug offenders and the mentally ill. Citizens have become both more brutal in meeting these tactics and more calloused in general. An example would be the proliferation of Special Weapons and Tactics (SWAT) teams and paramilitary style law-enforcement that engages in home invasions on suspected drug houses. Even though they periodically force their way into the wrong house and kill innocent individuals, these incidents are forgotten within weeks and the drug war continues. The brutalizing effects of the criminal justice system extend to the correctional industry with its supermax prisons, longer sentences, mandatory minimums, and capital punishment.

The problem with brutalization is that it thrives in a feedback loop. As one party, in this case the government, enforces approval policies, the other party, citizens, react by becoming more brutal, requiring even more stringency from the first party. Usually, in a brutalization contest, the better armed party wins, which is usually the State. However, in the case of the prison, where inmates will eventually be released back into free society, the brutalization effects experienced by the inmates are potentially passed on to the rest of us through serious violent crime. Is there a way to make prison less brutal? Is it possible to incarcerate inmates without placing them in an atmosphere that robs them of the ability and the inclination to treat others with dignity and respect? Before we offer suggestions in this regard it is useful to consider what some experts have said about the social role of the prison.

In 1958, Gresham Sykes published his groundbreaking book, *The Society of Captives*, where he describes what he calls the "defects of total power." Sykes argues that even though it appears that the prison administration and staff have total power in the prison; this is clearly not the case. The day-to-day functions of the prison cannot be accomplished without the tacit cooperation of the inmates. According to Sykes, an analysis of power within the prison can be briefly described as:

- Power based on authority. In most institutions, power is based upon authority. By this we mean that the legislature, board of directors, or voters have ceded power to a particular individual or group because they believe that it is an effective way to accomplish the agency's goals. Because this individual is given the authority to occupy this position, the power that he or she exercises is considered legitimate. In addition to legitimacy, another factor that is crucial to power based on authority is the moral obligation to obey that is experienced by agency personnel. For instance, in the military a captain commands a platoon, and the members of that platoon recognize the legitimacy of that command and feel obligated to carry out the captain's orders because they believe in and accept the mission of the military and the chain of command. In the prison, although the inmates might recognize the prison administration's legitimacy, they do not feel the moral compulsion to obey all the rules. In fact, in this situation, in which power is based on authority, the inmates consider the power structure to be something to defy rather than something to be obeyed. If power based upon authority does not work in the prison, or does not work very well, then how should power be exercised?
- Power based on force. If prisoners will not obey because they are supposed to, then they must be forced to obey. Prison administrators have the tools necessary to make inmates obey; they have guns, steel bars, brick walls, and can call on reinforcements at any time. Prison administrators should potentially have enough power in the prison to maintain good behavior; however, this is not always the case. It is expensive to maintain an adequate level of force at all times. Consequently, correctional officers will often find themselves responsible for a hundred inmates at a time and have very little in terms of adequate backup if trouble should arise. In many prisons, and at any time, if the inmates acted in concert, they could overtake large areas of the institution. Accomplishing tasks such as feeding the entire population three times a day requires inmate cooperation. Although selective force can be employed at any time against any inmate, it is simply not feasible to maintain an atmosphere of force on a 24-hour basis. Instead, prison administrators must devise other ways of dealing with inmates.
- Power based on rewards and punishments. Sykes contends that when power based on authority does not work, prisons resort to rewards and punishments. Inmates who obey receive extra rewards, and those who disobey are punished. However, this common sense philosophy cannot keep the prison in order. The problem with power based upon rewards and punishment in the prisons, according to Sykes, is that the courts must in-

tervene to such an extent that the prison administration does not have an adequate range of rewards and punishments with which to induce good behavior. Legal cases have greatly restricted the ability of prison administrators to induce or coerce behavior from inmates. The courts have addressed the quality—and quantity—of prison conditions in great detail, including the amount of sunlight a prisoner is to see each day, the number of square feet that should be allocated to each inmate, the caloric intake each prisoner should be given, and the degree of force that correctional officers can use in subduing unruly inmates. Sykes argues that the prison administrator does not have the ability to make life either a good deal better or a good deal worse for inmates.

- Let's make a deal. If power based on authority, power based on power, and power based on rewards and punishment all do not work, how is the prison supposed to maintain a safe working and living environment? Sykes says that, in reality, what happens is that the prison administration and the inmates come to an agreement. This agreement entails the correctional officers not enforcing every rule to its full extent, leaving some rules and policies as negotiable. Correctional officers and inmates are in constant negotiation over a wide variety of issues. The power of noncooperation enables the inmates to frustrate correctional officers when tension arises. This "let's make a deal" attitude allows for a relatively smooth daily routine, but also comes at a stiff price for the correctional officer. Once any nicety or favoritism is shown toward the inmate, that inmate will use that instance of civility as a wedge in which to undermine the correctional officer's power. The inmate might tell the correctional officer's superior that the officer bent the rules, thus blackmailing the correctional officer into further transgressions. So, in short, Sykes (1958) argues that power is diffused and contested in the prison.

Although Sykes' book was written over 50 years ago, it still has currency. With the exception of some of the supermax prisons that are able to totally control every movement of the inmate, prisons today are still faced with the defects of total power. Supermax prisons are expensive to build and maintain, and can be used for only the most dangerous inmates (Irwin, 2005). For all others, a reduced level of security is necessary in order to effectively handle large numbers of inmates. The vast majority of inmates in this country's correctional institutions, then, are willing participants in the negotiation of power with correctional authorities. The important question that arises is how to best equip correctional officers and administrators with the verbal tools necessary to effectively deal with a large and unruly inmate population.

The Job of the Correctional Officer

The job of correctional officer has changed over the years in a number ways, most specifically in the use of technology. Correctional officers are equipped with better communication systems allowing them to both monitor inmates and be monitored by administrators. Another change in the correctional officer's job is the direct result of prison overcrowding. The relationships that correctional officers make with inmates are highly circumscribed by the bureaucratic routine necessitated by prison overcrowding. Correctional officers are unable to interact with inmates on a personal basis simply because of the sheer number of inmates. Finally, there are real constraints in the nature of the correctional officers' job due to the rules and regulations under which they labor. Officers are discouraged from forming any type of interpersonal relationships with inmates due to perceived security issues and because it is considered unprofessional (Whitehead, Jones, & Braswell, 2008).

The nature of the correctional officer's job changes as correctional philosophies change. John Irwin and James Jacobs provide interesting histories of the changing nature of the correctional officer's job as it relates to the atmosphere within the prison. For instance, Irwin identifies three types of prisons that operated in the twentieth century. In the early part of the century, the "big house" was the term given to the prisons of the day because they operated in a totalitarian manner that allowed correctional officers very little freedom to engage the inmates. The model for this type of prison was Statesville where Warden Joe Reagan ran every aspect of the prison. Officers who did not follow his rules were quickly dismissed. Inmates who violated regulations were severely punished. For the most part, the prison ran smoothly because the rules were clear, and everybody knew what was expected of them (Irwin, 1980; Jacobs, 1977).

In the 1950s and 1960s, a new philosophy entered corrections. Irwin calls this the era of the correctional institution because it was based upon rehabilitation. This can be visualized by the changing of the name of the institution from a penitentiary to the correctional institution. This meant the prison attempted to reform the inmate through rehabilitative practices. Psychologists and caseworkers focused on inmates' needs and often clashed with the traditional custodial force. There was little opportunity for correctional officers to exercise discretion within such a philosophy. Inmate rehabilitative counseling was done by the professional staff, and gradually the corrections officer was reduced to providing only security services. The net effect of this new rehabilitative philosophy was to strip from the correctional officers the "clean work" of helping inmates, leaving them the "dirty work" in which they focused purely on security. In the 1980s, the rehabilitative ideal was discarded partly because of the unfounded prevailing sentiment that "nothing works." Irwin claims that the rehabilitative efforts were only token in nature and that the rehabilitative idea was never given a fair chance due to lack of resources and lack of commitment on the part of many correctional administrators (Irwin, 1970, 1980).

The 1980s ushered in a different type of prison atmosphere. The involvement of federal and state courts in prison administration established a new legalistic environment. The bureaucratic rules and regulations were codified into policy and standard operating procedure to the extent that most discretion was taken away from not only the correctional officers, but also from correctional administrators. The courts established policies on a vast range of correctional practices including food, cell size, recreation, and access to the outside world. This new bureaucratic and legalistic atmosphere established a routine within the prison that structured how the correctional officers interacted with inmates. The legalistic atmosphere meant that correctional officers could hide behind the rules and claim little or no authority to grant concessions. Grievance processes were instituted and even the smallest decisions had to be adjudicated by authorities higher than the correctional officer. In the contemporary prison, the separation between guard and inmate has increased because of the artificial nature of their interactions flowing from the bureaucratic nature of the institution (Johnson, 2002).

> The gulf between staff and prisoners is still wide. The culture of the guards, as the culture of the police, with its negative images of the "criminal," persists. In the contemporary prison, this gulf is more a function of the particular institutional arrangement than the personal values and meanings that employees bring to the workplace. Controlling persons who are in a position of extreme deprivation and who are antagonistic toward their overseers promotes negative attitudes. In their job training, new staff members are taught to mistrust prisoners. The outcome of new employees and inculcation with the existing informal guard culture and their interactions with prisoners—most of whom hate the guards and many of whom attempt to manipulate them to increase their levels of privilege and material means—results in guards and staff distrusting, demeaning, and often hating prisoners. (Irwin, 2005, p. 65)

It is the bureaucratic and legalistic nature of the contemporary prison that is problematic today. Although much of this artificial environment exists for good reason, it should be recognized that the rehabilitative ideal has been jettisoned and that administrative efforts at controlling inmates are purely concerned with security (Goffman, 1961). This is inevitable, in part, because of prison overcrowding. However, this has not made the prison safer, and it has not met inmates' rehabilitative needs. The modern-day prison, therefore, is a place of tension, violence, and tragic human waste. Given the lack of progress in finding humane and effective ways of changing criminal behavior, perhaps the rehabilitative ideal of the 1950s, 1960s, and 1970s should be reconsidered. In part, this can be done by revisiting how correctional officers and administrators treat inmates. Two books published by the American Correctional Association, *The Art of the Con: Avoiding Offender Manipulation*, by Gary Cornelius and *Game Over! Strategies for Redirecting Inmate Deception*, by Bill Elliott and Vicki Verdeyen (2002), provide the operating philosophy of the contemporary prison. In the first book, Cornelius (2001) provides potential correctional officers with an acronym, CHUMPS, that encapsulates how they can interact with inmates.

C = controlling yourself and not being complacent
H = helping offenders to help themselves
U = understanding the offender subculture and understanding yourself
M= maintaining a safe distance
P = practicing professionalism in adhering to policies and procedures
S = stopping yourself from being stressed out so you are not vulnerable

Some of Cornelius's advice is worth analyzing. Offenders like to spin a staff member out of control and will pick the busiest time to try to approach staff (artful/unfair means). Staff should use the power of paper. As one jail officer says, "Working around offenders is like being tugged in 20 different directions. When offenders approach me when I'm too busy to deal with them, I tell them to put it on a request form and send it in. By doing so I am controlling messages to me in a manageable way" (Cornelius, 2001, p. 76).

Cornelius suggests that correctional officers maintain an adequate professional and emotional distance from inmates. According to him, an inmate should not be allowed to call correctional officers by their first names or to engage in any kind of flattering behavior or to hurry an officer. Cornelius is adamant in his argument that correctional officers are not there to make friends and that their professional responsibilities preclude them from treating inmates in a familiar way. Although officers should be courteous to inmates, the correctional officer must also adhere to institutional rules to be firm in denying requests for exceptions. The correctional officer always has to be on guard for inmates crossing the line and becoming too friendly. It is not unheard of for correctional officers to be seduced by inmates into smuggling contraband into the prison, smuggling messages out of the prison, or being enticed into romantic relationships.

According to Cornelius, correctional officers can use the CHUMPS strategy to maintain a professional attitude on the job. But does this come at a price? When correctional officers must treat inmates in highly structured, bureaucratic ways, they lose something of their own humanity, and they deny the humanity of the inmates. An example of this can be gleaned from George Ritzer's *The Mc-Donaldization of Society* (2007), in which he writes about sales techniques used in fast food restaurants. The suggested sales technique is most recognizable when a counter person asks, "Would you like fries with that?" This is a counterfeit interaction in that the counter person is relying on training to structure the interaction so that customers will buy more products. Rather than having an authentic conversation, the counter person uses their experience in sales to manipulate the customer into buying more. This might not be objectionable in such a short interaction based upon commerce, but when dealing with inmates who need experience in having honest and open interactions, this preprogrammed response on the part of correctional officers is disingenuous and dysfunctional. It is accomplished for the convenience of the institution and the correctional officers, with little regard for the effects on the inmates.

So what kind of message are we giving inmates when we have such insincere conversations with them? On one level, the inmate is learning that he or she is not worthy of a real dialogue (McCullough, 1998). On the other hand, we are giving the message that there is much to keep away in terms of secrets or resources, and that the only way the inmate will gain access is through duplicity. To be honest here it is reasonable to assert that the rules of the institution are designed to show the inmate boundaries. Each of us has to negotiate our way through the world within certain strictures of acceptable behavior, and inmates who have demonstrated that they are unable to do this need firm and unwavering guidelines and policies to dictate how they are to act. The prison, in which administrators presumably have complete control, is an environment where inmates can learn how to follow orders and bend to the rules of the institution. If they cannot behave in prison, it is reasonable to expect that they will not be able to return to free society. Therefore, the prison environment in which inmates are allowed a little discretion or freedom can be viewed as training for life in free society.

This logic is flawed, however; once the state has complete control over the quality of life of the inmate, it is not difficult to coerce compliance. The real test as to whether the prison's rules or regulations are effective in changing behavior comes when the inmate returns to free society. When inmates are deprived of the ability to make decisions, they undergo a process called prisonization. Here, the inmate is incapable of making decisions based upon sound judgment, even when he or she is released from prison. Deprived of the opportunity to use judgment while incarcerated, the inmate is ill-equipped to use it in free society in which the rules are ever-changing and less visible. It can be argued that one reason the recidivism rate is so high in U.S. prisons is that inmates are not adequately prepared to return to a life in which they must make all their own decisions. When every aspect of inmates' lives are completely controlled by an outside force (the prison administration), and the inmates have no personal responsibility because they have been told when to get up, when to eat, what to eat, where to work, when to go to sleep, and when to go to the bathroom every single day for an extended period of time, it will be extremely difficult for them to overcome this institutionalization once released back into society where they are the only ones responsible for every aspect of their lives. The amount of freedom and responsibility can be too much for some to handle.

The multiple mandates of the prison produce an inherent tension. First is the mandate of custody and security. Prisons are required to keep inmates inside and to maintain security for both staff and inmates. There is, however, another mandate and that is attempting to rehabilitate the inmate. According to Elliott and Verdeyen (2002), the treatment staff must learn their proper role in the prison.

> The safe containment of inmates and the management of their risk for violence takes precedence over therapeutic and programmatic initiatives. In fact, psychiatrists, psychologists, counselors, and the like often have a peripheral role in the overall operation of the prison ... it behooves the treatment staff to demonstrate how their knowledge and expertise can benefit custody in security objectives ... the bottom line is that treatment staff must first accept where they sit within the "big picture," and then demonstrate how they can significantly contribute to the broader mission of the institution. (Elliot & Verdeyen, 2002, p. 172)

When the custody and security demands in the prison completely dominate the rehabilitative efforts of treatment personnel, it fosters an atmosphere of paranoia, distress, and hopelessness. Again, while realizing that the treatment of security functions of the prison are important, room must be made for the opportunity to engage in positive behavioral change for the inmate. It is important to remember that prisons are communities. Although they are confined communities behind walls with varying levels of security, they are nonetheless the communities within which convicted offenders may spend a significant portion of their lives. The interactions inmates have with correctional personnel on a daily basis can greatly influence their behavior during confinement. Negative interactions beget negative behavior. Although prison has been criticized as a place where inmates learn criminal behavior from other inmates, it is also a place where there is the opportunity to get the inmates' attention and set them on a path of effective functioning and law-abiding behavior. When correctional officers are systematically trained to believe that all inmates are engaged in lying and deception, the culture of the entire institution becomes socially poisonous, and inmates are unable to progress in developing the social skills necessary to survive in the free world.

It is the authors' contention here that this poisonous atmosphere of the prison is something that is useful to prison administrators and correctional officers and that it makes their jobs more predictable and easier. This philosophy does not consider the effects it has on future inmate behavior. Inmates who are treated as if they are liars, cheats, and dangerous often act in ways to make those judgments come true. What would an institution that treated inmates as valuable human beings look like?

Civility in Prisons

We have tried to present a new and radical program for altering the social culture of the prison. We do this with some trepidation because, not being correctional professionals, our comments might appear not only to be utopian and naïve, but to disregard the practical aspects of the prison. This is a challenge we gladly accept because the current atmosphere in prison fails to positively affect inmates and is often counterproductive. Therefore, we submit the following suggestions for changing the prison:

- Inmates are human beings also. Rather than treating inmates as socially undesirable, the prison should recognize that they are individuals who will most likely one day return to free society. As human beings, they are deserving of respect—one of the basic aspects of civility (Forni, 2002). Attention should be focused on how to best prepare them to live in the free world. This would entail giving inmates some type of actual control over their lives in prison and allow them to make decisions both individually and as a group. Many functions of the prison that are not custody- or security-related could be turned over to inmates. For instance, one of the most contentious areas is food. By giving inmates control over which days certain meals will be served, they get a chance to have some control over their lives.
- Inmates can work together. Many institutions have some form of inmate governance. Individuals are elected to an inmate council that represents the inmates' interests to the administration. These inmate councils ac-

complish two important goals within the prison. First, they give inmates an opportunity to choose those who speak for them. In doing so, it fosters a positive culture in which, rather than being at each other's throats, the inmates are required to work together and cooperate in dealing with prison administrators. Secondly, inmate councils actually relieve the prison administrators and correctional officers from dealing with many mundane issues for which they have little concern. For example, prison administrators have little interest in whether hotdogs are served for lunch on Tuesday or on Wednesday. To the inmates, however, having this control over what they will eat gives them experience in group decision-making. This is a valuable social skill.

- Correctional officers can be change agents. It is wise to recognize that correctional officers actually do have quite a bit of discretion in how they do their jobs. Although on paper it looks like prison policies and procedures dictate all interactions between prison personnel and inmates, the fact is that front-line officers routinely make discretionary judgments that are outside the purview of correctional administrators. By selecting who is inserted into the correctional grievance bureaucracy, the front-line correctional officer exerts a tremendous amount of power over inmates. By deciding when a behavior amounts to an infraction, the correctional officer is a gatekeeper. This gate-keeping function should be openly recognized and encouraged. This not only empowers the officer, but it also demonstrates to the inmates that the prison administrators value the officer's ability to make important decisions. Furthermore, it allows for civil, reciprocal relationships or acts between the prison's correctional officers and inmates. This would provide for an environment that is more conducive for rehabilitation.

- Inmates should be allowed to personalize their cells. In order for inmates to resist prisonization, we suggest that they be allowed to have a greater range of personal items in their cells, including books, posters, and televisions. Additionally, they should be allowed to wear a limited range of civilian clothing that is reflective of their personality and individual taste. Certainly, this would be limited to some degree by security concerns and would obviously vary by the type of prison. However, the austere and rigid rules and regulations of the present prison can be modified and relaxed to give inmates a greater sense of control over their captivity. It could be expected that by giving inmates this flexibility, the underground black market, including goods and services, would be diminished.

- Coeducational prisons should be reconsidered. At one time back in the 1960s and 1970s, several jurisdictions experimented with coeducational prisons (Ortiz, 1980). Although this is not a politically popular policy, it did have some positive effects on the social world of the prison. Confinement in single-sex societies deprives human beings of a significant audience. One of the observations of coed prisons was that homosexual rape was reduced. When women are present, men define their masculinity in terms of attracting female attention. When women are absent, men demonstrate their masculinity by domination and threats of violence. The civilizing effect that men and women have on each other can be a useful tool in the contemporary prison. This has benefits not only for the atmosphere of the prison, but also for the rehabilitative effects that could put inmates in a better position to successfully adjust to the free world. These benefits accrue not only to male inmates but also to female inmates because they are able to maintain a more natural social world than is possible in a single-sex society.

- Blended rehabilitative programs. Many such programs exist both in prison and in the free world. For example, Alcoholics Anonymous and other drug and alcohol treatment programs as well as educational programs exist in the prison and in the community. However, these programs are often limited in the prison because of lack of resources and conservative political winds. Bringing community resources into the prison makes it possible to increase the effectiveness of the progress. We would like to see this benefit extended even further by either bringing civilian clients into the prison for a couple of hours to take advantage of these programs with prisoners or allowing prisoners very limited release time to attend programs in the community. Obviously, this has great security implications, but with carefully screened inmates and outside clients, it might be possible to blend these two populations together to take advantage of the limited resources and allow for the positive effects their association could produce. In some countries, particularly Scandinavian ones, the philosophy is not so much to isolate offenders in prison where they are surrounded by other problematic individuals, but rather to immerse offenders in community programs where they can benefit from the example of law-abiding citizens.

Our proposals here are not exactly modest. In fact, they might fly in the face of conventional correctional wisdom. If we have overstepped common sense in some places, it is because the contemporary prison is dysfunctional. The recidivism rate in many prisons is so high that the institution might as well have a revolving door. Furthermore, the rate of violence in prisons is steadily increasing. In order to better prepare inmates for a productive life on the outside, it is suggested that the social world of the prison be more like the one that the inmates will face when they regain their freedom.

Limitations and Qualifications

We are not so naïve as to expect that these unusual suggestions will be implemented wholesale. This new philosophy of civil prisons might be inappropriate, particularly in maximum security prisons. However, on any experimental basis, in carefully selected institutions with specially trained correctional officers and administrators, these ideas deserve a chance. The social world that is created in what Goffman (1961) calls "total institutions" guarantees that there will be adjustment problems once the inmate is no longer confined and must negotiate relationships in a less structured environment. Additionally, this new philosophy of civility in prisons will be a difficult sell in today's political atmosphere of accountability and punishment. Politicians vie to see who can appear to be the toughest on crime, and the public demands retribution for the transgressions of offenders. It will take a substantial public relations effort that highlights the promises and possibilities of the new philosophy we are proposing in order to promote a change. Additionally, society should be prepared for the inevitable setbacks that occur in any new program.

If prisons were more effective, this new philosophy of civility would not be necessary. If prisons were more effective, inmates would return to society prepared to hold down a job, be a good parent, and become a productive citizen. Obviously, this is not the case, and after decades of ever-increasing failure, it is apparent that something new and radical deserves the opportunity to be tested on an experimental and limited basis.

References

Cornelius, G. (2001). The art of the con: Avoiding offender manipulation. Lanham, MD: American Correctional Association.

Elliott, B., & Verdeyen, V. (2002). Game over! Strategies for redirecting inmate deception. Lanham, MD: American Correctional Association.

Forni, P. (2002). Choosing civility: The twenty-five rules of considerate conduct. New York: St. Martin's Griffin.

Goffman, E. (1961). Asylums: Essays on the social situation of mental patients and other inmates. Garden City, NY: Anchor.

Irwin, J. (1970). The felon. Englewood Cliffs, NJ: Prentice-Hall.

Irwin, J. (1980). Prisons in turmoil. Boston: Little, Brown.

Irwin, J. (2005). The warehouse prison: Disposal of the new dangerous class. Los Angeles: Roxbury.

Jacobs, J. B. (1977). Statesville: The penitentiary in mass society. Chicago: University of Chicago Press.

Johnson, R. (2002). Hard time: Understanding and reforming the prison. Belmont, CA: Wadsworth.

McCullough, D. (1998). Say please, say thank you: The respect we owe one another. New York: G. P. Putnam's Sons.

Ortiz, J. O. (1980). Coed prisons. New York: Human Sciences Press.

Ritzer, G. (2007). The McDonaldization of society. Thousand Oaks, CA: Pine Forge Press.

Sykes, G. M. (1958). The society of captives: A study of a maximum security prison. Princeton, NJ: Princeton University Press.

Whitehead, J. T., Jones, M., & Braswell, M. C. (2008). Exploring corrections in America. (2nd ed.). Newark, NJ: Matthew Bender.

CHAPTER NINE

VARIETIES OF RESTORATIVE JUSTICE: THERAPEUTIC INTERVENTIONS IN CONTEXT

Lana A. McDowell, University of Southern Mississippi
John T. Whitehead, East Tennessee State University

Restorative justice offers numerous approaches as therapeutic interventions within the realm of criminal justice. Restorative justice has been defined in many ways by criminologists as well as practitioners. It is suggested by such individuals that criminal action, aside from being a violation of state or federal code, also creates a wound in the fabric of social relationships, which is in need of mending (Clark, 2005; Cook & Powell, 2003; Roche, 2001). More specifically, criminologists and practitioners in the criminal justice field are interested in utilizing underlying restorative justice values in order to practice restorative justice as a process. Restorative justice practices are viewed as informal processes (Bazemore, 2005; Roche, 2006) often held outside of the traditional criminal justice system locations (Calhoun & Borch, 2002; Dzur & Wertheimer, 2002). Restorative justice practices focus on the criminal action committed rather than placing the focus on the offender (Hayes & Daly, 2003; Tyler, 2006). Likewise in restorative justice practices, the focus is geared toward all individuals involved rather than simply focusing on the offender (Gavrielides, 2005; White, 2000). Restorative justice practices are also thought to be proactive and preventive (Morrison & Ahmed, 2006).

The values within restorative justice therapeutic interventions suggest the community has a collective responsibility to involve themselves in the restorative process. One reason for this is based on the contention that crime does not occur in a bubble. In other words, it is important for community members to consider their role in the commission of criminal behavior such as the lack of social connections between the offender, victim, and those who make up the community (Goren, 2001). The idea of collective responsibility requires community members to provide assistance and support to the offender and the victim as well as others affected by offenses. Another aspect of collective responsibility emphasizes the importance of members of society collaborating to create resolutions, which ideally take into consideration the needs of all involved, including society as a whole.

Needs of the Offender, Victim, and Community

From the restorative justice perspective, victim needs include compensation through an apology (Calhoun & Borch, 2002; O'Mahony & Doak, 2004), monetary restitution (Maxwell & Hayes, 2006; Rodriquez, 2005), and service to the community (Calhoun & Borch, 2002; Rodriquez, 2005). Other types of restitution may come in the form of fines and educational guidance as well as psychological measures such as counseling (Rodriquez, 2005). Another need of victims includes the ability for the individual to feel as though the offender is remorseful for his or her actions. Restorative justice therapeutic interventions provide a greater ability to offer remorse on the part of the offender than in the traditional system within the courtroom (Szmania & Mangis, 2005). Additional needs of victims within restorative justice therapeutic interventions include the ability to tell their story (Cook & Powell, 2003; Dzur & Wertheimer, 2002), to be part of the process that creates an agreement (Strang, 2004), to feel a sense of support from the community in which they live (Schwartz, Hennessey, & Levitas, 2003; Smith-Cunnien & Parilla, 2001), and to question the offender as to why he or she committed the crime and why the victim was chosen as the target (Strang et al., 2006).

Restorative justice therapeutic interventions also take into consideration the needs of the offender. Such needs include the need to be forgiven by both the victim and the community for his or her actions (Clark, 2005; Maxwell & Hayes, 2006; Roche, 2001), the need to feel as though the community is present in order to provide a sense of positive relationships among all involved (White, 2000), and the ability to gain a more positive perception of themselves by increasing their personal level of dignity (Parkinson & Roche, 2004).

Needs of all parties—the offender, victim, and community—include the ability for all to be empowered (Bazemore, 2005; Morrison, 2006; van Wormer, 2004). The offender, victim, and community also need a sense of reparation, meaning the harm caused by the action should be repaired to the greatest extent possible (Harris, 2006; White, 2000). It is important for all involved parties that a resolution be forged through the process of collaboration (Hillian,

Reitsma-Street, & Hackler, 2004). By creating appropriate paths to reparation and resolution, all involved move towards the ability to restore the harmed relationship back to the needed equilibrium (Burford & Hudson, 2001). The process of restoration leads everyone to reconcile their differences (Calhoun & Borch, 2002). It is important for all those involved to assist in the reintegration of both the offender and the victim (Gavrielides, 2005; Karp & Conrad, 2005). Lastly, all have a need to increase the safety of citizens by engaging in the restorative process (Goren, 2001).

The Restorative Justice Therapeutic Invention Process

Within restorative justice therapeutic invention processes, a number of aspects are viewed as important. The rationale for such processes suggests there is power in all parties coming together in an encounter phase (Calhoun & Borch, 2002). Within the encounter process, equality of all participants must be ensured (Boyes-Watson, 1999; Parkinson & Roche, 2004) as well as protection of all involved (Rundell, 2007). All individuals who attend the restorative justice encounter must do so through their own will. No participants may be forced to take part in restorative justice therapeutic intervention processes (Ryals, 2004; van Wormer, 2004). Additionally, participation of all parties regarding the resolution is important (Adams, 2004; Boyes-Watson, 1999). Further, it is paramount that individuals who are affected by the harm should ultimately be involved in the restorative justice therapeutic intervention (Roche, 2006; White, 2000).

Such core persons or attached actors may consist of the offender (Hillian et al., 2004; Rodriquez, 2005), the victim (Dzur & Wertheimer, 2002; Smith-Cunnien & Parilla, 2001), community members (Goren, 2001; Grauwiler & Mills, 2004), family members of both the offender and the victim (Maxwell & Hayes, 2006; Parkinson & Roche, 2004), friends of the offender and victim (Goren, 2001; Maxwell & Hayes, 2006), supporters (Boyes-Watson, 1999; Karp & Conrad, 2005), as well as volunteers (Bazemore, 2005). In addition, officials from criminal justice administrations such as court officials (Hillian et al., 2004), defense attorneys and prosecutors (Calhoun & Borch, 2002), Department of Corrections administration (Bays, 1999), judges (Hillian et al., 2004), juvenile case workers (Rundell, 2007), youth advocates (Maxwell & Hayes, 2006), police officers (Bazemore & Griffiths, 2003; Strang et al., 2006), and probation officers (Schwartz et al., 2003) may be involved in such processes. Additional individuals who may be included within restorative justice therapeutic interventions include guidance counselors (Ryals, 2004), psychologists (Rundell, 2007), school principals (Calhoun & Borch, 2002), social workers (van Wormer, 2004), teachers (Goren, 2001), and college administrators (Karp & Conrad, 2006). Restorative justice encounters are often guided by a facilitator (Rundell, 2007; Strang et al., 2006), mediator (Szmania & Mangis, 2005), or a coordinator (Dzur & Wertheimer, 2002).

Together, the actors and the encounter phase of the restorative justice process open the door for a re-education of social values for all participants. This has been noted as the ability to provide a sense of moral education (Adams, 2004; Gavrielides, 2005). The encounter creates the opportunity for a decision-making process among all who are present (Schwartz et al., 2003). The outcome of this decision-making process is based on the discussion of the storytelling phase in which the offender declares the reasons for the commission of the crime and the victim(s) has/have an opportunity to explain how the offense personally affected them (O'Hear, 2005; Yeager, 2004). After the storytelling process, the parties work to formulate a negotiation or agreement that suggests the necessity of compensation, reparation, and prevention of future crimes in order to repair the social relationships and harm created by the action at hand (Cook & Powell, 2003; Gavrielides & Coker, 2005).

Peacemaking Circles

The concept of peacemaking circles has been derived from Native American thought (Parkinson & Roche, 2004). Like all restorative justice therapeutic intervention programs, peacemaking circles operate on the premise that all parties in a community have a responsibility to restore the harm created by a particular member of the society in which they live (Ryals, 2004). Due to the Native American framework of thought, within peacemaking circles there is a distinct emphasis on the importance of ritual (Parkinson & Roche, 2004). Peacemaking circles, sometimes referred to as sentencing circles, often begin and end with prayer (Parkinson & Roche, 2004; Smith-Cunnien & Parilla, 2001) and also utilize symbolic items such as a talking stick or feather which embodies the relevance of only one member of the community speaking at a time (Parkinson & Roche, 2004). Such processes do not necessarily occur separately from the traditional criminal justice system; rather, the agreements made may be utilized in formal sentencing decisions (Smith-Cunnien & Parilla, 2001). Moreover, members of the formal criminal justice system, including judges and attorneys, are often involved in the circle process (Boyes-Watson, 1999).

It is not uncommon for a judge to become adapted to the position of a community elder who is given the task to oversee the circle process (Hillian et al., 2004). However, when actors from the traditional system are included in the circle process, it is important for such persons to remove their professional trappings to the extent possible. After all, restorative justice therapeutic interventions require a sense of equality between all parties (Boyes-Watson, 1999).

One example of peacemaking circles takes place in Canada and is known as an Aboriginal sentencing circle. Aboriginal sentencing circles are attended by the offender and the victim, members of society, supporters of the offender and the victim, administration of justice personnel, judges, or an individual in the community who resides over the circle and is known as the community elder (Hillian et al., 2004). As the name implies, participants are arranged in a circle format and the goal of the process is to allow storytelling to take place, as well as the ability for parties to create a resolution together which will be forwarded to the formal criminal justice system regarding the case (Hillian et al., 2004).

Another example of peacemaking circles includes those persons who have been or are entangled in domestic violence. Intimate Abuse Circles may begin after an arrest has taken place or when it is brought to the attention of the community that such abuse is transpiring with the lack of an arrest (Grauwiler & Mills, 2004). Such circles are utilized when both parties in the relationship have made the decision to remain a couple and work through the underlying issues. Additionally, Intimate Abuse Circles may be utilized when a couple has decided to separate, yet are interested in creating a break that is best for their children (Grauwiler & Mills, 2004). Unique to the Intimate Abuse Circles is the direct accountability of both the offender and the victim. Both the offender and victim select supporters who make up a community of care. Such circles are led by individuals who are experts on domestic violence, and the underlying goal is to cease the violent behavior rather than ultimately ceasing the relationship completely (Grauwiler & Mills, 2004).

One downfall of peacemaking circles is that they require a great amount of time and there is a need to tap into numerous resources (Hillian et al., 2004). However, when putting forth appropriate effort, all involved parties have the ability to reshape relationships, reconcile differences, and reintegrate both the victim and the offender into the community.

Group Conferencing

The idea of conferencing can be traced to its development within New Zealand (Parkinson & Roche, 2004). Conferencing processes within restorative justice therapeutic interventions are informal and guided by a facilitator or coordinator (Maxwell & Hayes, 2006). Individuals who attend conferences include the victim and the offender (Smith-Cunnien & Parilla, 2001), family members (Goren, 2001; Ryals, 2004), police (Goren, 2001; Maxwell & Hayes, 2006), probation officers and social workers (Goren, 2001), lawyers (Maxwell & Hayes, 2006), judges, school principals, and guidance counselors (Calhoun & Borch, 2002). Family group conferences do not include the general population of community members; such processes instead are family centered (Smith-Cunnien & Parilla, 2001). Family group conferencing is a voluntary process that requires both the victim and offender to agree to participate (Maxwell & Hayes, 2006).

Family group conferences may be utilized after a guilty plea has been received; when juveniles do not deny their involvement in a crime (Goren, 2001); in elementary and secondary school systems independently from the traditional or juvenile justice systems (Dawson & McHugh, 2006); and when personal responsibility is taken by the offender (Calhoun & Borch, 2002; Hayes & Daly, 2003). Many jurisdictions provide different opportunities for restorative justice family group conferences. In South Australia, restorative justice programs utilize the process for minor offenses as well as offenses against persons such as sexual offenses. In Adelaide, Australia, drug offenses, acts of shoplifting, and cases of public order utilize the family group conference process. However, in other jurisdictions, for instance Western Australia, only offenses of minor magnitude have the ability to experience the family group conference process (Hayes & Daly, 2003).

In South Australia, attendants are informed of their responsibilities and what the purpose of the conference entails prior to attending a conference. Next, in the storytelling phase, the offender explains his or her actions and the victim explains the effects of the actions. Family or supporters explain the effect of the crime personally for them. The offender speaks again and responds to what has been brought to light in the storytelling phase, which often elicits some form of personal responsibility from the offender as well as remorse. Lastly, the entire group tries to come to a compromise regarding how the harm may be repaired (Maxwell & Hayes, 2006). However, this is not always the case. In some family group conferences, the offender and supporters develop an action plan, which is then presented to the rest of the group for input (Maxwell & Hayes, 2006). Such resolutions or action plans may include an apology and remorse (Hayes & Daly, 2003), restitution in the form of money or time, forms of rehabilitation such as classes taken by the offender (Maxwell & Hayes, 2006), and agreeing to strive to refrain from criminal or delinquent behavior in the future.

The Children, Young Persons, and Their Families Act of 1989 in New Zealand brought about the implementation of family group conferencing, which today is utilized frequently with juveniles in Australia. In such conferences, encounters are administered by community members who receive training (Maxwell & Hayes, 2006). Family group conferences have been implemented within the walls of prisons where correctional educators conduct such practices (Halstead, 1999). The family in this instance includes those within the structured prison family. Conferences are also headed by police in what are known as police-based conferences (O'Mahony & Doak, 2004). In Ballymena, Ireland, offenders who shoplift may be asked to attend a police-based conference. In such cases, the direct victim may not want to be present; therefore, other retailers may act as the victim. In these conferences, a police officer who has been trained in restorative justice values and family group conferencing acts as the facilitator (O'Mahony & Doak, 2004).

In Canada, the Youth Criminal Justice Act of 2003 provides the option of conferencing for juveniles (Hillian et al., 2004). Victims are not included in all conferences within Canada; rather, they are only included in those conferences which have specially trained probation officers (Hillian et al., 2004). Another example of group conferencing includes Calgary Community Conferences, which hear noncriminal cases from public schools and from community members (Calhoun & Borch, 2002). The majority of Calgary Community Conferences are related to property offenses or offenses against the person (Calhoun & Borch, 2002). Family group conferences and police-based conferences widen the community of concern when an offender or delinquent has created disequilibrium in relationships. By bringing together those persons who are most affected by the offense, attached actors have the ability to be active participants in the justice process.

Reparative Boards

Reparative boards are made up of individual members of society. Reparative boards may be utilized as an alternative to the traditional system (Ryals, 2004) and may also be utilized once guilt has been established as an aspect of probation. The difference between reparative boards and other restorative justice therapeutic interventions is that citizens are in charge of such programs (Dzur & Wertheimer, 2002). Obviously, cases which enter the reparative board process are court referred, and the majority of such cases are not serious offenses (Boyes-Watson, 1999).

Victims' needs take priority in reparative boards. The encounter includes the victim explaining the suffering caused by the harm and then questioning the offender as to the motivations of his or her actions, as well as the offender detailing his or her history in order to better understand what circumstances may have led to the offense at hand (Dzur & Wertheimer, 2002). Next, the victim and offender create an understanding of what should be done to right the wrong. Victims also play an integral part in allowing the offender to show remorse and in providing the choice to the victim to decide to forgive the offender. The remorse and forgiveness stage usually occurs after a plan has been fully implemented by the offender. The completion of a plan offers a sense of closure to all involved (Dzur & Wertheimer, 2002).

Although the focus of reparative boards is on the victim, the offender is in need of becoming educated on ways to curb future offending and often needs to move beyond his or her transgressions (Dzur & Wertheimer, 2002). However, in certain reparative board processes, the victim is not so intimately involved and the board members act as the victims (Parkinson & Roche, 2004). One example of reparative boards is known as Project Turnaround in New Zealand, and it is utilized with adult offenders (Maxwell & Hayes, 2006). Reparative boards are also utilized with juveniles as found in Canada within Youth Justice Committees. Also in Canada, Family Court Committees work with the traditional youth services to provide recommendations for custody and issues regarding separations (Hillian et al., 2004).

Another program in Maricopa, Arizona, has created reparative boards referred to as Community Justice Committees. Each committee is made up of no more than five community members who decide what needs to be done to repair the harm that is a consequence of an infraction (Bazemore, 2005). Vermont has implemented Community Reparative Boards and has more than 60 such boards across the state. These boards were developed due to focus groups held by the Department of Corrections with citizens in order to gain a greater understanding of what members of the community think should be done in cases of harm (Dzur & Wertheimer, 2002).

Once guilt has been accepted by the offender in Community Reparative Boards, the case is redirected from the formal system to the probation process. Before taking part in the encounter phase, the offender is first told what will happen in the process, such as the importance of the offender explaining the crime at hand as well as an overview of his life situation. This information will be passed on to the members of the board (Dzur & Wertheimer, 2002). The encounter allows board members to establish that the action of the offender went against communal culture and the offender is in need of community moral re-education (Dzur & Wertheimer, 2002). In Vermont, the victim plays an important role in the process, unlike in some other reparative board processes. The victim leads the discussion, asks questions of the offender, participates in making an action plan, and attends a closing meeting (Dzur & Wertheimer, 2002).

Another example of restorative justice therapeutic interventions is Community Accountability Boards. For instance, a citizen in Oregon called the Islamic Cultural Center in his town after the 9/11 attacks and suggested all Muslims should die (Umbreit, Lewis, & Burns, 2003). The caller sought forgiveness from the formal criminal justice system and the victims expressed a desire to meet with the offender. The victims were interested in the offender making a public apology to the Muslim community. In addition, the victims requested the offender take part in Islamic thought lectures. The agreed plan also encouraged the offender to participate in media coverage of the event, receive psychological counseling, and meet with juvenile delinquents to discuss his crime and the harm he created (Umbreit et al., 2003). One interesting outcome of this encounter was that the victim also attended the Islamic lectures and learned of the offender's interest in becoming more educated regarding Islamic thought. This led to the attendance of additional lectures beyond the requirements stated in the agreement (Umbreit et al., 2003).

At one university, the Skidmore Integrity Board was created, which is made up of faculty, students, and staff. An example of the types of cases handled by the board includes a drug dealer who was given a prison sentence and wanted to re-enter school upon release from the correctional facility. The board required the offending student to speak to groups of students regarding his crime. Furthermore, the offender/student was asked to make an educational video for the university to be utilized for future prevention and general deterrence. The board requires violators to say they are sorry for the wrongdoing via letter format, to provide restitution, and to take part in community service activities. Offenders are also asked to write an essay focusing on their particular infractions, including means for prevention, and must provide academic research on aspects of the offense at hand. The offender/student may be asked to participate in campus activities or to utilize assistance, such as gaining educational help or visiting the counseling center; however, the board cannot require psychological treatment (Karp & Conrad, 2005). The ability for community members to act as boards that deal with criminal or delinquent actions provides a unique approach to distributing justice.

Victim Offender Mediation/ Reconciliation Programs

The restorative justice therapeutic intervention process of victim offender mediation differs from other practices in that the encounter was initially only attended by the offender, the victim, and a mediator. However, as restorative justice expands, such processes have begun to include supporters of the victim and offender as well (Parkinson & Roche, 2004). The encounter begins with both parties speaking, usually beginning with the victim, one at a time about the harm created. The storytelling phase includes the victim personally explaining the consequences of the harm, followed by the offender communicating his or her upbringing, and lastly the offender provides explanations as to why he or she committed the crime (Browning, Miller, & Spruance, 2001). The ability to show remorse for one's actions is another important aspect in the victim offender mediation process. Lastly, the victim and offender work together to create a restorative plan that will rebalance the harm created by the action (Ryals, 2004).

The mediator is encouraged to remain an impartial entity in the process. In addition, the mediator does not act as a citizen member, but rather as an expert within mediation (Boyes-Watson, 1999). The mediator's job is focused on setting the process in motion, but the actual encounter requires the focus of the discussion to be between the victim and the offender (Szmania & Mangis, 2005). Victim offender mediation may be utilized by viewing family members as indirect victims of crimes as well. For instance, spouses, children, parents, or grandparents could meet with the offender in order to help restore the social bonds which have been broken among family ties due to harm (Browning et al., 2001).

One example of the encounter process within victim offender mediation involved a couple who were frightened because a juvenile pretended to have a gun in order to scare them. The storytelling phase allowed the victims to learn the offender had recently lost a sibling due to a car accident. The victims felt this underlying tension in the offender's life had created a sense of unease and rage. A sense of connectedness was found because the victims had recently lost a child as well. The victim and offender came to understand they were not so different, and the victims wanted to become positive role models for the offender (King, 2002).

Szmania and Mangis (2005) conducted a case study relating to one offender's quest to express remorse to those individuals affected by his actions. The offender had been responsible for the deaths of two individuals while he was driving under the influence. The mother of one of the victims agreed to meet with the offender in a face-to-face meeting, which was carried out through the

Texas Victim Offender Mediation Dialogue (VOMD). VOMD processes are geared towards persons who have been involved in serious crimes (Szmania & Mangis, 2005). In this example, we see the importance of the willingness of both the victim and the offender to meet. Only one of the victims felt the process should be conducted. This may be because the Texas VOMD process requires a commitment from both parties. Both the offender and the victim are required to take part in a lengthy process before meeting, which includes writing letters to one another. Texas VOMD programs always occur after sentencing has taken place (Szmania & Mangis, 2005); therefore, it is less likely the offender will feel the encounter will have an impact on the outcome on his or her punishment. In the case of serious violent crimes, it may be important for time to first heal the wounds of the victim which may lead to a request of being involved in a mediation process. In the above example, the encounter occurred four years after the offender was sentenced (Szmania & Mangis, 2005). Although such programs as the Texas VOMD processes are geared toward serious crime, it has been suggested the general public believes victim offender mediation is more appropriate for less serious offenses (Roberts & Stalans, 2004).

In Canada, victim offender reconciliation programs include only the victim, the offender, and a mediator. The encounter may act as a replacement for sentencing or may occur after adjudication as part of an offender's probation (Hillian et al., 2004). Also in Canada, victim offender mediation has been utilized with individuals who have been involved in harm relating to the Roman Catholic Church. Students from Mount Cashel Orphanage created a union in order to legally have the ability to begin mediation between such victims and offenders (Gavrielides & Coker, 2005). The restorative justice therapeutic intervention process of victim offender mediation is thought to empower the victim and the offender of crime (Bazemore, 2005). This empowerment helps rebuild the ruptured social relationships by allowing the parties to work together to understand one another and to create a resolution that both parties feel is appropriate.

Victim Offender Panels

Victim offender panels are a unique addition to restorative justice therapeutic intervention processes. Within peacemaking circles, group conferencing, reparative boards, and victim offender mediation/reconciliation, the majority of cases involve a particular action in which the parties who attend have a personal stake. Victim offender panels differ in that the action focused upon is not based on one particular instance of harm. In victim offender panels, the victim of a particular crime, for instance aggravated assault, speaks to a group of offenders who have committed the action of aggravated assault. Numerous victims who have all been victimized by the crime of shoplifting, for instance, can speak with a group of persons who have committed shoplifting infractions. Victim offender panels may be important in cases where the victim cannot identify his offender, when the offender is not willing to meet with the personal victim of his or her crime, when the victim cannot be identified, or when the victim is uncomfortable with meeting the offender who caused the harm, yet has a desire to provide closure to the situation. This process allows the offender to understand how any particular crime affects numerous victims in substantial ways (Browning et al., 2001). An example of victim offender panels is found in elementary and secondary education. In Denver, Colorado, juvenile offenders who have stolen, vandalized, brought drugs on school premises, or who are harassing other students take part in listening to victims of their particular infractions (Karp & Breslin, 2001).

Additionally, offenders have the ability to meet with victims of the crime they committed without coming in personal contact with their own victims. Offenders can formulate a panel in order to explain their crime and why they believe they committed the crime, and they may also utilize the opportunity to answer questions from victims of the crime type at hand. Browning and colleagues (2001) contend victim offender panels may be useful for families in the sense that members of a particular family may better be able to understand what their offending family member is going through by listening, asking questions, and interacting with offenders not related to their family who have committed similar crimes. Furthermore, victim offender panels may be utilized by offenders who are interested in understanding the position, thoughts, and feelings of their personal families. An example may be a process of victim offender panels for a family whose current breadwinner is incarcerated for a period of time. The family could explain as a panel how they have been affected by the imprisonment of their family member to offenders who are in similar situations. In addition, the use of family panels may aid offenders in understanding how members of their own personal family feel regarding stigmatization, without being required to approach such a topic with their direct family members.

Social Justice Initiatives

Lotter (2005, p. 97) contends "injustices of the distant past are actually issues of the present." The values of restorative justice are slowly joining the fabric of the world today. One example relates to indigenous societies. Traditional forms of restorative justice are based on the idea that a sense of community needs to be created. However, indigenous justice holds the conception that a particular indigenous community was in existence prior to the restorative initiative (D'Errico, 1999). Restorative justice processes are becoming an avenue for communities to explore wrongs committed against the experience of a particular community (D'Errico, 1999). Indigenous justice is thought to be an extension of justice before the creation of codified law (Burford & Hudson, 2001). Zion (1999, p. 367) contends indigenous justice is viewed from the Navajo's perspective as "justice is respect in relationships." In addition, the "indigenous justice process and indigenous needs-based justice is feeling; it is relationship; it is active listening to others; and it is acting in response to the needs of others; it is groups of people depending on each other in arrangements we call a community" (Zion, 1999, p. 372).

In practice, indigenous justice has been set in motion to communicate wrongs towards certain populations. One such example is the South African Truth and Reconciliation Commission (TRC). Leebaw (2001, p. 275) contends, "The decision to investigate only those abuses classified as 'gross violations of human rights' has important implications for TRC's restorative aims." The basic idea supporting the South African Truth and Reconciliation Commission is that it provides the encounter of a hearing format where the group who has been unjustly treated may come into contact with groups that they feel are responsible for the community group harm (Minow, 2003; Roche, 2006). The universalization of restorative justice can be etched from the TRC creation. As explained by Leebaw (2001, p. 273), "Where restorative justice programs have typically operated as local alternatives to state-run justice systems, the TRC was constructed in part as a nation state-building and legitimating exercise."

The South African Truth and Reconciliation Commission came to fruition in order to mend broken relationships among citizens created by the era of Apartheid and the new democratic government within South Africa (Minow, 2003; Parkinson & Roche, 2004). Leebaw (2001, pp. 268–269) explains the fracture in relationships presented to the government of South Africa and the need for transitional justice in such occurrences. "The central question raised by transitional justice is this: given scarce resources and ongoing threats from remnants of the old order, how can a new state condemn mass violence and repression conducted under a prior regime while generating a normative basis for future co-existence and democratizing political reform?" At the hearings, it is obliviously difficult for particular victims and offenders to meet (Roche, 2006); therefore, it is also difficult for offenders to take responsibility and provide reparations to victims (Roche, 2006). Due to this lack of personal accountability, responsibility and reparation fall on the shoulders on the State (Roche, 2006). The hearings provide an opportunity for victims to explain how they were affected by the harm. Those individuals who were responsible and who took personal responsibility for their percentage of the harm were considered for amnesty regarding what could become a criminal violation (Minow, 2003; Roche, 2006). In order to be considered for amnesty, individuals were required to confess publicly and to admit the political ties that lead to the wrongdoing (Roche, 2006).

In Australia, principles of restorative justice therapeutic interventions may be viewed through the process of the Deliberative Poll of Canberra. Aboriginal Australians attended the poll to explain their feelings of unjust treatment throughout time and attempted to understand manners in which the harm could be reconciled (Cook & Powell, 2003). Two processes took place at the Deliberative Poll of Canberra. First, large discussions and storytelling were guided by a moderator who ensured only one person spoke at a time. Secondly, additional small groups met in order to more intimately discuss aboriginal harms of Australian indigenous people (Cook & Powell, 2003). Although the poll brought victims and offenders together, reconciliation was only achieved in a small number of instances between certain individuals. One issue which is in conflict with restorative justice values regarding the Deliberative Poll is that persons responsible for the harm did not necessarily or always accept their personal responsibility. An example of this follows:

> The topic of apology was raised by an aboriginal man participating as a representative Australian. He specifically confronted Minister Ruddock about why the government steadfastly refused to apologize officially. Ruddock replied: "We want to assist in the process; commitments have been made on this in terms of money. Apologies have been made by individuals, but a formal apology has been considered by the present government, and the decision not to offer a formal apology reflects our desire to move forward together." Then Aden Ridgeway responded: "The question is how are we to move forward from our current state? We have to judge the response from the aboriginal people, those who have been victimized. Do they feel satisfied in the present government's refusal to formally apologize? We all have to be part of the solution." (Cook & Powell, 2003, p. 285)

Within juvenile justice in the United States, the balanced restorative justice approach is believed by some to include an aim of social justice. The purpose of the balanced restorative justice approach suggests that the underlying philosophy of the traditional juvenile justice system should be reformulated to some extent (White, 2000). White (2000) contends the balanced restorative justice approach should consider the societal issues which are present in the infrastructure that create juvenile crime, such as the socio-economic standing of juveniles and their families.

Questions have been raised regarding the use of social justice initiatives to repair harm from instances of slavery in the United States. Kukathas (2006) explains such reparations are not plausible because offenses of one generation cannot be transferred to future generations. However, Winter (2006) contends current generations may be viewed as liable when setbacks are caused by past offenses and future generations do not deal with such issues in the proper manner. In other words, if one generation understands the harm caused by past generations, yet does nothing to correct for such transgressions through social capabilities, the current generation should be held liable in the aspect of reparation because such is the responsibility of the current generation. Lotter (2005) suggests it is important to remember injustices from history are almost always perpetrated by another group and brings up an excellent point regarding past injustices. He suggests it is not possible to calculate the harm done for financial reparation and contends not all descendants are harmed equally. Further, he contends individuals have a personal responsibility for how they behave currently, including overlooking injustices and current instances of injustices by omission as well as utilizing prejudice in their interactions. Social justice initiatives as described above are utilizing values of restorative justice in new and different ways. As restorative justice grows in popularity, citizens can expect additional creations of restorative justice therapeutic interventions over time.

Community Justice

There are questions and arguments among restorative criminologists that center on the idea that combining the conception of restorative justice and community justice is inappropriate. This topic will not be considered in this discussion of community justice. This section will provide examples of how restorative justice values and principles may be embedded in the fabric of a number of community justice programs.

One example of restorative justice values found in the community justice setting may occur within the institutionalized realm. In one prison, inmates were provided access to a prison computer lab; however, a hard drive went missing. The educational staff spoke with groups of inmates in order to explain the current circumstance and to suggest the inmates find a solution to the problem. Three weeks passed with no solution from the inmates. The educational staff suggested a resolution which included inmates could use the computer lab if they attended a computer class and if they promised not to take or harm the computers. Only a few inmates would not agree to this resolution and were therefore not allowed to take part in the computer room privileges. Within four years, zero damage occurred in this particular institution to the computers (Halstead, 1999).

Restorative justice principles are also found today in college classrooms. Holsinger and Crowther (2005) explain juvenile offenders are being invited to take part in one college course with students of a university in a restorative justice course. This initiative was created to allow juvenile offenders to feel they were part of a community, provide reparation through participation, and be reintegrated into the community by traditional college students. Likewise, it was believed traditional college students would gain a new perspective of juvenile offenders (Holsinger & Crowther, 2005). Upon interviewing, the researchers found delinquent youths gained a greater understanding of how their crimes affected victims and 100 percent of students suggested a desire for the needs of all involved in a particular harm to be considered and met. Some college students expressed the importance of the ability to better understand the histories of juveniles as well as the labels placed on such persons. Other students commented on their increased knowledge of connectedness with the juveniles and expressed the opinion that juveniles had an ability to create change in their lives (Holsinger & Crowther, 2005). This example notes the ability for community members to come together in order to better understand one another without a formal or informal restorative justice therapeutic intervention process taking place.

Restorative justice initiatives are also making their way into secondary education. Morrison and colleagues (2005) note that in the past when delinquent activities arose in schools, the offender was transferred to the traditional system; however, today initiatives are being made to transform the mindset into the ability for school administration and teachers to utilize restorative justice principles as their central philosophy. Karp and Breslin (2001) studied restorative justice-based philosophies in schools in Minnesota, Colorado, and Pennsylvania. In Minnesota, chemical health coordinators received training on restorative justice and utilized it with juveniles who were found to be plagued with substance abuse issues. In Denver, Colorado, teachers may call circles to discuss inappropriate behavior in the classroom. As discussed previously, teachers in Denver have the opportunity to create victim offender panels where offenders hear from victims of the type of offense committed in order to gain a better understanding of the consequences of such behavior. In one Denver school, the traditional system may be utilized with serious offenses, yet upon returning to the school environment the student may take part in restorative justice processes to curb re-offending (Karp & Breslin, 2001). In Pipersville, Pennsylvania, Buxmont Academy has an environment structured for teenage students with disciplinary problems, and restorative justice principles are woven into the school philosophy. When a student is known to have possession of illegal substances, they are provided the opportunity to explain to their classmates why they have been found guilty of such charges (Karp & Breslin, 2001). In other words, students are provided the opportunity to take personal responsibility for their actions not only to the administration of the school but to the community to which they belong.

In Illinois, the Taylorville Correctional Center and Lake Land College have teamed up to formulate a program where inmates build modular homes under the supervision of a construction trades instructor (Bays, 1999). One benefit of this program is that many of the homes built are delivered to the communities in which the offenders were raised. This provides a sense of giving back or reparation to the community along with a sense of accomplishment and empowerment (Bays, 1999). Another form of social initiatives related to restorative justice therapeutic interventions includes community accountability programs as discussed in the section regarding reparative boards. Such programs are in existence in Canada and are made up of community members. Police have the ability to refer an offender to one of around 65 programs when offenses are not considered as serious (Hillian et al., 2004).

It should come as no surprise that restorative justice values and principles blur the line between community justice initiatives and restorative justice therapeutic interventions. As restorative justice principles become embedded in the mindset of practitioners, criminologists, and citizens, one should expect to recognize a greater number of such values within aspects noted and defined as community justice in the present and future.

Results of Restorative Justice

An early meta-analysis of restorative justice programs found that on average they reduced reoffending by eight percent. Recent meta-analyses of restorative justice programs have found significant results for restorative justice programming with effect sizes ranging from .03 to .30 (for more details, see Bergseth & Bouffard, 2007).

One example of a program with positive effects is the Maricopa County, Arizona, Community Justice Committee program. These committees were considered a type of family group conferencing program, in which victims and family members attempted to respond to the harm that a juvenile offender committed. More than 75 percent of the juveniles were ordered to perform community service and pay restitution. The juveniles had from 60 to 90 days to complete the terms of the agreements.

A simple examination seemed to show no difference in recidivism rates; 34 percent of the restorative justice program subjects recidivated compared to 36 percent of the comparison group. However, when controlling for legal and extralegal factors, after 24 months, juveniles in the restorative justice program were less likely than offenders in the comparison group to have a new petition (Rodriguez, 2007).

A recent study of a restorative justice program in Ohio is noteworthy because it included offenders with prior offenses and current violent offenses, not just first-time non-violent offenders. Program staff tried to match offenders with the most appropriate restorative justice program, including victim offender mediation, victim impact panels, or a community panel. Offenders in the program had significantly lower prevalence of official contacts within six months, one year, two years, and three years of referral, and significantly lower total numbers of contacts. Most of these significant findings held up controlling for other variables in multivariate analyses (Bergseth & Bouffard, 2007).

In summary, there is evidence available that restorative justice programs can reduce recidivism. Given the comparatively high victim approval of restorative justice programs and the extremely high satisfaction of offenders with restorative justice programs (Braithwaite, 1999), this positive evidence on recidivism reduction is additional support for restorative justice programming. Restorative justice not only produces positive feelings in victims and offenders, it also reduces reoffending.

Conclusion

Restorative justice therapeutic interventions are providing new avenues for those who offend in the criminal justice and juvenile justice systems. The processes of circles, group conferencing, reparative boards, victim offender mediation, and victim offender panels work to heal social relationships that have been disrupted due to offenses. As restorative justice therapeutic interventions become more popular, we begin to see an increase in restorative processes among social justice initiatives on a larger national and global scale. Likewise, restorative justice values are being intertwined within community justice efforts. Restorative justice processes may be thought of as therapeutic interventions because family members, supporters, and community members, as well as offenders and victims, all take part in an encounter phase. These activities provide a method of storytelling, which is hoped to aid those who offend to recognize the wrongs they have committed, to take responsibility for such actions, and to work towards rebuilding the broken relationships. Restorative justice processes are therapeutic for victims because they may come to better understand the history and circumstances of the offender, have the ability to express their personal feelings, and be provided the ability to forgive the offender for his or her actions. Restorative justice processes are therapeutic for community members because citizens are provided the opportunity to take part in the justice process and to make a difference in the lives of both offenders and victims. As restorative justice therapeutic interventions grow in number and popularity, it is obvious the values embedded within restorative justice are finding their way into the perceptions and hearts of offenders, victims, and community members, which will increase the utilization of such processes in the future of criminal justice.

References

Adams, P. (2004). Restorative justice, responsive regulation, and democratic governance. Journal of Sociology & Social Welfare, 31(1), 3–5.

Bays, B. (1999). Habitat at Taylorville: One example of how prisons can successfully partner with outside agencies for restorative justice. Journal of Correctional Education, 50(2), 48–50.

Bazemore, G. (2005). Reaction essay: Whom and how do we reintegrate? Finding community in restorative justice. Criminology & Public Policy, 4(1), 131–148.

Bazemore, G., & Griffiths, C. (2003). Police reform, restorative justice, and restorative policing. Police Practice & Research, 4(4), 335–346.

Bergseth, K. J., & Bouffard, J. A. (2007). The long-term impact of restorative justice programming for juvenile offenders. Journal of Criminal Justice, 35(4), 433–451.

Boyes-Watson, C. (1999). In the belly of the beast? Exploring the dilemmas of state-sponsored restorative justice. Contemporary Justice Review, 2(3), 261–281.

Braithwaite, J. (1999). Restorative justice: Assessing optimistic and pessimistic accounts. In M. Tonry (Ed.), Crime and justice: A review of research (pp. 1–127). Chicago: University of Chicago Press.

Browning, S. L., Miller, R. R., & Spruance, L. M. (2001). Criminal incarceration dividing the ties that bind: African-American men and their families. Journal of African American Men, 6(1), 87–102.

Burford, G., & Hudson, J. (2001). Guest editors' introduction. Contemporary Justice Review, 4, 259–266.

Calhoun, A. J., & Borch, D. (2002). Justice in relationships: Calgary community conferencing as a demonstration project. Contemporary Justice Review, 5(3), 249–260.

Clark, M. E. (2005). Skinner vs. the prophets: Human nature and our concepts of justice. Contemporary Justice Review, 8(2), 163–176.

Cook, K. J., & Powell, C. (2003). Unfinished business: Aboriginal reconciliation and restorative justice in Australia. Contemporary Justice Review, 6(3), 279–292.

Dawson, N., & McHugh, B. (2006). Commentary: A systemic response to school-based violence from a UK perspective. Journal of Family Therapy, 28(3), 267–271.

D'Errico, P. (1999). Restorative indigenous justice states and communities in tension. Contemporary Justice Review, 2, 383–394.

Dzur, A. W., & Wertheimer, A. (2002). Forgiveness and public deliberation: The practice of restorative justice. Criminal Justice Ethics, 21(1), 3–20.

Gavrielides, T. (2005). Some meta-theoretical questions for restorative justice. Ratio Juris, 18(1), 84–106.

Gavrielides, T., & Coker, D. (2005). Restoring faith: Resolving the Roman Catholic Church's sexual scandals through restorative justice (Working Paper I). Contemporary Justice Review, 8(4), 345–365.

Goren, S. (2001). Healing the victim, the young offender, and the community via restorative justice: An international perspective. Issues in Mental Health Nursing, 22(2), 137–149.

Grauwiler, P., & Mills, L. G. (2004). Moving beyond the criminal justice paradigm: A radical restorative justice approach to intimate abuse. Journal of Sociology & Social Welfare, 31(1), 49–69.

Halstead, S. (1999). Educational discipline using principles of restorative justice. Journal of Correctional Education, 50(2), 42–47.

Harris, N. (2006). Reintegrative shaming, shame, and criminal justice. Journal of Social Issues, 62(2), 327–346.

Hayes, H., & Daly, K. (2003). Youth justice conferencing and re-offending. Justice Quarterly, 20(4), 725–764.

Hillian, D., Reitsma-Street, M., & Hackler, J. (2004). Conferencing in the youth criminal justice act of Canada: Policy developments in British Columbia. Canadian Journal of Criminology and Criminal Justice, 46(3), 343–366.

Holsinger, K., & Crowther, A. (2005). College course participation for incarcerated youth: Bringing restorative justice to life. Journal of Criminal Justice Education, 16(2), 328–339.

Karp, D. R., & Breslin, B. (2001). Restorative justice in school communities. Youth & Society, 33(2), 249–272.

Karp, D. R., & Conrad, S. (2005). Restorative justice and college student misconduct. Public Organization Review: A Global Journal, 5, 315–333.

King, D. (2002). Reconciliation is a gift and a task ... and we can work for it in doing restorative justice. Network News, 22, 3–4.

Kukathas, C. (2006). Who? Whom? Reparations and the problem of agency. Journal of Social Philosophy, 37(3), 330–341.

Leebaw, B. (2001). Restorative justice for political transitions: Lessons from the South African truth and reconciliation commission. Contemporary Justice Review, 4(3/4), 267–284.

Lotter, H. P. P. (2005). Compensating for impoverishing injustices of the distant past. Politikon: South African Journal of Political Studies, 32(1), 83–102.

Maxwell, G., & Hayes, H. (2006). Restorative justice developments in the Pacific region: A comprehensive survey. Contemporary Justice Review, 9(2), 127–154.

Minow, M. (2003). Foreword: Why retry? Reviving dormant racial justice claims. Michigan Law Review, 101, 1133–1140.

Morrison, B. (2006). School bullying and restorative justice: Towards a theoretical understanding of the role of respect, pride, and shame. Journal of Social Issues, 62(2), 371–392.

Morrison, B., & Ahmed, E. (2006). Restorative justice and civil society: Emerging practice, theory, and evidence. Journal of Social Issues, 62(2), 209–215.

Morrison, B., Blood, P., & Thorsborne, M. (2005). Practicing restorative justice in school communities: Addressing the challenge of cultural change. Public Organization Review: A Global Journal, 5(4), 335–357.

O'Hear, M. M. (2005). Is restorative justice compatible with sentencing uniformity? Marquette Law Review, 89, 305–325.

O'Mahony, D., & Doak, J. (2004). Restorative justice: Is more better? The experience of police-led restorative cautioning pilots in Northern Ireland. Howard Journal of Criminal Justice, 43(5), 484–505.

Parkinson, J., & Roche, D. (2004). Restorative justice: Deliberative democracy in action? Australian Journal of Political Science, 39(3), 505–518.

Roberts, J. V., and Stalans, L. J. (2004). Restorative sentencing: Exploring the views of the public. Social Justice Research, 17(3), 315–334.

Roche, D. (2001). The evolving definition of restorative justice. Contemporary Justice Review, 4(3/4), 341–353.

Roche, D. (2006). Dimensions of restorative justice. Journal of Social Issues, 62(2), 217–238.

Rodriguez, N. (2005). Restorative justice, communities, and delinquency: Whom do we reintegrate? Criminology & Public Policy, 4(1), 103–130.

Rodriguez, N. (2007). Restorative justice at work: Examining the impact of restorative justice resolutions on juvenile recidivism. Crime & Delinquency, 53(3), 355–379.

Rundell, F. (2007). "Re-storying" our restorative practices. Reclaiming Children & Youth, 16, 52–59.

Ryals, J. S., Jr. (2004). Restorative justice: New horizons in juvenile offender counseling. Journal of Addictions & Offender Counseling, 25(1), 18–25.

Schwartz, S., Hennessey, M., & Levitas, L. (2003). Restorative justice and the transformation of jails: An urban sheriff's case study in reducing violence. Police Practice & Research, 4(4), 399–410.

Smith-Cunnien, S. L., & Parilla, P. F. (2001). Restorative justice in the criminal justice curriculum. Journal of Criminal Justice Education, 12, 385–403.

Strang, H. (2004). The threat to restorative justice posed by the merger with community justice: A paradigm muddle. Contemporary Justice Review, 7(1), 75–79.

Strang, H., Sherman, L., Angel, C. M., Woods, D. J., Bennett, S., Newbury-Birch, D., & Inkpen, N. (2006). Victim evaluations of face-to-face restorative justice conferences: A quasi-experimental analysis. Journal of Social Issues, 62(2), 281–306.

Szmania, S. J., & Mangis, D. E. (2005). Finding the right time and place: A case study comparison of the expression of offender remorse in traditional justice and restorative justice contexts. Marquette Law Review, 89(2), 335–358.

Tyler, T. R. (2006). Restorative justice and procedural justice: Dealing with rule breaking. Journal of Social Issues, 62(2), 307–326.

Umbreit, M. S., Lewis, T., & Burns, H. (2003). A community response to a 9/11 hate crime: Restorative justice through dialogue. Contemporary Justice Review, 6(4), 383–391.

van Wormer, K. (2004). Restorative justice: A model for personal and societal empowerment. Journal of Religion & Spirituality in Social Work, 23(4), 103–120.

White, R. (2000). Social justice, community building, and restorative strategies. Contemporary Justice Review, 3(1), 55–72.

Winter, S. (2006). Uncertain justice: History and reparations. Journal of Social Philosophy, 37(3), 342–359.

Yeager, P. C. (2004). Law versus justice: From adversarialism to communitarianism. Law & Social Inquiry, 29(4), 891–915.

Zion, J. W. (1999). Monster slayer and born for water: The intersection of restorative and indigenous justice. Contemporary Justice Review, 2(4), 359–382.

Section III

Humanistic Themes in Offender Treatment

CHAPTER TEN

CORRECTIONAL TREATMENT AND THE HUMAN SPIRIT: THE CONTEXT OF RELATIONSHIP[1]

Michael Braswell, East Tennessee State University
Kristin Wells, East Tennessee State University

The evolution of the study and practice of corrections in America has moved within the historical pendulum between the principle of retribution as endorsed by such sacred writings as the Upanishads, the Koran, and the Law of Moses, and the more peacemaking/restorative and rehabilitative philosophy of the New Testament as expressed in various reform movements. The tension between the two has been considerable in the inevitable ambiguity of our democratic society. Such ambiguity recognizes the need for social order and control, yet at the same time stresses individual liberties, human potential, and the value of a community at peace with itself. Punishment and rehabilitation, emotion and reason, and incarceration and restoration reside together as our system of justice attempts to reach a more effective synthesis—a synthesis that will provide order and stability in the community in a humane way without diminishing the possibilities for positive change in most of the individuals who offend the community.

To be a part of a justice system that is more humane for both the community at large and for the offender, correctional treatment will need to refocus on the power of relationship as a priority for positive change. Such refocusing will require treatment staff to more clearly view treatment strategies as a means to an end rather than as an end in themselves. In other words, corrections should place greater emphasis on the capacity and abilities of offenders to develop and maintain meaningful relationships with themselves, family, and staff.

---

1. This chapter is a substantial revision of "Correctional Treatment and the Human Spirit," previously published in the *Federal Probation Quarterly* in June 1989.

One could suggest that such a goal is more natural or common sense and some-what less clinical than others. Within this framework, the counselor or other professional uses the power of the counseling relationship to become the pri-mary model for demonstrating self-discipline, empathy, and compassion to the offender.

In trying to bring the nonconforming offender to an accommodating point within the order of an established democratic community, corrections has run the gamut of treatment strategies and philosophies. Historically, most of the various treatment phases were somewhat fallacious; often we find a substan-tial difference between the claims surrounding new treatment programs and the reality of their implementation and results. From the more coercive pro-grams of correctional hardliners who deny the value of rehabilitation and other humanistic approaches to correctional liberals who are inclined to confuse a busy inmate services agenda with an effective one, legitimate treatment pro-grams have often been replaced more quickly than new fall television shows.

Early efforts inspired by the Quakers attempted to influence offenders through religious instruction and reform. Post-Civil War efforts evolved from teaching inmates to read the Bible to mass liberal arts and vocational education programs. The congregate work environment, as exemplified by the Auburn prison model, spawned an emphasis upon the work ethic of the prison industry era. Starting in the 1950s, the medical model was implemented as the treatment approach of choice wherein criminality was to be treated in the same manner as a physical dis-ease (i.e., diagnosis of problem, prescription, treatment, and cure). In reaction to this trend, the behavioral science movement emerged, embracing some ele-ments of the medical model but perhaps being more compatible with the tech-nology and engineering orientation of the hard sciences. Through scientific methods applied to human behavior, behavioral scientists contended that crim-inality could be eliminated. Some critics accused the behaviorists of "methodolatry," the worship of the scientific method, or at least placing too much confidence in its infallibility (Braginsky & Braginsky, 1974). The more enthusiastic and even blatant claims attributed to behavioral treatment are demonstrated by McConnell's (1970) comments concerning a person possessing an antisocial personality:

> No one owns his own personality. Your ego, or individuality, was forced on you by your genetic constitution and by the society into which you were born. You had no say about what kind of personality you ac-quired, and there's no reason to believe you should have the right to refuse to acquire a new personality if your old one is antisocial. (p. 3)

Therapeutic communities in and out of prison also enjoyed some degree of popularity in the 1970s as evidenced by the success of such programs as Daytop, a drug treatment program. Common goals, personal sacrifice, and responsibility were advocated, notwithstanding outside criticisms ranging from charges of suspect qualifications of supervising staff to claims that some therapeutic communities encouraged a cult-like dependency in their members. For better or worse, each movement in turn started with a high level of enthusiasm and energy, only to be eventually overshadowed by the institutions of confinement themselves and the accompanying business and bureaucracy of corrections. Regarding the historical lessons of evolving American prison policy (which includes treatment), Sherman and Hawkins (1981, p. 118) suggest, " ... it is at periods of the most excessive claims that the greatest indignities have been wrought."

Although remnants of each correctional movement may remain, over the years the rhetoric of correctional treatment seems increasingly to bear little resemblance to its realities. Treatment programs that start out as an innovation seem to inevitably become assimilated into this or that correctional treatment hierarchy. Such a course of action often does not seem to make much sense, yet we have followed this approach faithfully for decades, pausing every now and then to slap on a fresh coat of legislation and policy mandates—usually around election time. It often appears as though our correctional efforts are more the result of political and social fashion than of serious, long-term program commitments. Each new treatment program, like that of popular diet and self-help movements, is heralded as the "one-and-only" model to solve the majority, if not all, of our crime problems. Less sensational programs that may be viable for a smaller portion of the inmate and offender population are less conducive to extensive press coverage and, as a result, are inclined to be ignored even when they prove to be effective (Andrews & Bonta, 2006; Cullen & Gilbert, 1982; Van Voorhis, Braswell, & Lester, 2007). Somehow we have continued to believe that we can isolate the majority of offenders from the social arena of relatively normal community life to confinement in the abnormal world of the prison in order to teach them how to become more humane and well-adjusted to the outside world. Of course, given enough time in such an environment, many offenders do learn to become fairly well-adjusted, not to the outside world, but rather to the world inside walls designed to confine them and to protect us. Perhaps their confinement becomes as much a symbol as anything else— one which restricts their intellectual and emotional possibilities as much as their physical movement, and one which also restricts our community and economic resources in order to keep them there, especially during more recent years when prison construction and privatization have been such a growth industry. In the context of worldwide incarceration, our country has become the McDonalds of imprisonment. All we are missing are the "golden arches."

A "just desserts" approach to correcting, or at least maintaining, offenders emerged (Fogel, 1975; von Hirsch, 1976) during the 1970s. As reassuring as "making the time fit the crime" sounded, it proved to largely be another exercise in futility. What looks good on paper can easily prove to be as illusive in practice as, for example, justice is to the bureaucratic necessity of plea-bargaining. It appears that we have continued to lose confidence in our ability to rebuild human lives, and have instead decided to focus on building more prisons.

Accompanying our loss of confidence in rehabilitating and restoring offenders is a crisis mentality regarding correctional policy issues and decision making. Such a problem-solving orientation forces the policy debate out-of-balance with an increasing emphasis on short-term, quick-fix solutions (Sherman & Hawkins, 1981; Benekos & Merlo, 2006). As a result of our crisis mentality, our policy and problem-solving focus appears to have become increasingly narrow to the point where it might be restricting us from seeing the long-term consequences of our short-term solutions. As our questioning of the process becomes less relevant, the issues and subsequent policies will inevitably follow suit. Solutions, short- or long-term, to inaccurately defined problems are not solutions at all, but rather become significant problems in themselves, adding another layer to the confusion that already exists. An example of this is the perennial, politically popular "get tough" movement in corrections. It may get the governor votes on Election Day, but such policies have little correctional value in terms of encouraging inmates to change. It does, however, make life much tougher for prison administrators, correctional counselors, and correctional officers. Reintroducing chain gangs, taking televisions out of cell blocks, and eliminating educational and recreational programs may actually serve to dehumanize offenders and staff members alike, rather than to encourage inmates to take responsibility for their humanity.

This introduction to correctional treatment, although somewhat bleak, is not intended to discount the value of current or past treatment programs, but rather to address a contemporary theme in corrections; one which places more emphasis on probabilities than possibilities; on the "hard facts" of science more than on the open possibilities of the human spirit; on maintaining offenders in prison rather than developing creative ways to encourage them to change. The point we seem to have come to in correctional treatment is related to the broken promises of various treatment movements. Such promises are silent in policy-making arenas and cost-benefit budget analyses. The importance of a healthy sense of skepticism appears to have evolved into the narrower tunnel vision of the political or Orwellian inspired behavioral/pharmacological cynic. Martinson's (1974) original negative assessment of much of the correctional treatment effort during a limited time span seems to have become the exaggerated symbol and political battle cry of such cynics — no more country club prisons; no more coddling inmates; no more "touchy-feely" treatment programs.

It seems important to remember that no matter what emotional benefit such thinking may enjoy, the essential elements of Scharf's (1983) classic list of prison realities continues 25 years later to bring the present state of corrections into a clearer focus:

1. Prisons continue to be overcrowded.
2. Many prisons have abandoned rehabilitation, restoration, education, and vocational training.
3. The level and quality of interaction between professional, correctional, and academic disciplines continues to be inadequate and in some instances, largely nonexistent.
4. Correctional practice in the context of correctional treatment continues to decline.
5. Prisons remain largely unable to protect the safety of their inmates.
6. There continues to be little experimentation in corrections in the area of correctional treatment.
7. There continues to be resistance in viewing corrections as a social intervention requiring an ongoing review and reinvention.
8. There is still little consensus as to a rational correctional purpose in a moral context. (pp. 114–124)

What should our response be to revisiting Scharf's list of prison realities? Traditional answers might point to increased treatment budgets, more personnel, more government grants to encourage research and evaluation, greater interaction between practice and theory development, and, of course, numerous task forces to make recommendations to the commissioner, governor, or president. While these and related responses may have their legitimate place in addressing Scharf's correctional dilemmas, this chapter will attempt to suggest an approach that, while it may benefit from such traditional solutions, does not depend on them. This approach can work in both institutional and community-based settings. It is an approach that focuses not on another grand technological design or technique, but rather on the fundamental relationship process itself. This is not to suggest that improving technology is not important or that traditional education and vocational skills programs aren't essential for helping offenders to have a decent opportunity to support their families, afford comfortable housing, and engage in satisfying vocations. Rather, it is about priorities. It is about taking what is "on one's plate" and trying to find meaning and purpose. This approach suggests that the qualities of the relationship process itself are at the center of positive or destructive decision-making—that the inner work of an offender or counselor relationship needs to take priority in order that external expressions in the context of family and work can be positive and sustaining. Even Martinson, who was so critical of the results of the general correctional rehabilitative effort, wrote "the only such benefit may flow not from intensive supervision itself but from contact with one of the 'good people' who are frequently in such short supply" (1974, p. 31). Prison activist Bo Lozoff contends that " … we may despise an offender's crime, but still want to help him or her put what's left of their life back together" (in Lozoff & Braswell, 1989, p. 20). Perhaps Daniel Van Ness states in best (cited in Braswell, Fuller, & Lozoff, 2001, p. 154): "When we speak of restorative justice, we run the risk of saying more than we know. And if we are honest, we must admit that we know more than we live."

The Lost Art of Relationships

More than any specific systematic approach to treating offenders, the quality and credibility of relationships that offenders have with treatment staff and significant others have the greater correctional influence. For example, historically speaking, it is too easy to overlook the critical treatment impact of the humanity of some of the early correctional pioneers like John Augustus or Alexander Maconochie in favor of their respective treatment methods and procedures. A description of Augustus' interaction with offenders in the police court attests to the genuineness and intensity of his sense of relationship with offenders: "It is probable that some of them know him, for as he walks to the box two or three turn their blood-shot eyes toward him with eager glances … In a moment he is with them, gently reproving the hardened ones, and cheering … those in whom are visible signs of penitence" (in Dressler, 1959, p. 25).

Likewise, Maconochie, in responding to inmate Charles Anderson of Norfolk Penal Colony, who had become little more than an unmanageable "wild animal," placed him in a position of responsibility for a flock of animals. Greater freedom of movement, personal responsibility, and separation from jeering fellow inmates and guards brought him a substantial degree of confidence and personal stability. Although he later became emotionally disabled and was hospitalized, Anderson never forgot Maconochie. "He was out of touch with reality most of the time, unaware of what was going on about him, but when Maconochie, his wife, or their children visited, he returned to reality, recognized his callers. He showed affection for them to the day he died" (in Dressler, 1959, p. 67). In other words, one could suggest that what really made the innovative treatment approaches of Augustus, Maconochie, and numerous others since then work, was the quality, credibility, and creativity of the their relationships with their staff and charges.

While kindness and compassion may seem old-fashioned compared to modern treatment strategies more inclined toward subtle or even overt coercion, such human and peacemaking qualities continue to offer a timeless testimony to the power of human connection and relationship. Mother Teresa (cited in de Bertodano, 1993, p. 48) wrote, "I do not agree with the big way of doing things. To us what matters is the individual."

Effective correctional relationships then are centered on respecting where the other currently is and potentially can be. An attempt is made not to focus on how an offender, correctional officer, or administrator ought to be, but rather on how they really are and what they can become. In a correctional setting, the art of relationships includes interactions between offenders, between offenders and correctional staff, between offenders and family or significant others on the outside, and between correctional staff and the families and significant others of offenders. It is true that not all offenders will make positive changes. Some have chosen crime as a career, some are experiencing severe emotional disturbance, and others are angry or confused.

While we cannot be certain who will or will not respond to more meaningful and effective relationships, we can be assured that such a relationship environment can increase the possibilities for more offenders to learn self-discipline. Unfortunately, many academic and professional training programs in such areas as counseling, psychology, and social work have placed more emphasis on clinical diagnosis, therapeutic technique, and research replication and less emphasis on basic communication, experiential, and relationship skills. The art of relating concerns both the needs of the immediate relationship as well its long-term aspects. A well-known counselor/educator, Robert Carkhuff (1969), conducted substantial research that indicated the further students progressed in clinical help programs, the more proficient they became in diagnostic and assessment skills. At the same time, however, they appeared to become increasingly less effective in meaningful and effective communication skills. We come back again to the point of relationship in a community; a point where we are connected to each other; the community within the prison to the community without; the keepers to the kept; and the part of each of us the world sees to our private world within. How do we restore the quality and credibility of relationships? We know that many offenders and non-offenders may become assaultive, suicidal, or on the other hand, try very hard to do the "right thing" in response to their relationships with others. How do we attempt to transform the energy of negative, destructive relationships into positive ones? We do it through working on ourselves—through our own attitudes as correctional counselors and treatment professionals. We cannot give inmates attitudes or values we do not possess. If we want to change the world for the better, we have to start with ourselves.

Discipline and Obedience

Bo Lozoff (1985, p. 398) writes, "A staff person who's calm and strong and happy is worth his or her weight in gold. People who are living examples of truthfulness, good humor, patience, and courage are going to change more lives— even if they're employed as janitors—than the counselors who can't get their own lives in order." Such staff persons have reached a place of discipline in their own lives. This sense of discipline involves one who has internalized his or her personal and professional values. These values, forged through a lifetime of experiences, come from a wellspring deep within the core of the person's being.

On the other hand, obedience typically reflects a process that encourages us to respond to external cues regarding decisions we choose to make. As correctional counselors, we may place a higher priority on choosing the appropriate treatment strategy, whether it be cognitive/behavioral, person-centered, or some other therapeutic system, than on the potential relationship we might have with the offender we are trying to help. We may choose to look outside our relationship for some therapeutic technique other experts have written about. While it may certainly prove useful to consider others' professional expertise, the correctional power of relationships requires counselors to look within themselves and the relationships with their clients for the primary therapeutic value regarding positive interpersonal changes. It is important to have a "beginner's mind." Suzuki Roshi (cited in Braswell et al., 2001, p. 1) believes, "In the beginner's mind, there are many possibilities. In the expert's, there are few."

It is hard to trust oneself in a life where from childhood on, obedience has been the order of the day; from home to school to work, being a good boy or girl has been an important force in our lives. And while to some extent obedience' is a necessary and valuable dimension of social living and control, it can become a destructive power when applied too strenuously to the human spirit. Simply "following orders" has gotten a lot of individuals and societies into serious trouble. War crimes trials offer ample examples of such folly. If we continue to look outside ourselves for meaning and direction, we may in time lose our capacity to think and feel for ourselves.

Looking back over the years when working as a correctional psychologist, one of the authors can remember how surprised and disappointed he was when a particular smiling, cooperative, congenial inmate who never gave a moment's trouble returned to prison so quickly. His hopes for the inmate in question had been as high as the inmate's apparent failures were for himself deep. It eventually began to occur to him that it may well be that the more assertive, even somewhat cantankerous inmate has the best chance to sustain himself or herself in the free world. An inmate or correctional counselor whose primary emphasis is on obedience is looking for orders to follow. Those orders may result in positive or destructive outcomes depending on the environment and who gives them; the bank robber in search of a driver or the community service worker in search of a volunteer may equally hold the key to a parolee's future. Perhaps that is why teaching or imparting a sense of personal discipline that includes moral responsibility to an offender is such an important part of the relationship process. Through discipline, the offender can look within when there are hard choices to be made. As Lozoff (1985) suggests, discipline cannot be taught only through the intellect, but must be demonstrated as well by people who are living examples of truthfulness, good humor, patience, and courage.

Another noteworthy point concerns the professional mandate of maintaining distance from one's client. "Don't get personally involved" is a relatively common attitude among many correctional treatment professionals. It seems reasonable to suggest, however, that the very qualities Lozoff (1985) identifies as essential to teaching the offender discipline (e.g., truthfulness) cannot be adequately imparted through such a detached attitude. Neither being too close nor too removed in a counseling relationship seems appropriate. It is more a question of balance than of distance.

So much of correctional treatment efforts are by definition inherently coercive, and with several decades worth of litter on the therapeutic landscape, it seems safe to conclude that the success of coercive efforts is dismal. While we can imprison the body, the mind and heart are not so easily restrained. It seems true enough that we can coerce certain appropriate behaviors in highly structured environments through external rewards and punishments. Unfortunately, recidivism and other evidences of correctional failure suggest that such coercive efforts often do not translate into internal controls—into a sustaining sense of self-discipline outside such environments. Crime does in fact often pay both in and out of prison.

It appears to be more an internalized sense of personal morality and discipline than a fear of legal action that encourages persons to act in socially responsible ways. For example, Kohlberg (1976) demonstrated that offenders can learn to act and feel in a morally responsible fashion. Yet for such learning to result in a sustained change of attitude and behavior, it would seem that the human will or spirit must be at the center of a person's commitment to act. The heart and the mind always have a choice in a relationship to remain hidden or to be open. In a genuine relationship between counselor and offender, the opportunities increase for the heart and mind to remain open and for positive change to occur from within the offender.

Through the therapeutic process of relationship between the counselor and the offender, what each does matters to the other. Other than encouraging the offender to continue working on himself or herself, one additional suggestion involves the counselor's efforts to maintain an attitude of "therapeutic intention" (Braswell & Seay, 1984; Van Voorhis et al., 2007). As treatment professionals, or for that matter as human beings, we are not guaranteed the results we desire. Our intentions—what we are trying to act upon in order to encourage positive change—are all that we have. There are no guarantees regarding treatment outcomes. We know a lot more about what does not work than what does. Nonetheless, it is important that we keep trying, that we continue doing the best that we can. At this point a familiar saying might occur to the reader that goes something like "the road to hell is paved with good intentions." We would amend that to say " … good intentions not acted upon." Our sense of therapeutic intention may not seem like much in an age of high technology, but in matters of the human spirit such perseverance more often than not makes the price we pay for relationships worthwhile.

PACTS: An Existential Model for Change

In keeping with our focus on the primary therapeutic value of relationships, a brief overview of an experiential model referred to as PACTS is offered as a catalyst for exploring the positive potential of the human spirit in correctional relationships (Braswell & Seay, 1984). PACTS is an acronym for Paradox, Absurdity, Choosing, Transcending, and Significant Emerging. These five existential themes follow in sequence to some extent and attempt to help the counselor and offender better understand the mind and heart both in terms of their internal feelings and external actions—what Parker Palmer (1966) refers to as "whole-sight." This approach is experience- rather than expertise-based. The focus is on the experience at the center of the relationship between counselor and offender, not on the expertise of the counselor whom can hold such a relationship at arm's length. The counselor needs to personally consider and examine each of these themes in his or her life if they are to be effectively shared with an offender. What is important is that the essence of each theme is addressed in ways that are relevant to persons engaged in a meaningful relationship, not

Table 10.1: Themes of PACTS

1. *Paradox*: "When things are not what they seem."
2. *Absurdity*: "When life doesn't add up." or "When my world is out of control."
3. *Choosing*:
    a. Commitment — "Deciding to try to change and persevering in my efforts."
    b. Non-commitment — "Deciding not to change" or "pretending to change," which is, of course, essentially the same decision.
4. *Transcending*: "Trying to accept responsibility for where I am, but at the same time having a vision of where I can be — being responsible and hopeful at the same time."
5. *Significant Emerging*: "Understanding more clearly the costs of the choices I am making and making more meaningful and positive choices."

whether the actual conceptual labels are necessarily discussed. In other words, rather than talk with an offender/client about the nature of paradox, the counselor may instead talk about "when things are not what they seem." Table 10.1 provides a brief description of the five themes.

Paradox

The following passage from the Tao Te Ching by Lao Tzu (1972) captures the qualities and truths of paradox, the initial theme:

> A man is born gentle and weak. At his death he is hard and stiff.
> Green plants are tender and filled with sap. At their death they are withered and dry.
> Therefore the stiff and unbending is the discipline of death. The gentle and yielding is the discipline of life.
> Thus an army without flexibility never wins a battle. A tree that is unbending is easily broken.
> The hard and strong will fall.
> The soft and weak will overcome. (p. 139)

Sometimes what seems to be true does not turn out to be, and what appears to be wrong in fact may turn out to be right. Defending a girlfriend's honor at a bar may seem to be the right thing to do, yet serving two years for a conviction on assault and battery charges make little sense. The offender who attempted armed robbery looked forward to a leisurely life at the bank's expense, not to the despair of a 15-year sentence in a maximum security prison. In other words, our most fool-proof, best-laid plans for success may often result in failure. On the other hand, sometimes positive personal growth may come from a bad experience. The student who fails a test may then study harder than ever and earn a better grade for the course than he or she expected. A couple may become closer after the tragic loss of a child. The appearance of a teenager before a juvenile judge may help clarify a family's priorities. What this theme can mean to the counselor is that it is important for the offender to understand that, unlike basic math, life often does not add up, that one's best success can turn sour with failure, and that good can come from bad experiences. It may also be more important to ask "why" regarding life than "how."

The lessons of life's paradox include:

1. Pay close attention to what is going on around you and the choices you are making—things are not always what they seem;
2. Stay humble—there are no guarantees and you do not absolutely control anyone or anything; and
3. If you work at being conscious of numbers one and two and keep trying, life often does work out and even when it does not, you can still gain insight and wisdom from the bad times and become stronger.

Absurdity

Absurdity is basically negative paradox. When we expect something bad to happen, but something good happens instead, we are inclined to be overjoyed with our good fortune. On the other hand, life seems most absurd when the end-result of our fool-proof plans is that we end up feeling like a fool. Absurdity shatters the illusions of the security upon which we have relied. The "tough guy" in prison, who relied on a waiting, faithful wife as his symbol for hope in the future, feels the hopelessness and despair of his world reeling out of control when served with divorce papers. A typical drug sale that had succeeded a hundred times before now turns sour, resulting in a young adult male for the first time in his life being confined to a maximum security prison. A loving, law-abiding wife, and mother of young children is diagnosed in the prime of her life with inoperable cancer. These and countless other examples acknowledge that no matter what we do, sometimes bad things happen to good and bad people.

It is in times of our absurdity that we are most vulnerable and most likely to seek help. The feelings of absurdity the offender is experiencing usually comprises his or her presenting problem (e.g., depression) to the counselor. "My wife has left me," "I can't stand the pressure of prison any longer," or "My parents don't really love me," all portray someone whose sense of relationship to his world has become broken (May, Angel, & Ellenberger, 1958). Alienated, alone, and separated, offenders may feel confused and empty. It is as though sometimes we have to lose ourselves in order to begin finding ourselves. The psychotherapist, Sheldon Kopp (1972, p. 31) writes, "Sometimes the heart has to be broken before it is opened." The emptiness the offender is feeling during his or her times of absurdity is often feared and rebelled against because it represents the unknown. When we feel isolated from those relationships which are most important to us, we may indeed feel that we have nothing to live for. Yet it is during such a time of personal crisis that we are most open to the potential of a helping relationship, of seeking new ways of relating to ourselves and others.

Feeling empty also has the potential to be more than the anxiety and fear of being abandoned and without hope. Emptiness can also become openness. For example, a container has to be emptied before it can be refilled. Emptiness can also encourage us to feel greater compassion for others, learning not to be attached to the illusions that we have depended on for our purpose and meaning. Being empty can also mean being open and receptive to new, more positive experiences. It is at this point of the relationship process that the offender must choose the way of commitment, being open to new ways of thinking and feeling, or the other darker side of emptiness, the way of non-commitment and hopelessness.

The lessons of absurdity include:

1. Where your tragic and absurd experiences lead is more important than where they come from (Kushner, 1981); and
2. All the experiences in your life, both good and bad, are part of the growing-up process; if you keep trying, even your most absurd and despairing times can, in the end, work for your own good and for the good of others.

Choosing

Choosing is a crossroads experience. Realizing and accepting that life does not always add up, that sometimes the result is painful, even tragic, offers each of us a time of expressing our intentions through the choices we make. For the offender it may be a decision to genuinely commit himself or herself to learn how to read and write or perhaps to participate in group therapy or vocational training. For the perplexed counselor, it may be a decision whether or not to risk trying something different in a relationship with a frustrating client or to just go about business as usual. Each time we recognize some part of our existence as being absurd, we find ourselves at the crossroads of choosing. We may choose either the way of commitment or non-commitment.

When we become committed to trying to put our good intentions into action, we are not promised success; there are no guarantees. So the inmate who commits to learning a vocation may be more or less successful. Likewise, the counselor's commitment to a new treatment approach may or may not improve his or her therapeutic relationship with the frustrating client. Such efforts could, of course, result in the client becoming even more difficult. While the way of commitment does not provide guarantees for any particular relationship outcomes, it can encourage us to engage in creative responses to whatever the outcomes are, even when they are the most disappointing. "This lesson is ... the promise of most religious teachings: not a promise to take away all of our pain and anxiety, but to help us through it—to help us grow and gain a more meaningful perspective concerning who we are and why we are" (Braswell & Seay, 1984, p. 29). Kurtz and Ketcham (2002, p. 80) write that we learn life's essential lessons " ... not reading about them or thinking about them but by doing them."

Being more fully committed to a relationship with an offender/client, the counselor can more clearly understand and remember what is really important to the client and become less concerned with defending a particular therapeutic or political ideology. If our relationship is to matter in a significant way to the client, we must first enter his or her world. Before we can expect them to seriously consider an alternative reality—an alternative way of perceiving and relating to society at large—we must first acknowledge their world with our presence in relationship. Our presence in the world of the client must be first as the person who we are rather than a symbol of the therapy we represent. Our relationship with the offender/client then may become an experimental and experiential model that, perhaps in time, can become enlarged to include others as well.

Confession and service are also important elements of commitment that have evolved from ancient spiritual traditions. Voluntary confession offers the offender the opportunity to put a human face on the suffering he or she has initiated and is forever connected to. Through such confession, what was a barrier can become a bridge, a bridge to becoming more responsible and more compassionate. In becoming more compassionate, the focus can move from the offender to the victim as well as to others who are in need. This, unfortunately, is not the case with some rehabilitation or punishment philosophies that continue to maintain the primary focus on the inmate or offender. A compassionate attitude can be expressed through service to others. Examples include prisoner-tended gardens growing food for homeless shelters, inmate volunteers translating books into Braille for the blind, and maximum security offenders building playground equipment for low-income day care centers (Bartollas & Braswell, 1993).

Genuine commitment to a helping relationship can be both frightening and exhilarating at the same time. The intimacy that evolves from such a relationship will inevitably include both positive and negative experiences. It is important that the counselor continue to try to help the offender translate both "high" and "low" experiences in terms of his or her ongoing existence; of "what can be" for that person. In serving as translator and interpreter of experiences found in a relationship, the counselor must share a part of his or her world by telling his or her stories, and receiving the presence of the other by carefully listening to the client's stories, which range from childhood memories to hopes for the future.

The counselor or client does not have to choose the way of commitment. One or both may instead choose non-commitment. Choosing non-commitment becomes self-evident through acted-out intentions. Such evidence may be found equally in the client who refuses to even give treatment a "try" or who tries all the treatments as a means of manipulating or conning the counselor for favors and other special considerations. Likewise, the counselor whose office walls are littered with professional membership and in-service training certificates, and who sees more clients each day than any other counselor, may be no more committed to helping clients than the counselor whose bare walls reflect a similar level of disinterest.

Three traps counselors can easily fall into with clients are mutual admiration and gratification, professional advancement and recognition, and burnout. Mutual admiration and gratification is a subtle relationship trap where the correctional counselor can find himself or herself working with clients who are appealing. The story line goes something like, "You make me feel good about myself as a counselor and I won't require you as a client to really examine where you are as a person and where you need to be." As counselor and client, we risk little, preferring to keep our relationship slick and simple. If we become too genuine, we may have to face uncomfortable aspects of our personal identities as well as conflicts within our relationship. We may even have to become more responsible to each other.

Professional advancement and recognition is a reasonable goal for the correctional counselor but not at the expense of one's relationship with one's clients. Does our professional advancement and recognition naturally emerge from the center of our relationships with clients, or are such relationships pe-

ripheral to our advancement and recognition efforts? If our answer is the former, then we are committed to the service of others. If our answer is the latter, then we are committed to the service of ourselves. Service to ourselves
leaves little or no room for relationships with those we are supposed to be helping. It is an easy enough trap to fall into for the counselor who has the energy
and ambition to substitute professional growth for personal growth. Of course,
one does not have to exclude the other, but it does seem to happen in many
instances. The correctional counselor who starts his or her career seeking creative ways to motivate and encourage positive change in offenders through relationships may find himself or herself several years later more interested in
promotions, publications, and presentations. The challenge then becomes how
to remain mindful and centered on our commitment to our relationships with
clients, which comes from within, while gracefully accepting whatever promotions, rewards, and other recognitions that come from without. If we are
not careful, our own professional advancement and recognition may become
our vocation at the expense of our personal work. To the extent that this happens, we will have more, but be less—have more pieces of the pie, but be less
at peace with ourselves.

Burnout is a reality each of us faces regarding vocations and relationships
in which we choose to participate. It is well documented (see, e.g., Whitehead,
1987; Van Voorhis et al., 2007). Disappointing experiences with coworkers and
clients, as well as the effects of working in bureaucracies, from time to time restrict our focus and close our hearts to the possibilities of a relationship. Nar-
row-mindedness evolves into cynicism and from cynicism we are but a short
step away from despair. The burned-out counselor or client is more concerned
with surviving than with growing. Playing it safe becomes a priority. Their
thinking is, "If I risk nothing, at least I won't lose anything." Of course, life
teaches us that nothing could be further from the truth. The lessons of life
suggest, "If I risk nothing, I will lose everything."

What does the correctional counselor do when the client he or she is trying
to work with continues to demonstrate non-commitment in a variety of ways?
After all, most correctional counselors have too few hours in the day and too
many clients to see. One suggestion is to respect the client's right not to try to
change or grow and share such feelings with him or her in an appropriate way.
And while leaving the door to your office and heart open to a relationship
should the client decide to become committed at some future time, focusing
most of your energy instead on those persons who seem to be committed to
trying appears to make more sense. It would seem such an approach would
decrease one's potential for burnout and increase the possibilities for meaningful, helping relationships. Finally, as important as commitment is for the

counselor and client's relationship, trying alone is often not enough. Such relationships also need hope and a sense of vision.

The lessons of choosing include:

1. Try to become more responsible for who you are and who you really want to be;
2. Persevere in trying to put your good intentions into action;
3. Make an effort to work through relationship traps of which you are a part; and
4. Forgive yourself when you fail so that you can keep trying.

Transcending

Transcending refers to the ability to become aware of and accept responsibility for where one is presently, while at the same time, having the capacity to envision and hope for what they can become. The theme of transcending includes not only the present, but the awareness of a possible future found hidden in the present. D.T. Suzuki (1972, p. 92) once wrote, "It is for this reason that we say that we are far greater than the universe in which we live, for our greatness is not of space, but of the spirit." In other words, while the small cubicle of a windowless prison office may provide the apparently insignificant meeting space between the counselor and offender, the spirit of their relationship is not necessarily limited to that space. Their relationship encompasses both past experiences and visions of the future (good and bad) as realized in the present moment of their meeting. For such a meeting to be transcendent, counselor and client will have to encourage their relationship to move beyond their physical confinement.

Too often, the weight of restricted space also restricts the relationship's possibilities for personal growth and change. However, commitment to a helping or therapeutic relationship can enable the counselor and offender to take the necessary "leap of faith," which is essential to developing a transcendent attitude. Such an attitude does not depend on a "blind leap. It is, rather, a leap filled with vision and purpose ... and struggle" (Braswell & Seay, 1984, p. 38). The transcendent attitude takes full responsibility for what I have done and where I am. Yet, at the same time, it seeks a vision of where I can go and what I can become. For a juvenile offender on probation, it may involve recognition that his family life is dysfunctional—that he is a part of a larger family problem—and that his parents will probably get divorced no matter how good or bad he is. And still, with all the pain and confusion, he can continue to care for his parents and have a life of his own, a chance to find his own way and feel good about the journey. For an adult offender on death row, it may require his acceptance that regardless of the circumstances, in taking someone's life, he took something that cannot be given back—that on an appointed date according to the laws of the state, the cost of his crime will be his own life.

Even with such a desolate example as this, transcendence is a gift the human spirit offers. Perhaps the guiding vision that the offender follows is one in which he accepts a limited sense of time and space and yet struggles through his sense of isolation and remorse to find forgiveness for the pain given and the pain received. His actions, though limited by the constraints of death row, do not reflect his thoughts and feelings, which can be freely expressed to guards and fellow prisoners and secretly in the openness of his own heart. Dietrich Bonhoeffer, a theologian imprisoned by the Nazis, completed some of his most inspirational work through his letters to friends and family while in prison. His execution was carried out just days before his prison camp was liberated by allies. Jarvis Masters (1997), an inmate on death row at San Quentin State Prison, experienced a transformation that allowed him to influence and encourage inmates and correctional officers alike to become more mindful and peaceful.

Part of the process of developing a more transcending attitude involves understanding the difference between attachment and nonattachment in relationships. From a young child's attachment to his or her blanket to a senior executive's attachment to his or her career and the assumed power that goes with it, attachment to persons and things comes in all shapes and sizes. Most of us, in one way or another, are inclined to be attached to such elements as status, money, youthfulness, good looks, and other persons that for whatever reason appeal to us. If we can just make enough money, be accepted in the right circles, be more attractive, and have the right friends, we will be able to create a good life for ourselves. Unfortunately, the truth is that most of us occasionally make bad career decisions and financial investments, friends do not always stay friends, and no matter what we do, we eventually grow older and die. Yet our attachments allow us to prolong the attachments that we can control in our lives; that we can somehow earn intimacy and closeness. Such a focus inevitably requires us to develop an increasingly more narrow and restrictive view of our lives as we attempt to predict and control the empty promises of our illusion. I may become correctional counselor-of-the-year, but is such recognition gracefully received as a symbol of my inner work which is expressed through meaningful relationships with clients, or is it a political reward, another piece of external evidence I have collected to strengthen the illusion that I am somebody, that my life is in good order? I may become the most respected inmate in prison, but is such recognition based upon my attachment to power and intimidation or is it more of a reflection of the respect I feel inside? Am I simply the strongest of the strong or am I centered on the reality of what it means to be in prison, yet with a vision of how such a reality, even with its hard edge, can be improved in more humane ways? If we continue to cling to the illusions of our attachments, we will find ourselves increasingly in fear of our future and missing out on the significance of the present. When addressing a group of inmates at a maximum security prison, Bo Lozoff (1985) indicated that the prison they currently lived in was their neighborhood. He asked them if their neighborhood was a better place because they lived there.

Nonattachment offers us another way to relate to each other. Nonattachment invites us to struggle with our need to give to a relationship with "no strings attached." Nonattachment encourages us to give for the significance of giving rather than simply as a condition for receiving something in return. Nonattachment does not mean being detached in a negative or noninvolved way. It is more of a process of acknowledging that we cannot in fact control anyone's mind and heart or, for that matter, absolutely control their behavior. It is a process through which we try not to perceive ourselves or others as objects or things to be manipulated. Nonattachment can help us to sit and relate to someone in an atmosphere as free of stereotypes and biases as possible—through an attitude of respect and empathy for where they are in their lives, yet nurturing a vision of where they can be and who they can become. Nonattachment is a vital attribute for all meaningful relationships. To place such a quality in the context of parent-child relationships, do we "love our children to death," binding them forever to us through our need for attachment, or do we "love them enough to let them go," freeing them to find their own way—a way that will ironically allow us to join them in a deeper, more loving relationship? The same can be said of the correctional counselor who is relating to an offender or the relationship between a teacher and a student. Do we care enough to struggle with being real in the relationship we share with our client, or do we demand that the relationship conform and be limited to our perceptions and attachments of what we think a counselor and offender are?

Encouraging a transcending attitude in ourselves and our clients is not easy and requires practice. Meditation in its diverse and various forms provides such a way of practice. Meditation is essentially the ability one has to move into a state of "relaxed concentration." John Main (1982) contends that meditation is a process of liberation through which we activate our spirit. The practice of meditation attempts to quiet both the body and the mind, afterwards allowing one to think more clearly and act in more meaningful ways. Forms of meditation can include breathing exercises, physical exercise such as jogging, prayer, and silence (Lewis & Streitfeld, 1970; Lozoff, 1985; Braswell, 1990). The practice of meditation can help us become more aware of ourselves and increase our ability to become more attentive and receptive to what is going on inside us and around us. A form of breathing or silent meditation can be a particularly useful way for the counselor to begin and/or end a session with a client. Becoming quiet and centered can help both counselor and client begin a session on a more common plane, more closely attuned to the relationship they share. In addition and perhaps more importantly, such a meditation practice teaches the counselor and client self-control. Lozoff (1985) writes:

> An uncontrolled mind—no matter how much it knows, how smart it becomes, or how many pleasures it experiences—will never find peace or satisfaction ... we have to learn the delicate art of allowing a thought or feeling to be whatever it is, but without getting sucked into it; we can't let it control us. (pp. 37, 39)

Developing a transcending attitude can help us become more aware of the feelings and moods with which we often victimize others and make ourselves victims as well. Through such an attitude we can learn to nurture a sense of humor, taking ourselves and others less seriously, yet taking our commitment to grow more seriously.

The lessons of transcending include:

1. Accept responsibility for where you are in your life, but be committed to a vision of hope in who you can become;
2. Care enough to struggle with whatever you are attached to—hate, power, another person, etc; and
3. Practice meditation to quiet your body and mind so that you can make clearer and more meaningful choices about your life.

Significant Emerging

The final theme, significant emerging, provides a cumulative reference point for the other themes we have examined. Significant emerging is most fundamentally concerned with the costs of our life choices. Through examining and exploring each of these themes, which are found primarily in our relationships, perhaps we can become more aware of the price we are paying for our lives. The juvenile who decided to go along with friends and commit a crime for a thrill had no forethought of the possible legal consequence and did not really want to embarrass his or her family. The inmate in prison who killed someone in a drunken quarrel wanted respect, not the burden of someone's death. The correctional counselor with the cynical attitude and the burned-out disposition now wears the institutional label of being ineffective. At one time that counselor wanted to be effective and appreciated before he or she became convinced administrators and offenders would always be incorrigible. Each of these persons and each of us have chosen pathways to follow that have led us to places we did not realize we were going, at emotional and physical costs we were not aware we would have to pay.

The lessons of significant emerging include:

1. Put the other themes into practice;
2. Learn how to experience synthesis; and
3. Keep trying.

Conclusion

The purpose of the PACTS model is to help the correctional counselor and client become more informed and aware of the directions in which our choosing leads us. From the paradox of things not always being what they seem, to the absurdity of our world being out of control, to the point of self-confrontation where we choose a way of commitment or non-commitment, to the development of a transcending attitude for those who are committed, separately and together, each theme in the context of relationship points to a whole greater than the sum of its parts—to a point of significance that gives our lives meaning and authenticity. Rollo May (1975, p. 220) states, "Psychologically and spiritually man does not live by the clock alone. His time, rather, depends on the significance of the event." Good and bad experiences offer both counselor and client an opportunity to grow and experience greater significance in their lives. As we attempt to develop a transcendent attitude, we may find that we become more free as we persevere in trying not to control or manipulate other persons.

Experiencing synthesis is an important part of our search for significance. Synthesis is essentially our attempt to come to grips with both the good and the bad that is within each of us. Synthesis can allow us to live more fully with the highs and the lows, the joy and the pain of everyday living. We can simultaneously acknowledge that which is worst about us and that which is most positive. Sam Keen (1974, p. 22), when interviewing Robert Assigioli, writes, "There may be a reconciliation between warring opposites—reason and emotion, duty and desire, mind and body. I am tired of warfare. But reconciliation between the contradictions … makes sense only when the contradictions have been experienced … I have to reverence my anger and fear before they become civilized." Such a reconciliation allows one to become more than his or her fear and anger. The pain and fear do not necessarily disappear and cannot be pushed away, but by becoming larger than the wound that encompasses such feelings and memories, one can move beyond the "stuck place" and be liberated from the prison of the spirit, free to be something more.

Prisons are full of unreconciled contradictory feelings. Rationalization and denial abound in both the cell of the inmate and the office of the counselor. Restoring the lost art of relationships creates an environment where such unreconciled feelings as love and hate and despair and hope can be acknowledged and respected for what they are. Such a therapeutic environment can help reconcile these "warring opposites," which can result in so much damage both within and without the individual. Experiencing a greater sense of synthesis in our search for significance is an integrating function, making us more accountable for the quality of our relationships, rather than a separating function which estranges us both from ourselves and other persons. The correctional relationship is fundamentally the counselor and client seeking significance through the struggle for synthesis. We should remember as counselors, or as anyone who is trying to be a helping person, that the treatment process we most need to utilize in order to be effective is not in a book, expert, or some other place outside of ourselves; the most powerful treatment process is within— within the midst of the relationship we share with the one we are trying to help; the one inside our own heart and mind and the one looking at us across the desk in our office. For better or worse, we are the treatment. The treatment is us. As correctional counselors, or for that matter as human beings, we are the point through which the therapeutic process comes alive in relationship with another person. The time for such a relationship is now. The place for such a relationship is wherever we find ourselves. The basic requirement for our being effective is that we keep trying. And in our trying, we may find that "the keeper and the kept, the offender and the victim, and the incarcerator and the liberator that is within each of us" (Lozoff & Braswell, 1989, p. iii) may find a sense of peace and wholeness and meaning.

References

Andrews, D., & Bonta, J. (2006). The psychology of criminal conduct (4th ed.). Cincinnati: Anderson.

Bartollas, C., & Braswell, M. (1993). Correctional treatment and the New-Age Movement. Journal of Crime and Justice, 16, 43–58.

Benekos, P., & Merlo, A. (2006). Crime control: Politics and policy. Cincinnati: Anderson.

Braginsky, B., & Braginsky, D. (1974). Mainstream psychology. New York: Holt, Rhinehart, and Winston.

Braswell, M. (1990). Journey homeward. Chicago: Franciscan Herald Press.

Braswell, M., & Seay, T. (1984). Approaches to counseling and psychotherapy. Chicago: Waveland.

Braswell, M., Fuller, J., & Lozoff, B. (2001). Corrections, peacemaking, and restorative justice. Cincinnati: Anderson.

Carkhuff, R. (1969). Helping and human relations (Vol. 2). New York: Holt, Rhinehart, and Winston.

Cullen, F., & Gilbert, K. (1982). Reaffirming rehabilitation. Cincinnati: Anderson.

de Bertodano, T. (Ed.). (1993). Daily readings with Mother Teresa. London: Fount.

Dressler, D. (1959). Practice and theory of probation and parole. New York: Columbia University Press.

Fogel, D. (1975). We are the living proof. Cincinnati: Anderson.

Keen, S. (1974). Voices and visions. New York: Harper & Row.

Kohlberg, L. (1976). Moral stages and moralization: The cognitive-developmental approach. In D. Lickona (Ed.), Moral development and behavior (pp. 31–53). New York: Holt, Rhinehart, and Winston.

Kopp, S. (1972). If you meet the Buddha on the road, kill him. Palo Alto, CA: Science and Behavior Books.

Kurtz, E., & Ketcham, K. (2002). The spirituality of imperfection. New York: Bantam.

Kushner, H. (1981). When bad things happen to good people. New York: Schocken.

Lewis, H., & Streitfeld, H. (1970). Growth games. San Diego: Harcourt Brace Jovanovich.

Lozoff, B. (1985). We're all doing time. Durham: Human Kindness Foundation.

Lozoff, B., & Braswell, M. (1989). Inner corrections. Cincinnati: Anderson.

Main, J. (1982). Christian meditation. Montreal, Canada: Benedictine Priory.

Martinson, R. (1974). What works? Questions and answers about prison reform. The Public Interest, 10, 22–54.

Masters, J. (1997). Finding freedom. Junction City, CA: Padma.

May, R. (1975). Love and will. New York: W. W. Norton.

May, R., Angel, E., & Ellenberger, H. (Eds.). (1958). Existence. New York: Basic Books.

McConnell, J. (1970). Criminals can be brainwashed—now. Psychology Today, 3, 14–18.

Palmer, P. (1966). To know as we are known. San Francisco: Harper & Row.

Scharf, P. (1983). Empty bars: Violence and the crisis of meaning in prison. The Prison Journal, 63, 114–124.

Sherman, M., & Hawkins, G. (1981). Imprisonment in America. Chicago: University of Chicago Press.

Suzuki, D. (1972). What is Zen? New York: Harper & Row.

Tzu, L. (1972). Tao te ching (G. Feng & J. English, Trans.). New York: Vintage.

Van Voorhis, P., Braswell, M., & Lester, D. (2007). Correctional counseling & rehabilitation (6th ed.). Cincinnati: Anderson.

von Hirsch, H. (1976). Doing justice. New York: Hill and Wang.

Whitehead, J. (1987). Probation officer job burnout: A test of two theories. Journal of Criminal Justice, 15, 1–17.

CHAPTER ELEVEN

Psycho-Spiritual Roots of Adolescent Violence: The Importance of Rites of Passage

Drake Spaeth, Chicago School of Professional Psychology

This chapter endeavors to establish a justification for the establishment of "rites of passage" programs as an approach to treating violent adolescents and as an adjunctive intervention that buttresses the effects of more conventional approaches to psychotherapy. The link between the lack of mentoring in the context of healthy rites of passage and the phenomenon of violence seems to be an increasingly popular notion. Yet to date, reports in the literature regarding implementation of such programs and systematic testing of their efficacy is sparse at best. After exploring some conceptual formulations and studies that seem to have much in common with the idea of rites of passage as a means of addressing and positively transforming adolescent violence, this chapter will outline a general approach to constructing a rites of passage experience that could conceivably be investigated through quantitative and qualitative research.

Dispositional vs. Contextual Factors

Violence among human beings is certainly a difficult and troubling social problem. For the hundred or so years that psychology has existed as a recognizable field, researchers have sought to identify and understand the biopsychosocial sources of violence and influences that impact it. These efforts have given rise to a persistent debate about the extent to which biological, characterological, and dispositional factors are chiefly responsible for violent acts that an individual may perpetrate, as opposed to the extent to which situational, social, or contextual factors need to be taken into account in order to understand the phenomenon of violence. The infamous fundamental attribution error often arises in discussion of this issue—namely, the idea that human beings typically overly attribute responsibility for a phenomenon to the individual and underestimate contextual influences. The perspective outlined in this chapter is somewhat in sympathy with this view, not to mitigate the need for violent offenders to take responsibility for their actions and to realize their power to make different choices—a pillar of existential ideology! However, taking responsibility depends on greater awareness of choices, and increased awareness may not be possible without addressing the social context in which choices are made or not made.

Dispositional factors seem to interact with contextual factors in complex ways with regard to the phenomenon of violence. For instance, Kakar (2005) found that adolescent gang members who have delinquent friends and at least one family member with a criminal background were more likely to engage in a significantly higher rate of offending than gang members who did not possess these characteristics; and yet gang members committed significantly more violent and delinquent acts than did comparative groups of youths who had delinquent friends. Such research sheds light on the limits of reductive explanations of violence. However, it is possible that gaps remain. Given the vast amount of literature devoted to this issue, relatively little attention and consideration has been paid to the idea that violence is as much a spiritual phenomenon as it is a biological, psychological, or social concern. This chapter will hopefully show how, with regard to violence—adolescent violence in particular—spiritual factors and issues dovetail closely with psychological variables and should not be ignored.

Adolescent Violence and Psychological Interventions

In some ways, violence among adolescents provides a focus of even greater concern than violence among adults, given that a strong investment in the physical and psychological well-being of youths seems critical during what is perceived as the emotional vulnerability of the adolescent transition into adulthood. Today's adolescents are the legacy carriers of hopes and dreams for the future. Quinsey and colleagues (2005), in an extensive review of psychological efforts to assess and manage violence risk, conclude that the majority of violent offenders are male adolescents who begin their pattern of violent offenses in their teens and typically stop before their mid-20s. The disproportionate

number of males identified as violent compared to the number of females similarly identified, is an important issue that certainly needs to be understood;
however, that discussion is unfortunately beyond the scope of consideration in
this chapter.

Psychological interventions seem to be largely responsible for helping adolescent offenders end their violent patterns before they persist later into the
lifespan—a fortunate consequence, since antisocial adults typically do not
demonstrably benefit from psychotherapy (Quinsey et al., 2005). Moreover,
the growing emphasis on a more holistic understanding of the biopsychosocial factors that comprise the phenomenon of adolescent violence seems to be
a sensible consideration. This emphasis has illuminated a need for circular or
systemic interactive models that are more satisfying and offer more possibilities for intervention (or prevention) at various and multiple points. Efforts to
reduce this phenomenon to testosterone excess or to history of abuse, while
offering compelling causative explanations, are simply too linear.

While encouraging, the evidence that adolescents can and do benefit from
psychological treatment does not obscure the frequency of instances of adolescent violence or the enormity of the issue, as anyone living in urban gang
territories can attest to. Clearly, a widening of the holistic lens of psychotherapy seems not only possible, but necessary. For adolescents, the psychological
experience of transition to adulthood is fraught with psychological challenges,
even if rigid adherence to traditional concepts of "adolescent storm and stress"
has been rightly called into question (see, e.g., Arnett, 1999; Hines & Paulson,
2007). Improving therapeutic efficacy in addressing violent behavior patterns
remains a critically important objective, but the search for ways to prevent violence is even more critical. The media coverage of eruptions of violence at
Columbine, Virginia Tech, and Northern Illinois University sadly spotlights
this need.

Humanistic-existential Approaches

As with adults, the psychological issues that adolescents face are frequently
linked to deeper, existential struggles for a sense of meaning and purpose—
struggles that may be sharply defined by the confusion associated with this
major life transition. At such times, a feeling of being bereft of a sense of connection to family, to others, to the global dimension, or to a unified sense of
identity or self is common. This author has previously reviewed the work of
researchers who identify a sense of connection as an essentially universally held
definition of spirituality (Spaeth, 2006). "Third force" approaches to therapy

and counseling—those guided by humanistic-existential and transpersonal theories—have long been respectful of these psycho-spiritual strivings and phenomena in clients' lives. These strivings are inextricably tied up with the psychological experience of moving from fragmentation of the psyche into wholeness and integration; from incongruence toward congruence; from inauthenticity toward greater genuineness; from polarized, black-and-white thinking to a greater comfort with complexity and ambiguity; from thesis and antithesis to an ever-evolving synthesis in dialectical process; from simple constructions of personal world to larger and more complex constructions of global experience; and from death to rebirth in the experience of rites of passage. With these dichotomies firmly in mind, the appeal of third force approaches for use with adolescents is immediately apparent. Their struggle for identity and belonging frequently embodies these extremes in various ways. Their inability to balance or resolve them may be evident in violent engagements with others. This idea is important in connection with discussion of mentoring and rites of passage later in the chapter.

Humanistic-existential and transpersonal approaches have traditionally been undervalued by clinicians who favor cognitive-behavioral approaches as a consequence of the significant amount of quantitative, empirical support for their use, as well as significant contributions to positive and measureable psychotherapeutic outcomes. Despite the fact that qualitative research, often more amenable to third force approaches, is able to provide unique information about clients' experiences in psychotherapy, the difficulty in operationally defining complex concepts such as "meaning" or even "authenticity" has posed a challenge to widespread utilization of such approaches. Relevant third force approaches include Rogers' client-centered therapy, gestalt therapy (popularized by Fritz and Laura Perls), Gendlin's focusing approach, emotion-focused psychotherapy, Frankl's logotherapy, Boss's daseinsanalysis, May and Yalom's respective approaches to existential counseling, or more integrative approaches such as Greenberg's process-experiential psychotherapy or Bugental's global humanistic-existential style. Jung's theory of individuation also belongs with these approaches, perhaps even more than with the psychodynamic paradigm, given his emphasis on the evolution of the limited ego into a more comprehensive "self" that is more open to universal experience.

In the past decade, some research has challenged the idea that the use of third force approaches cannot be empirically supported. For instance, Elliott (2001) performed a meta-analysis of psychotherapy outcome studies that encompassed a wide range of clients in outpatient and inpatient settings; a wide range of treatment modalities (i.e., individual, couple, and family therapy); a wide range of therapist experience; and a wide range in the therapist's level of allegiance to the approach under consideration. He found that more directive humanistic-existential approaches such as gestalt, process-experiential, focusing, and emotion-focused approaches actually compared favorably to cognitive-behavioral approaches in traditional measures of positive psychotherapeutic outcomes. Even though Elliott (2001) admittedly did not provide data that separated results for adolescents and adults, his conclusions seem to support the use of these approaches in a wide range of settings. Elliott's research bodes well for the potential increased utilization of more directive approaches with adolescents who may not respond as quickly to non-directive reflection and supportive encouragement to change on their own initiative. With all due respect to Rogers' belief that the actualizing potential inherent in every human being will inevitably emerge if the therapist shows sufficient genuineness, empathy, and unconditional positive regard, adolescents—even more so than most adults—may occasionally benefit from more directive encouragement toward personal growth.

Rogers' approach should, however, not be dismissed out of hand. Miller and Rollnick's (2002) "motivational interviewing" strategy deserves special mention. Based largely on Rogers' reflective listening approach, motivational interviewing emphasizes the importance of reflecting accurately a client's level of motivational readiness to change, which can fluctuate at various times during the therapeutic process. The effective therapist is able to utilize his or her own awareness of the client to determine what therapeutic conditions can maximize the probability for the client's readiness to change. The skillful therapist thus not only uses empathy, genuineness, and unconditional positive regard in traditional ways to allow the client's natural desire for authenticity and greater self awareness to emerge, he or she also maximally reflects those parts of the client's personality and cognitions that are indicative of a genuine desire to change. Miller and Rollnick's emphasis on behavior change represents a subtly more directive departure from more traditional models, a facet that even a staunch cognitive-behavioral therapist might conceivably find appealing. The unique balance of non-directive and directive elements inherent in motivational interviewing is similar to that achieved by process-experiential therapy, which syncretically blends elements of client-centered therapy and gestalt therapy. This approach also offers promise in therapeutic work with adolescents and the prospect of their changing violent behavior patterns.

Rites of Passage

The possibility that psychotherapy has been effective in helping adolescents to successfully cease patterns of violent offending was mentioned previously.

Perhaps what has worked well for youths in these instances was the presence of the therapist as a mentor, who acted as an adult guide through the confusion and vicissitudes of transition into adulthood. Bratter (2006) articulates a perspective that seems to be in strong agreement with this idea. He describes his experience of over 40 years as a psychotherapist, during which he worked with many adolescents who engaged in patterns of self-destructive, aggressive, dangerous, or addictive behaviors. His description of his work, grounded in reality therapy, seems reminiscent of Perls's abrasive, confrontational style of gestalt psychotherapy. He describes frequently engaging in verbally aggressive, even angry confrontations with adolescents, as well as a high therapeutic success rate. He further relates that when confronted with their poor choices and attendant social consequences, the adolescents that he worked with also independently confronted their own underlying shame, guilt, and self-loathing. According to Bratter, in doing so, they became better able to take responsibility for decisions, becoming more aware of their power to make different choices. Bratter also describes actively advocating for the adolescents to have preferential treatment in the clinic and to arrange adjunctive services for them. What is not stated clearly but certainly implied is that his authenticity and advocacy fostered trust and a strong therapeutic alliance. He is a role model and mentor for the adolescents as much as a therapist.

The "normal" struggles of adolescence are compounded by the violence itself, which may have in large part been a consequence of a "normal" desire for a rite of passage that was denied. The natural emphasis of third force approaches on the importance of confrontation of anxiety, conflict and suffering in the search for meaning and purpose, and the attainment of balance and wholeness suggests that they may be ideal vehicles for an experience of initiation for a violent adolescent. Initiation as an experience of death and rebirth is consistent with these important themes in third force psychology. In this context, "initiation" encompasses both initiation into positive change as well as an initiation from childhood into adulthood. In both cases, the symbolic death of one state of being and the rebirth of the next should be evident. This idea will be further discussed later in the chapter.

From a Jungian standpoint, the rite of passage into adulthood may be "archetypal" or universally characteristic of human beings across time and cultures. In contemporary religious contexts, the passage into adulthood is still ritually honored through ceremonies and revered traditions. Catholicism espouses confirmation, in which a young adolescent ritually chooses to follow Catholic teachings as an adult and who shares in the community of the Church. Judaism offers the bar-mitzvah and the bat-mitzvah, which are ceremonies of welcoming into adulthood for young Jewish boys and girls, respectively. Contemporary Pagans are attempting to construct (often in highly creative and imaginative ways) modern rituals and rites of passage—frequently reflecting their own ancestral traditions and mythological motifs found in folklore associated with their cultures (Adler, 2006). A comprehensive and systematic study of the extent to which such initiatory ceremonies seem to "ward off" or ameliorate violence among adolescents who experience them has yet to be undertaken. Such a study would be helpful in evaluating the extent that this idea, which is becoming increasingly popular in open-minded treatment contexts, has actual merit.

Tick (2005) has done extensive work with veterans of the Vietnam War. Based on numerous interviews with veterans, he has found that the experience of traumatization shared by many Vietnam veterans seems to be strongly associated with the fact that as adolescents and young men they were thrust into the role of a soldier or warrior without any initiatory preparation for that role. Tick points out that historically, adult men often became warriors and served their nations or tribes in war after an involved period of initiation from boyhood into manhood (e.g., warriors among Celtic tribes, Greek soldiers, and Roman centurions, to name a few). According to Tick, war was regarded as a necessary evil but also as a training ground where true heroism was achieved as the culmination of freely given service. He further describes how American veterans of the Vietnam War show excessive traumatization due to the fact that they were compelled to be violent with no prior preparation or initiation into the role of warrior. Instead of regarding themselves as heroes or being lauded as such by their peers, they often perceived themselves to be criminals. Sadly, being trained as killing machines and being encouraged to engage in violent acts in an unfamiliar country, many Vietnam veterans did not know how to do or be anything else upon their return to hearth and home (Tick, 2005).

A Jungian depth psychologist might also be tempted to view gang activity or violence among groups of adolescents as the expression of this archetypal need for an adulthood initiation. Unfortunately, without the presence of an adult guide or mentor, their adolescent foray into individuation may become directionless and vulnerable to the influence of the Shadow, which represents the darker, repressed, or rejected pieces of the personality. The bizarre and highly aggressive initiation practices frequently employed in such contexts become more understandable.

As the previous paragraphs have alluded, the idea that mentoring and rites of passage may have value in promoting psychological and spiritual health among adolescents and may possibly diminish, eliminate, or prevent violent or other negative behavior patterns is not new. For instance, Axelman and Bonnell (2006) emphasized that for impoverished adolescents in inner cities and rural areas of America, who are often disenfranchised from parents and families, gangs offer an appealing sense of belonging based on obedience and loyalty. Axelman and Bonnell seemed to imply that gangs act as substitute parents or families. Perhaps gangs offer a context for a rite of passage into adulthood that would normally be facilitated by parents of origin.

Kimmel (2007) conducted interviews with Swedish and American adolescents in their mid- to late-teens who claimed to be ex-neo-Nazis. Kimmel was interested in determining what these teens initially found to be appealing about neo-Nazi groups. What were the "dynamics of entry" as well as the "dynamics of leaving" (Kimmel, 2007, p. 203)? How did their experiences relate to their sense of masculinity? What were the roles of ritual and ideology?

Kimmel found several common themes from the interviews. Nazi groups seemed to attract young adolescent males who experienced a sense of being emasculated under threat of bullying. These adolescents also came from backgrounds of poverty, lacked an experience of familial support, and often suffered outright abuse from their families. Nazi groups provided such boys an experience of belonging or being connected to a community. They helped them establish a masculine identity structured around a view of the young man as a strong, patriotic hero. Perhaps most importantly, the groups appeared to establish rites of passage in which the young men could continually evoke and focus rage and then ritually discard it (Kimmel, 2007). The yearning to leave childhood behind and solidify an identity as an adult man, to establish a sense of connection to other like-minded men, and to cathartically purify themselves is evident. Having experienced little or no positive parenting or mentoring in their homes or communities of origin, they intuitively sought alternatives. What the young men found and ultimately engaged was a warped initiation and twisted sense of spiritual connection.

Howell and Egley (2005) reviewed several longitudinal studies of risk factors for gang membership and proposed a developmental model that attempted to account for findings of the studies they reviewed. Their observations correspond with those of Kimmel (2007). Howell and Egley (2005) noted that studies converge on observations that during preschool years, "concentrated disadvantage at the community level, family problems, and certain child characteristics lead to early childhood problems (aggression and disruptive behavior), and each of these four variables in turn increases the likelihood of delinquency in childhood and gang membership in adolescence" (Howell & Egley, 2005, p. 341). During school years, aggressive and disruptive behaviors are associated with dysfunctional families and result in rejection by peers. During later childhood, earlier rejection by peers seems to engender a tendency to socialize with delinquent and antisocial peers from which gang membership is an easy step.

By early adolescence, family influences begin to fade in favor of peer influences and neighborhood risk factors, such as availability of drugs, lack of a feeling of safety, high community arrest rates, and neighborhood disorganization, play a role in increasing risk of gang membership. Poor school performance, low academic aspirations, low attachment to teachers, diminished parental expectations of college, and little commitment to school, all play a role. In terms of individual risk factors, previous history of delinquency, excessive alcohol or drug use, and experience of life stressors have predictive value (Howell & Egley, 2005). Howell and Egley also state the primary reasons (identified by prior research) that youths are typically drawn to gangs include family member involvement and safety and protection—even more than selling drugs or making money (Howell & Egley, 2005). Howell and Egley's research illustrates the value of systemic models that consider biopsychosocial factors. They also illustrate the tendency of gangs to become substitute families and vehicles of connection to what adolescents experience as a community that keeps them safe—an important feature of rites of passage experiences. Again, without healthy adult mentoring, these experiences are illusory at best and extremely harmful at worst.

Menzise (2006) examined the impact of culturally-specific rites of passage on cognitions and behaviors of adolescents who were considered to be "at risk." Menzise gathered a sample of 275 African-American adolescents ranging in age from 12 to 22 years of age, with a mean age of 17.96. The sample included 128 males, 146 females, and one transgendered individual. Participants came from foster care settings, the juvenile justice system, middle schools, and low-income communities. All participants met criteria on various measures for being at risk for delinquency, violence, substance abuse, and other criminal offenses. He then implemented what he describes as a rites of passage program that was based on indigenous African traditions and compared pre-test and post-test performance on various measures of cognitions about familiarity with African cultural traditions, ethnic identity, school interest, family communication, substance abuse, and sexual behaviors (Menzise, 2006).

Menzise's results partially supported a hypothesis that the correlation between culturally-specific beliefs and risky behavior variables would be significant in pre- and post-test conditions. He discovered significant correlations between cultural knowledge and perceptions of risky sexual behaviors and substance abuse. Menzise also found partial support for his second hypothesis—that upon completion of the rites of passage program, participants would show an increased commitment to a drug-free lifestyle and safe sexual practices. He found that participants' perception of the negative impact of using drugs significantly increased. His third hypothesis that participants who had actually reported engaging in substance abuse would have a greater sense of perceived harm resulting from said abuse upon completion of the rites of passage program was not supported. Apparently, actual abuse patterns require psychological interventions above and beyond a process such as this rite of passage program. His fourth hypothesis that participants who had reported more than one sexual partner would not show a significant change in perceptions about risky sexual behaviors was supported. His fifth hypothesis that the rites of passage process would significantly increase knowledge of African-centered traditions was also supported. Overall, Menzise interpreted the results of his study as supporting the notion that rites of passage can have a constructive influence on the cognitions of at-risk adolescents regarding substance abuse and risky sexual behaviors, as well as increase their knowledge of their ethnicity and cultural heritage. As an adjunctive treatment to psychotherapy for at-risk adolescents, such a program could potentially be very useful (Menzise, 2006).

Implications and Considerations

The need for systematic studies of the possible impact of rites of passage programs in the treatment of violent adolescents seems clear. It is an exciting idea that requires well-documented implementation and investigation through quantitative and qualitative research. Nevertheless, as adjunctive programs, rites of passage processes could offer a number of benefits that enhance the value of traditional approaches to psychotherapy and counseling. Combining such programs with humanistic-existential or transpersonal treatment approaches in particular makes sense because rites of passage have a number of elements in common with these approaches. Research that is undertaken regarding the efficacy of rites of passage programs should endeavor to determine the extent to which such programs may serve better as a preventive strategy for at-risk adolescents (see, e.g., Menzise, 2006) or as adjunctive intervention strategies for adolescents who show a history of violent behaviors. Menzise's study suggests that the former group may benefit more, but the question is not by any means resolved.

Culturally-specific rites of passage programs could effectively ground adolescents in their cultural history and ethnic traditions, instilling or restoring a sense of connection to their communities and continuity with family and ancestors, even if only in a symbolic way. This connection could instill a sense of meaning and purpose, allowing an exploration of spirituality. Given the demonstrable impact of situational and contextual factors on the phenomenon of violence, instituting such a dramatic contextual change which also appeals to a revered history, could help to maximize these adolescents' readiness for change. This maximizing of conditions for change is consistent with the approach of Carl Rogers and that of Miller and Rollnick described earlier.

Mentors who facilitate rites of passage programs also serve as representatives of the community and provide tangible feedback on choices made and actions undertaken by adolescents participating in the program. They are visible bridges to the outside world for the participants. In the immediate context, adolescents learn that their choices and behaviors impact the community and that the community influences them in turn. In the longer term, the circularity between the positive reaction of the community at large to the successful graduates of the rites of passage program and the long-lasting respect and satisfaction derived by the adolescents in their accomplishment would hopefully be evident as well.

Moodley and West (2005) discuss the value of incorporating into psychotherapy indigenous healing practices that are germane to the culture and ethnicity of clients who are open to such modalities. They note that many traditional methods of healing, some of which date back over a thousand years, are being revived and recreated for contemporary times. Adherents embrace these methods for their ability to help them connect in a meaningful way to cultural symbols and archetypes that are often outside the boundaries of traditional counseling and psychotherapy (Moodley & West, 2005). Culturally-specific rites of passage programs could serve a similar purpose—even for those of European descent, whose heritage reaches back to the old Celtic, Norse, Germanic, Greek, and Roman nations. As mentioned earlier, contemporary Pagans could also be considered the "lore-keepers" of the remnants of customs and stories that could serve as a source for the creative design of such programs.

From a person-centered perspective, adolescents who take part in rites of passage programs find support, compassion, and acceptance by mentors who understand that they come as flawed human beings. They encounter in mentors and facilitators the notion that everyone begins life as a child who finds it difficult to take irrevocable steps into adulthood. Empathy abounds, encouraging them to allow into full expression their "actualizing tendency," or their desire to achieve balance and congruence between who they wish they could be and who they actually are to the rest of the world.

From a Gestalt psychology perspective, rites of passage programs could enable adolescents to discard their "false selves," their projected rage, the introjections of power and aggression of the gang or peer context, and the confluence of their identity with that of the gang or delinquent peers. The mentor/facilitator serves to help them identify and confront the part of who they are that wishes to remain an angry, rebellious, selfish adolescent that refuses to assume the mantle of responsible adulthood. In becoming more aware of their individual somatic experience and bodily reactions to events, adolescents may learn to express emotions with genuineness and authenticity. They can become more able to listen to their own intuitive "felt experience" as a guide to understanding the incongruence of violent choices.

From an existential perspective, rites of passage programs could help adolescents confront their fear and awareness of their mortality that comes through their fear of being victimized, which in turn manifests as their pre-emptive desire to inflict harm on others. They may become more aware of how they fill the void left by abusive or dysfunctional families and communities through a superficial identification with gang identity or delinquent peers. They can learn that past choices do not have to determine present decisions and behaviors— that every moment is a new opportunity to decide to be somebody different. They may realize that the power and freedom for which they have been searching is in their grasp as individuals who are free to define their role within their communities.

From a transpersonal perspective, adolescents who undertake rites of passage programs could become aware that they are more than their physical bodies and that they are free to transcend limited notions of identity defined by criminal and delinquent peers. They may learn that they are participants in a mystery associated with being and living—one that is much greater than the cynical perspective to which they have been formerly subjected. Their imaginative capacity to design possibilities for themselves and their lives could increase dramatically.

Smith (1997) links Jungian psychology with indigenous shamanic practices, identifying a call to shamanism as an archetypal initiation involving a symbolic death and rebirth experience. In the "typical" or archetypal shamanic initiation, dismemberment dreams, or visions of dying or being ritually destroyed, precede an awakening or rebirth as a shaman (Smith, 1997). The one who experiences this calling may also encounter in dreams or visions, a guardian or challenger figure of some sort that attempts to keep the shaman-to-be from achieving the objective of becoming a shaman. In Jungian terms, this guardian encounter constitutes an experience of the Shadow, or the repository of the qualities, emotions, beliefs, images, and constructs that are not expressed in conscious, day-to-day behavior. These pieces tend to take on a personified, frightening, or dark aspect, as they are associated with the parts of the psyche with which a person is least comfortable. If the prospective shaman successfully encounters the Shadow and resolves the encounter in a successful manner, or if the shaman actually reconstitutes a new experience of self from an experience of death or destruction, then the new shaman emerges with extraordinary skills and an ability to balance dichotomies. The shaman is able, as it were, to "walk between the worlds." These abilities also include the capacity to alter consciousness, experience travel in non-ordinary reality, ally with animal spirits, indulge in shape-shifting, and help those who have lost pieces of their soul or psyche through trauma or illness.

The archetype of this "initiatory ordeal" also seems to be inherent in rites of passage in general. Any experience of successfully navigating a transition involves a symbolic death of one way of being and a rebirth into another. If there was not a chance of failure, the initiation would hold no power and meaning. The assumption of shamanic power seems like an excellent metaphor for the psycho-spiritual transformation undertaken by the violent adolescent in a rites of passage program. In the course of the initiatory experience, the adolescent transmutes the energy of rage into a constructive resolution of the initiatory challenge, setting the stage for adult problem-solving.

In light of the discussion throughout this chapter, a rite of passage should include several elements in order to meet the archetypal requirements of initiation. It should have a supportive, empathic guide or mentor—or perhaps several—who are not afraid to confront and actively challenge adolescents when needed. The mentor thus combines a non-directive and directive approach, embodying the best qualities of both a person-centered and gestalt therapist. The rite of passage should involve a ritual separation or removal from the former environmental context into a liminal space of isolation that is ideal for transformative, psycho-spiritual work. It should entail a ritual ordeal of some kind or an encounter with a challenger or guardian figure that intentionally impedes the progress of the adolescent through the ordeal. The challenger should enable them to discard pieces of their psyche that are no longer useful, like the butterfly that leaves behind the cocoon woven in its caterpillar incarnation. It could perhaps also include an encounter with opposite gender representatives, to provide what Jung refers to as an experience of anima (for men) or animus (for women), the opposite gender complex that also resides in the unconscious. Such an experience might allow for greater possibilities, balance, and choice with regard to gender issues. It should include an integration stage—some kind of space in which the adolescent may reflect on or process newly acquired information or awareness. Finally, a rites of passage should entail a symbolic restoration to the community, perhaps with a commitment or promise to the community made out of newfound strength and resolve.

By virtue of their archetypal nature, the elements of a rites of passage initiation outlined above are conducive to adaptation within a variety of cultural contexts. According to Eliade (1951/2004), most cultures around the world have, far back in their history, some version of tribal practices and shamanism. The act of creating or recreating rites of passage that evoke the spirit of these ancient traditions would seem to combine the archetypal power of the initiation with the uniqueness of a given cultural tradition in a relevant, modern-day context. As contemporary Pagans are fond of saying, "Let the circle be open, but never broken."

References

Adler, M. (2006). Drawing down the moon: Witches, druids, goddess-worshippers, and other pagans in America. New York: Penguin Books.

Arnett, J. J. (1999). Adolescent storm and stress, reconsidered. American Psychologist, 54(5), 317–326.

Axelman, M., & Bonnell, S. (2006). When the peer group becomes the parent: Social and developmental issues associated with youth gangs. In T. G. Plante (Ed.), Mental disorders of the new millennium (pp. 101–126). Westport, CT: Praeger.

Bratter, T. E. (2006). When psychotherapy becomes a war: Working with gifted, alienated, angry adolescents who engage in self-destructive and dangerous behavior. International Journal of Reality Therapy, 26(1), 9–13.

Eliade, M. (2004). Shamanism: Archaic techniques of ecstasy. Princeton, NJ: Princeton University Press. (Original work published 1951)

Elliot, R. (2001). Research on the effectiveness of humanistic psychotherapies: A meta-analysis. In D. Cain & J. Seeman (Eds.), Humanistic psychotherapies: Handbook of research and practice (pp. 57–81). Washington, DC: American Psychological Association.

Hines, A. R., & Paulson, S. E. (2007). Parents and teachers' perceptions of adolescent storm and stress. Family Therapy, 34(2), 63–80.

Howell, J. C., & Egley, A. (2005). Moving risk factors into developmental theories of gang membership. Youth Violence and Juvenile Justice, 3(4), 334–354.

Kakar, S. (2005). Gang membership, delinquent friends, and criminal family members: Determining the connections. Journal of Gang Research, 13(1), 41–52.

Kimmel, M. (2007). Racism as adolescent male rite of passage. Journal of Contemporary Ethnography, 36(2), 202–218.

Mensize, J. (2006). The use of culturally-specific rites of passage to influence thoughts, beliefs, and behaviors of "at-risk" youth. Unpublished doctoral dissertation, Howard University.

Miller, W. R., & Rollnick, S. R. (2002). Motivational interviewing: Preparing people for change. New York: Guilford.

Moodley, R., & West, W. (2005). Introduction. In R. Moodley & W. West (Eds.), Integrating traditional healing practices into counseling and psychotherapy. Thousand Oaks, CA: Sage.

Quinsey, V. L., Harris, G. T., Rice, M. E., & Cormier, C. A. (2005). Violent offenders: Appraising and managing risk. Washington, DC: American Psychological Association.

Smith, C. M. (1997). Jung and shamanism in dialogue. Mahwah, NJ: Paulist Press.

Spaeth, M. J. D. (2006). Core shamanism and kundalini yoga: Bridging concepts for lifespan psychology. Paper presented at the Annual Meeting of the Society for Scientific Study of Religion, Portland, Oregon.

Tick, E. (2005). War and the soul: Healing our nation's veterans from post-traumatic stress disorder. Wheaton, IL: Quest Books.

CHAPTER TWELVE

Developing Therapeutic Trust with Court-Ordered Clients

David Polizzi, Indiana State University

More than any specific systematic approach to treating offenders, the quality and credibility of relationships that offenders have with treatment staff and significant others have the greater correctional influence. (Braswell, 2000, p. 7)

In a small, quiet, simply furnished room, two people sit facing one another. One of them talks as the other listens. (DeYoung, 2003, p. vii)

Introduction

Before any attempt to apply theory, before any assumptions about the foundations of criminal behavior or one's criminal past, offender psychotherapy, like all types of psychotherapy, is predicated upon DeYoung's simple observation: one person is talking and one is listening. But therapy is more than the act of listening, more than a neurological transformation of sound into meaning. Rather, it is a way of listening that invites the patient, client, or offender into the shared psychological space of the therapeutic frame that can become the crucible for authentic growth and transformation. Implied in this process of change is the presence of two people committed to the belief that change is possible and the possibility that a trusting relationship can be built—two concepts difficult to apply when working therapeutically with offender populations.

What makes this application so difficult is two-fold. First, there remains the lingering belief that change is difficult to achieve with offender populations (Miller & Rollnick, 2002). Added to this perspective is the belief that all offenders are dispositionally unable to build a trusting relationship with a therapist or other staff person and are, therefore, poor candidates for insight-orientated psychotherapeutic interventions. Even though certain cognitive-behavioral approaches to offender treatment have shown some limited therapeutic success (Lipton, Pearson, Cleland, & Yee, 2002; Van Voorhis & Lester, 2004), there remain lingering biases which continue to threaten the very foundation of the therapeutic relationship and ultimately the possibility of witnessing lasting change.

The Building of Therapeutic Trust in Offender Psychotherapy: Is it Possible?

The possibility for authentic change is predicated upon the presence of trust in the therapeutic relationship between therapist and client (May, 1983; Polizzi, 1994; Rogers, 1946, 1967, 1989). Though more difficult to achieve with offender populations, this statement is no less true. Braswell's (2000) observation concerning the quality and credibility of relationships with inmates provides some insight into this problem. His focus is on the interaction between two individuals, one talking and one listening (DeYoung, 2003), that refuses to conceptualize this meeting within any other theoretical or conceptual frame of reference (Bozarth, 1993; Braswell, 2000). By proceeding in this way, both therapist and client are forced to focus on the here and now reality of their encounter and the possibilities for change that each individual brings to the relationship. Such an encounter demands that each individual be ready to lay down any preconceived notions or social construction of the other that may prevent this authentic meeting from taking place (Polizzi, 2007).

The immediate barrier to the creation of a successful therapeutic relationship with offender populations is the daunting presence of damaging preconceived assumptions about whom or what the offender really is. Much of the process related to the social construction of the criminal other is fueled by the belief that offenders are dispositionally or ontologically unable to take part in an authentic therapeutic relationship. Many of those attitudes or opinions concerned with working therapeutically with offenders have been driven by the lingering belief in the "nothing works" perspective, originally formulated by Martinson (1974). Though this idea has been challenged and revised over the last few decades (see, e.g., Andrews & Bonta, 1998; Lipsey, 1995; McGuire, 2001; McMurran, 2002; Van Voorhis & Hurst, 2004) certain attitudes remain that continue to have a negative impact upon the possibility for successful therapeutic work with offender populations.

In his important text, The Psychopathic Mind: Origins, Dynamics, and Treatment, Reid Meloy (1997) contextualizes these countertransference attitudes within the concept of therapeutic nihilism. Countertransference, a term originally coined by Freud, is generally defined as the way in which the patient influences the feelings or attitudes of the therapist at either the conscious or unconscious level (Laplanche & Pontalis, 1973). Therapeutic nihilism, an example of the therapist's countertransference feelings toward the offender, can be defined as the assumption that, as a group or class, all psychopathic or antisocial personality disorders are untreatable. Meloy (1997) asserts:

> I have most commonly observed this reaction in public mental health clinicians who are assigned patients on referral from probation, parole, or the court; and assume, because of the coercive nature of the treatment referral, that the patients must be psychopathic and any psychotherapeutic gain is impossible. (p. 325)

Meloy's observation outlines the way in which offender treatment becomes constructed through the countertransference perspective of therapeutic nihilism. Once the therapist has categorically accepted the assumption that therapeutic work with this population is absent, the inevitable failure of the offender/client in therapy is not far behind. The foundation of this belief lies with the false assumption that remanded offender/clients lack the motivation necessary to change based upon the coercive nature of their referral to treatment. Included here is the belief that motivation to change is somehow categorically different with offenders than it is with patients who enter therapy minus the baggage of a criminal justice referral. However, McMurran (2002, p. 8) points out that "this view ignores the evidence that many people enter treatment because of external pressure, and even apparent volunteers are there because of ultimatums from family, friends, or employers." In fact, she goes on to state that a legal mandate to treatment may be the necessary external motivator that allows the poorly motivated offender to achieve positive therapeutic results once involved in a treatment regime. The point raised by McMurran is an important one that needs further exploration.

The observation made by McMurran raises two rather obvious points. The first is that the relationship between the remanded offender and treatment success rates may be highly misleading and more indicative of an attitude of therapeutic nihilism than evidence of the lack of offender motivation to change. Secondly and perhaps more importantly, is the belief that treatment success with offender populations is much more tied to what occurs after the criminal justice referral than before it. Taken from this vantage point, the presence of therapeutic nihilism interprets the fact of the criminal justice referral as sufficient evidence to support the belief that change is impossible, thereby evoking in the therapist an anti-therapeutic stance toward the client. Once the offender recognizes this rather obvious and often aggressive attitude in the therapist, the result of the therapy is a forgone conclusion. Yet, this discussion still begs the question: Is trust in offender psychotherapy possible?

Of course, the answer to this question is predicated upon the theoretical frame of reference by which the question is asked. The assumption that the offender is categorically unable to participate in a therapeutic relationship because of the circumstances of the referral, becomes legitimate only if one accepts the image of the offender constructed by the perspective of therapeutic nihilism. Though one cannot discount the possible affect that such a referral may have on the patient's ability or desire to participate in therapy in a meaningful way, neither should we accept a priori that such a referral categorically guarantees a negative result. What McMurran's and Meloy's observations reveal is that the attitude and style of the therapist helps to either facilitate or hinder the offender's ability to become engaged in the therapeutic process (Williams & Hanley, 2005).

Therapeutic Trust and the Role of Resistance in Offender Psychotherapy

The concept of resistance was seen by Freud as an obstacle to treatment insofar as it attempted to block the clear elucidation of the patient's symptoms (Laplanche & Pontalis, 1973). In the Introductory Lectures on Psychoanalysis, Freud states:

> For resistance is constantly altering its intensity during the course of a treatment; it always increases when we are approaching a new topic, it is at its most intense while we are at the climax of dealing with that topic, and it dies away when the topic has been disposed of. (Freud, 1916/1966, p. 293)

Resistance, then, was seen by Freud as a mechanism that seeks to protect the analysand (client) from the power of his or her symptoms. From this perspective, the presence of resistance alerts the therapist to the way in which the client is responding to the unfolding of the therapeutic process. If we follow Freud's thinking on this matter, resistance increases as the client gets too close to certain psychological material that may be difficult for the client to accept and incorporate into his or her conscious experience. As the client finds that he or she is better able to confront this material, the intensity of the resistance will decrease. Perhaps most important to this discussion is the fact that resistance serves a protective function insofar as it protects the client from having to confront difficult and painful material before psychologically ready to do so.

The protective aspect of resistance also seems to present a challenge to the existing boundaries of the therapeutic frame. Taken from this vantage point, the presence of resistance is evoked by the uncertainty of the therapeutic alliance. If, as Freud asserts, the intensity of the resistance is relative to the material being explored, it may be possible to say that this intensity is connected to the level of trust the client has in the therapeutic relationship. The intensity of the emotional power of the resistance can only subside if the client has confidence in not only his or her own ability to confront this issue, but in the ability to recognize the supporting presence of the therapist. Though theoretical formulations of this concept differ based on the theoretical approach, the concept of resistance remains an important aspect of the therapeutic process.

Most theoretical models of psychotherapy offer some form of explanation concerning the dynamic of resistance. Cognitive therapies generally locate this dynamic within the context of the patient and his or her irrational beliefs (Ellis, 1985), whereas behavioral therapies are more likely to see resistance as the therapist's inability to understand the patient's reinforcement history (Harris, 1995). More experiential or psycho-dynamically oriented therapeutic approaches tend to understand resistance within a more interpersonal context (Braswell, 2000; Meloy, 1997; Miller & Rollnick, 2002; Polizzi, 1997). Regardless then, of the therapeutic perspective, resistance is generally seen as a construct of the process or experience of therapy that emerges within the relationship between patient and therapist. But how do we understand resistance when it is related to the therapy itself?

As Meloy (1997) describes, the concept of therapeutic nihilism is a form of resistance evoked in the therapist that is directly related to the way in which the therapist perceives the nature of court-ordered referral for treatment. However, what is left unexplored is the way in which the remanded offender/client takes up this same situation of being forced to enter therapy. The immediate socially constructed assumption of therapeutic nihilism is that the client has little interest in treatment and the nature of the referral will simply help to reinforce that stance, in a sense validating the "logic" upon which this concept relies, or perhaps more simply put, creating the self-fulfilling prophecy for treatment failure. However, there appears to be an important clinical distinction between one's resistance to the very idea of treatment due to the coercive nature of the referral and resistance to treatment related to the inability of the client to resolve certain difficult psychological issues.

Undoubtedly, anyone who has worked with court-ordered individuals has experienced the client's resistance to participate in treatment due to the nature of that referral. However, what is perhaps less obvious is how to understand this type of resistance in the context of clinical praxis. Said another way, what does this type of resistance mean, how does it differ from the more traditional understanding of this concept, and how will it affect the possibility for a positive therapeutic outcome? We will take each of these questions in turn.

How to Understand the Client's Resistance to Coercive Treatment

Too often, the refusal of the court-remanded client to engage genuinely in treatment is seen as proof of the individual's unwillingness to change. But is this the only possible clinical meaning for the client's stance toward treatment? By separating these two very different psychological positions or responses by the client, we may significantly transform the client's attitude and by so doing, greatly increase the likelihood of a successful treatment outcome. The reality for some offenders is that they are likely to be remanded to treatment as a stipulation for either their release from the penitentiary or for their continued participation with parole or probation (Blackburn, 2002). Their forced participation in treatment almost immediately evokes feelings of anger and frustration based on the fact of the referral and the impending consequences if the client fails to comply with the stipulations of that referral. Resistance to such a set of circumstances is not surprising but rather, is somewhat natural and legitimate given the situation. However, in the author's clinical experience working therapeutically with offender/clients, the presence of this type of resistance—resistance to court-ordered treatment—does not necessarily imply that the client is uninterested in treatment or that a successful treatment outcome will be impossible to achieve based on the presence of this type of resistance alone.

How Does Resistance to Coercive Treatment Differ from the Traditional Understanding of Resistance?

When resistance to engage in coercive treatment is separated from traditional understandings of resistance, that is, resistance related to some issue that emerges through the therapeutic process, a much different clinical picture comes into focus. Taken from this perspective, resistance to coercive treatment is understood as the result of the loss of agency represented by the fact and circumstance of the criminal justice referral itself (Polizzi, 1994). The client's initial refusal to participate in treatment is more related to the attempt to regain some semblance of this perceived loss of agency than it is an outright refusal to engage in the therapeutic process. Though resistance remains a choice insofar as it is a defiant response to the client's current situation, it is a choice that is driven by the sole desire to confront the referral process itself and one which provides the client only a limited sense of agency. In fact, it may be possible to say that the resistance which the therapist experiences from the offender/client, particularly in the beginning of the treatment process, is the same articulation of helplessness that one discovers with other types of mental health patients who are equally unable to realize their ability to effect meaningful change in their lives.

It is also important to note that the same helplessness experienced by the client through the process of the court-ordered referral is indirectly witnessed through the attitude portrayed in therapeutic nihilism, which of course, is not exclusive to the practice of forensic psychotherapy. What the therapist articulates when confronting this challenging clinical situation is that "I cannot or will not help you." Such a clinical stance limits the agency of the therapist insofar as it thwarts the very identity of the therapeutic process and calls into question the therapist's ability to facilitate lasting change with patients.

By refusing to recognize the psychological implications that such a referral has on the criminal justice client entering psychotherapy, the clinician misses a major opportunity by which to understand the experience of the client from his or her perspective. Too often, this experience is either ignored or rejected outright as being an aspect of manipulation on the part of the client who is simply making excuses for refusing to participate in treatment. When taken in this way, the client's experience of the situation is devalued and with it, his or her ability to create a genuine therapeutic bond with the clinician. How then, is authentic trust created in the face of this type of resistance?

How to Overcome the Client's Initial Resistance to Coercive Treatment and Create the Possibility for Success in Therapy

If it is true that the nature of the criminal justice referral is responsible for the type of resistance described above, then it is clinically essential that the therapist address this experience from the very beginning of treatment, if therapy is to have any possibility of success. What this implies is that the clinician takes seriously the legitimacy of the client's experience and begins to explore what meanings this experience has for him or her. Such an approach simply seeks to make explicit what is implicit in this encounter: the client's forced participation in treatment. The author's experience in working with criminal justice-referred clients has taught him that the most effective way to address this type of resistance is to address the problem directly.

All too often, certain clients will begin their initial meeting with the therapist by stating, "I don't know why I'm here, you'll have to ask my parole officer" or "I don't have a drug problem and I don't need treatment." By inviting the client to explore feelings concerning the nature of the treatment referral, the therapist immediately legitimizes those feelings and begins to build a therapeutic relationship that remains focused on the needs of the client. Such a focus helps to challenge the way in which the client has likely constructed the meaning of this interaction in advance of the actual session and helps to pave the way for the possibility of the client's authentic engagement in the therapeutic process. Given that this type of referral is often experienced by the client as a form of punishment, failure to address feelings related to the referral process will likely help only to reinforce negative attitudes about treatment in general and guarantee a poor treatment outcome. To include the client's experience of being forced to participate in treatment provides evidence of not only the therapist's desire to create a respectful therapeutic environment, but also reveals a realistic understanding of the client's current situation. Once the therapist recognizes that the resistant stance by the client is simply one more important clinical issue to address and not the cause of treatment failure, the treatment process can begin.

Problems with Trust: Socially Constructed Barriers to Working with the Criminal Justice Client

Though the nature of the criminal justice referral certainly evokes a host of difficulties related to the creation of a positive therapeutic environment, it represents only one of the barriers to successful treatment. As stated previously, the concept of therapeutic nihilism emerges as a socially constructed artifact from the process of court-ordered psychotherapy. The ability of the therapist to successfully address the coercive aspects of the court-ordered referral may help to alleviate some of the client's initial distrust of this process, and may also help the therapist to rethink his or her assumptions about the possibilities for court-ordered treatment. Regardless of how these initial obstacles are addressed, many doubts related to this process will likely remain. It is important to keep in mind that the social construction of offender psychotherapy is not unidirectional (Fruggeri, 1994). Just as the therapist constructs the image of the offender from a specific social perspective which evokes a specific set of socially generated meanings concerning who or what the offender is, so too does the client construct the therapist, case worker, or probation officer from a similar set of socially generated meanings (Berger & Luckmann, 1966; Cecchin, 1994). From this perspective, it is necessary to explore the way in which the client constructs the role of the therapist in court-ordered psychotherapy as well as the way in which the therapist "helps" the court-ordered client in justifying that construction.

The Client's Inability to Trust: The Social Construction of the Therapist in Offender Psychotherapy

Much has been written concerning the way in which preexisting attitudes toward the court-referred client affects the therapist's ability to engage in the therapeutic process (Meloy, 1997). Less focus, however, has been given to the way in which the client perceives this same encounter. Given the circumstances leading to the individual's involvement in court-ordered psychotherapy, there has been little interest in exploring the client's attitude toward his or her participation in the treatment process. The criminal behavior in question seems to be justification enough to ignore any possible concerns that the client may offer regarding this arrangement. The client's perception from an encounter with an aggressive or judgmental therapist is rejected or ignored even though it will likely provide justification for the client's belief that the referral process is more related to the continuation of his or her punishment than it is to the facilitation for positive change. Such a perspective assumes that the client, based on his or her involvement with the criminal justice system, forfeits all rights of complaint and must therefore stop making excuses and "get with the program." When the client fails to comply, the self-fulfilling prophecy for treatment failure is realized.

The roots of this self-fulfilling prophecy can be witnessed within the concept of institutionalization offered by Berger and Luckmann (1966, p. 54): "Institutionalization occurs whenever there is a reciprocal typification of habitualized actions by types of actors." What this dynamic implies for the social construction of offender psychotherapy is that each side of this encounter seeks to habituate or define the possible actions of the other actor or individual from a very limited perspective. To habituate the actions of the offender is to determine prior to any encounter with the individual, how he or she will act and how those actions will be defined by the therapist, counselor, or probation officer. For his or her part, the court-ordered client will likely come to the initial session with similar preconceived notions of the process and will act according to those predetermined meanings, particularly when those preconceptions are validated by experience. Any actions that fall outside of this preexisting schema of meaning will likely be taken with some suspicion given the circumstances of this context. It is therefore essential that the treatment provider not respond in such a way that will validate the client's perspective or expectation of a negative encounter with treatment staff or therapists.

By reducing the client to the socially constructed image of offender, the individual is left with little control and given no real opportunity to break free from the restrictions that this imposition provides, even if there exists a genuine desire to do so. The possibility of an authentic engagement with the therapeutic process is immediately thwarted by the legitimate stance of the client who refuses to invest in such a damaging and one-sided relationship. Much like the experience of the penitentiary, therapy becomes one more imposed stipulation that often articulates little authentic concern for the psychological needs of the client. Based on the circumstances of the court-ordered referral and the actual experience of court-ordered therapy, the client is provided ample evidence as to why this process cannot and perhaps should not be trusted (Williams & Hanley, 2005).

The possibility for the creation of trust in the court-ordered client seems predicated upon the ability of the treatment process to confront both sets of meanings that emerge through the social construction of offender psychotherapy. Given that the social construction of the face-to-face encounter always precedes its actual meeting, it is essential that the possibilities of this encounter remain fluid and not allowed to lapse into rigid and preconceived notions of the other. However, given the extreme imbalance in this relationship, it is important that the client's already potentially ambivalent stance toward the treatment process given the circumstances of the referral not become inadvertently strengthened by lingering assumptions about the court-ordered client.

The Limitations of Trust in Offender Psychotherapy

Though the creation of trust between therapist and client is essential to the very foundation of the therapeutic process, the limits of that trust should always be clarified, honestly explored, and discussed with the client before any therapeutic work is begun. These limits are particularly significant when placed within the context of offender psychotherapy, given the coercive nature of the criminal justice referral. Blackburn (2002, p. 152) states, "Whatever the limits on informed consent when employing strategies to change offenders, therapists have an obligation to provide information about any implications of the therapist's role as double agent, particularly the limits of confidentiality."

The reality of the logistics of offender psychotherapy is that the therapist is forced into the role of double agent: therapist as client advocate and therapist as representative of the criminal justice system. Blackburn is quite correct in recognizing the importance that this dilemma has on the therapist who is attempting to identify who the client is: the referred individual or the criminal justice system. Though this uncertainty may create a difficult obstacle for the therapist, it is not a barrier that is clinically insurmountable (Trotter, 1999).

In the author's work as a forensic psychotherapist either in the penitentiary or in the community, he has always recognized the referred individual as the sole client, regardless of setting or legal status. Every meeting with a new client would begin with a discussion of the limits of confidentiality and how the therapist would respond if the client in any way crossed those limits. Included in this discussion would be an explanation of the concepts of threat to self or others and any other specific situations such as child abuse, potential crimes within the penitentiary, or possible escape attempts. By clearly establishing with the client the limits of confidentiality, the therapist's role as double agent is honestly recognized and the duties of these two contradictory roles is clarified.

By directly confronting the issue of therapist as double agent with the client, the therapist immediately begins to set the foundation for the construction of an authentic therapeutic relationship. The circumstances of the referral process demand that this issue not be ignored, if one is serious about the possibility of providing effective treatment to this population of clients. Perhaps most important to this dynamic is the recognition that all relationships involve limits that cannot be crossed without consequences. Once the client understands the concept of confidentiality and its limits, the client may become much less reluctant to participate in the therapeutic process in an honest way. Too often, the court-ordered client enters therapy with the belief that this process is little more than a highly sophisticated sting operation intended to gather information that will be used against him or her at some later date.

Though the conditions under which court-ordered psychotherapy takes place are wrought with a variety of difficulties not often shared by other psychotherapeutic contexts, such difficulties do not preclude the possibility for psychotherapeutic success. It is clinically important that the psychotherapist not naïvely ignore the facts of the forensic environment or the process by which the forensic referral occurs. Even the most resistant forensic client can be reached if the therapist is open to the possibility that real, lasting psychotherapeutic change can occur. Such a position does not intend to assume that all forensic clients can be effectively helped with the assistance of psychotherapy; obviously they cannot. Such a position is also unwilling to accept at face-value many of the commonly held assumptions related to the practice of forensic psychotherapy. At this point, a forensic case will be discussed where the issue of client resistance was present, but was eventually overcome and real, lasting change was achieved.

Building the Therapeutic Relationship: The Case of D

D is a 41-year-old African-American male who the author worked with therapeutically for approximately 18 months. D came from a lower middle class background where drug use and involvement in the sales of illicit drugs became an all too familiar way of life for many of the individuals living in the community. D lived with his retired parents at the beginning of his time in therapy; however, soon after he began treatment, he decided to move in with his girlfriend with whom he had a monogamous relationship for approximately three years. He described his relationship with his parents as strong and stated that during his involvement with drugs, he was careful not to bring his drug use around them. He described a long history of substance abuse and a history of involvement with the criminal justice system due to his involvement in the sale of illegal substances. D would make constant reference to what he observed as the "senseless violence" all around him since his release from the penitentiary and his desire to find something more positive for himself.

D was remanded to outpatient psychotherapy by the criminal justice system for his continued use of crack cocaine. Though D had attempted to end his use of cocaine, his attempts in the past were not successful. He was also involved in the sale of crack cocaine which ultimately resulted in his arrest and subsequent incarceration at a minimum security facility in Pennsylvania where he served 18 months of a three-year sentence. Upon his release from that facility, he was directed by the court, as a stipulation of his parole, to participate in psychotherapy or face the possibility of returning to prison. Given his past history of drug use and the sale of crack cocaine, he was assigned to a special drug unit of the Pennsylvania state parole office, where he was required to provide two urine samples per week. He was also stipulated to participate in a case management program where he was required to provide a weekly urine sample, as an adjunct to his involvement in psychotherapy. Failure to comply with any of these stipulations would be grounds for the termination of his parole and his return to the penitentiary.

During his intake interview, D stated that he would not be involved in treatment if he had not been stipulated to do so. Though he was readily able to admit that he had a problem with cocaine and could benefit from treatment, he was uncomfortable with his forced participation in treatment and complied with the referral only because he did not want to return to prison. He added that if it were not for his current involvement with the criminal justice system, he would still be using crack cocaine today. D's ability to recognize that his involvement in the world of drugs was directly related to his difficulties with the criminal justice system made it slightly easier to address the issue of his forced involvement in treatment, but did not allow this issue to disappear immediately.

The most compelling aspect of D's resistance to treatment was the coercive nature of the referral itself and the total loss of agency that it represented for him. He was initially unable to reconcile his genuine need for drug treatment with the fact that he was being ordered to participate in therapy. Though D's continued use of crack cocaine directly affected his ability to articulate a clear sense of agency, he was unwilling to place sufficient emphasis on the role his own actions played in that loss. It was his choice to use drugs and therefore, he should be the one who decides when it is time to end that use. Though his attitude is not surprising given the circumstances, D's sole focus on the referral process prevented him from resolving the very issues that he stated were most important to him: a desire to end his use of cocaine and a desire not to return to the penitentiary. Ironically, it was his somewhat ambivalent stance toward his participation in treatment and not the need for treatment itself that became the main barrier to the therapeutic process. Once these two issues were separated and clarified, the process was able to move forward.

Though D's initial resistance to treatment was rather short-lived, his stance helps to clarify the clinical difference between resistance to the court-ordered referral and a resistance to treatment generally. Once his complaint about the nature of his participation in treatment was heard and legitimized by the therapist, he was able to formulate a strategy for treatment that was focused upon his drug use and not on the stipulations imposed on him by the court and parole board. Though the reality of his situation did not change, he was able to explore his feelings about that situation within a therapeutic context that did not attempt to invalidate his feelings or perspectives on the circumstances of his life.

D began our therapeutic work with the following question: "Is it possible for a black man to be happy in America?" The therapist's response was simply, "I don't know." What appears to have been most clinically significant for him was not so much the answer to this question, but the possibility that perhaps the therapeutic relationship could help him explore the depths of the question. The very idea that he was able to ask this question reveals an emerging desire to change his life and the realization that the defiant image of the drug dealer no longer provided a satisfactory answer to his question. An example of the emerging process of transformation is witnessed in the following experience D shared early on in therapy.

D stated that he was walking around his neighborhood one afternoon and witnessed a young woman offering to sell herself sexually in exchange for drugs. By his own admission, he had witnessed or participated in numerous transactions of this type in the past. However, much to his surprise, this particular experience was much different. D stated, "Though I knew that my drugs were not responsible for this little girl, I knew that I was responsible for other young women like her, so I was no better than the dude I watched selling." As he spoke, it was apparent that he was visibly shaken by the lingering image of this young woman and was truly aware of the consequences that his behavior had caused other people. So powerful was the experience for him that it shattered once and for all any possible rationalizations for his identification with the figure of the drug dealer and helped to clear the psychological space necessary for his therapeutic work to truly begin. Included in this process was the creation of the therapeutic frame that allowed for this powerful experience to be shared with the therapist (Cox, 1999).

D's sharing of this experience would have been possible if the therapist's stance toward him had been aggressive, confrontational, or judgmental. Though he clearly harbored some apprehension about being forced to participate in therapy, D was ready to confront the various aspects of his drug use and involvement in the criminal justice system. By respecting D's experience concerning his forced participation in therapy and his perspective on racism, D appeared better able to join with the therapist in the creation of an authentic therapeutic relationship. He relaxed his opposition to therapy once he felt that his perspective was being heard and not ignored simply because of his involvement with the criminal justice system. It was through this process of one person talking and one person listening that D was able to explore the depths of his experience in such a way that proved to be transformative and lasting.

Postscript

During D's 18 months in treatment, he was able to remain drug-free, return to school to complete his GED, and find gainful employment as well as confront a variety of issues related to friends and family. Upon completing his parole, D decided to end treatment. He stated that he wanted to put his prior involvement with the criminal justice system behind him, which required that he end his therapy as well. Though the therapist would have enjoyed working with him further, D had clearly accomplished the established treatment goals and had earned his successful discharge from treatment. Since his time in treatment, D has completed his associate's degree and is planning to enroll at a local four-year college to continue his education.

Conclusion

The building of therapeutic trust with offender populations remains predicated upon the quality of the relationship between therapist and client. Therapeutic success can only occur in an environment that is clinically safe, open, and free of judgment and aggression. Forensic psychotherapy, like all types of psychotherapy, must incorporate into its foundation, the belief that the patient or client can improve and that this process must always be respectful to the needs of the individual.

References

Andrews, D. A., & Bonta, J. (1998). The psychology of criminal conduct. Cincinnati: Anderson.

Berger, P. L., & Luckmann, T. (1966). The social construction of reality: A treatise in the sociology of knowledge. New York: Anchor.

Blackburn, R. (2002). Ethical issues in motivating offenders to change. In M. McMurran (Ed.), Motivating offenders to change: A guide to enhancing engagement in therapy (pp. 139–155). West Sussex, UK: Wiley.

Bozarth, J. (1993). Not necessarily necessary but always sufficient. In D. Brazier (Ed.), Beyond Carl Rogers (pp. 92–105). London: Constable.

Braswell, M. (2000). Correctional treatment and the human spirit. In P. Van Voorhis, M. Braswell, & D. Lester (Eds.), Correctional counseling & rehabilitation (4th ed., pp. 3–22). Cincinnati: Anderson.

Cecchin, G. (1994). Constructing therapeutic possibilities. In S. McNamee & K. Gergen (Eds.), Therapy as social construction (pp. 86–95). London: Sage.

Cox, M. (1999). Remorse and reparation: 'To double business bound'. In M. Cox (Ed.), Remorse and reparation (pp. 9–18). London: Jessica Kingsley.

DeYoung, P. (2003). Relational psychotherapy: A primer. London: Brunner Routledge.

Ellis, A. (1985). Overcoming resistance. New York: Springer.

Freud, S. (1966). Introductory lectures on psychoanalysis (J. Strachey, Trans.). New York: W. W. Norton. (Original work published 1916)

Fruggeri, L. (1994). Therapeutic process as the social construction of change. In S. McNamee & K. Gergen (Eds.), Therapy as social construction (pp. 40–53). London: Sage.

Harris, G. (1995). Overcoming resistance: Success in counseling men. Lanham, MD: American Correctional Association.

Laplanche, J., & Pontalis, J. B. (1973). The language of psychoanalysis (D. Nicholson-Smith, Trans.). New York: W. W. Norton.

Lipsey, M. (1995). What do we learn from 400 research studies on the effectiveness of treatment with juvenile delinquents? In J. McGuire (Ed.), What works: Reducing reoffending (pp. 63–78). Chichester, UK: Wiley.

Lipton, D. S., Pearson, F. S., Cleland, C. M., & Yee, D. (2002). The effectiveness of cognitive-behavioural treatment methods on offender recidivism. In J. McGuire (Ed.), Offender rehabilitation and treatment (pp. 79–112). Chichester, UK: Wiley.

Martinson, R. (1974). What works? Questions and answers about prison reform. The Public Interest, 35, 22–54.

May, R. (1983). The discovery of being: Writings in existential psychology. New York: W. W. Norton.

McGuire, J. (2001). What works in correctional intervention? Evidence and practical implications. In J. McGuire (Ed.), Offender rehabilitation in practice: Implementing and evaluating effective programs (pp. 25–43). Chichester: Wiley.

McMurran, M. (2002). Motivation to change: Selection criterion or treatment need? In M. McMurran (Ed.), Motivating offenders to change: A guide to enhancing engagement in therapy (pp. 3–13). New York: Wiley.

Meloy, J. R. (1997). The psychopathic mind: Origins, dynamics, and treatment. North Vale: Jason Aronson.

Miller, W., & Rollnick, S. (2002). Motivational interviewing: Preparing people for change. New York: Guilford.

Polizzi, D. (1994). Facing the criminal. Humanistic Psychologist, 22, 28–38.

Polizzi, D. (1997). Lacan, transference and the place of the criminal subject. Journal of Theoretical and Philosophical Psychology, 17, 32–44.

Polizzi, D. (2007). Social construction of race and crime. Intentional Journal of Restorative Justice, 3, 6–20.

Rogers, C. (1946). Significant aspects of client-centered therapy. American Psychologist, 1, 415–422.

Rogers, C. (1967). On becoming a person: A therapist's view of psychotherapy. London: Constable.

Rogers, C. (1989). A newer psychotherapy. In H. Kirschenbum and V. L. Henderson (Eds.), The Carl Rogers reader (pp. 63–76). New York: McGraw-Hill.

Trotter, C. (1999). Working with involuntary clients. London: Sage.

Van Voorhis, P., & Hurst, G. (2004). Treating substance abuse in offender populations. In P. Van Voorhis, M. Braswell, & D. Lester (Eds.), Correctional counseling & rehabilitation (5th ed., pp. 257–284). Cincinnati: Anderson.

Van Voorhis, P., & Lester, D. (2004). Cognitive therapies. In P. Van Voorhis, M. Braswell, & D. Lester (Eds.), Correctional counseling & rehabilitation (5th ed., pp. 183–207). Cincinnati: Anderson.

Williams, D. J., & Hanley, M. (2005). Thinking about thinking (errors). Journal of Forensic Psychology and Practice, 5, 51–58.

CHAPTER THIRTEEN

EPILOGUE: TOWARD A MORE HUMANISTIC FUTURE IN CORRECTIONS

David Polizzi, Indiana State University

The future of corrections in America is predicated upon not only the way in which the criminal justice system seeks to define its role, but also the way in which it defines those who will find themselves under its custody and control (Toch, 1997). Though it may be possible to refrain from providing any specific answers concerning the purpose of criminal justice, it does, however, remain essential that we adequately struggle with the question concerning the way in which the image of the offender is constructed by this process. It is, after all, the presence of that image to which we react and construct our systems of criminal justice (Arrigo, Milovanovic, & Schehr, 2005). Some will legitimately argue that once we have established a credible answer to this question, the more general concerns about the project of criminal justice will be addressed as well.

How then, do we instill these human qualities back into the enterprise of corrections, criminal justice, and offender treatment? The main purpose of this text has been fundamentally focused upon that question. However, its answer remains elusive and it is certainly not one that can be concluded within the pages of this text. What it can do is help to set the ground for another type of conversation concerning the theory, practice, and social meaning of corrections, criminal justice, and offender rehabilitation; one which is able to recognize the fundamentally human character of this practice. Given the complexity of the question and its answer, the notion of transforming corrections has sought to confront the issue from a variety of theoretical, conceptual, and disciplinary perspectives. The desire to focus the discussion on one specific aspect of this debate, though perhaps more appealing intellectually, is simply too narrow an examination to do justice to the problem before us.

The practice of corrections, criminal justice, and offender treatment presents a variety of questions unique to each of these disciplinary perspectives, while at the same time retaining an unmistakable confluence to each that should not be forgotten or ignored. Just as these practices represent an overlapping of a variety of social discourse concerning politics, economic status, and ethnicity, so too is there a juxtaposition of ideas between theory and practice, concept and method, that must be addressed as well. Just as it is difficult, if not misleading, to assume that the issues and concerns of the penitentiary are not relevant to the rehabilitation center, the parole office, or the community at large, the same degree of misunderstanding can and does exist between questions of theory and practice.

The idea of transforming corrections seeks to reconfigure the thematic limits of our conversations within criminology, criminal justice, and offender treatment at the level of both theory and practice. As has been demonstrated throughout this text, theory and practice are co-constituting principles of disciplinary praxis, which must be clearly articulated and explored but never viewed in isolation or as totally separate philosophical categories or positions. Essential to this integration is the belief that crime and those disciplinary practices which have been created to address it are unmistakably human in nature and are in need of a theoretical approach or vision that is able to recognize the human face of the offender, even when that image confronts us with the most unspeakable acts of predation, neglect, or self-destruction.

Individually and collectively, it is common for words such as these to evoke feelings of anger over the way in which offenders seemingly ignore the pain of the victims of crime. All too often, the more general perception of such a position is viewed with suspicion and seen as representing an alleged academic elitism, which allows itself to become little more than an apologist for the perpetrators of these unacceptable acts of criminality, cruelty, and violence. However, a humanistically-grounded theory of criminal behavior does not ignore the reality of that behavior, but neither does it seek to conflate such actions into an exclusive, constructed possibility for human existence.

Though there is a degree of flux within the various theoretical perspectives provided throughout this text, each approach represents a movement away from overly reductive structural or positivistic formulations concerning who or what the offender is. Included within this shared philosophical context is the belief that criminal behavior, like all other types of human experience, takes place within a shared cultural context that is not reducible to one specific or exclusively identified set of behaviors or perspectives and is almost always predicated upon variously constructed social meanings that rarely reflect an exclusively shared understanding across individual perspectives. Said another way, not all social perspectives share the same degree of social "legitimacy." Such perspectives may become overwhelmed by beliefs that carry more social currency due to constructed dynamics of influence and power that are unique to a particular cultural surround.

Given the reality of these incongruent dynamics of social power and influence, it is theoretically and practically essential that the study of criminology, criminal justice, and offender treatment effectively address the way in which these dominant narrative discourses influence and shape not only the conversation concerning the more general discussion, but also recognize specifically how these meanings about criminal justice relate to the construction of policy and the day-to-day involvement with various types of offender populations (Berger & Luckmann, 1966; Arrigo et al., 2005). Transforming corrections attempts to do just that. It is for this reason that our discussion has been somewhat broad. The points of entry to this conversation are many, but we must begin somewhere if any appreciable change is to be achieved.

Whether reflected in issues of theory, correctional training, or therapeutic involvement, transforming corrections seeks to expand the current discussion within these disciplinary conversations to include the human character of the process of criminology, criminal justice, and offender treatment. Fundamental to this project is the rejection of objectifying dynamics of control, which seeks to nullify the humanity of the offender based on the fact of his or her offense. Though such retributive solutions or attitudes concerning the problem of crime continue to enjoy a degree of cultural currency, their effectiveness as social policy remains in question. The desire to focus on the immediate act of criminality conveniently ignores the social context from which these behaviors emerge and presumes an undistractable rationality for all those individuals who have actively pursued a criminal lifestyle. Such an attitude is not surprising and is one whose reach extends far beyond the limits of theoretical inquiry or concern.

Criminology, through its inability or unwillingness to provide a clear theoretical understanding or definition of human experience that is separate from acts of criminal behavior, leaves itself open to a variety of abuses in everyday correctional practice. Such a gap invites or even encourages strategies of control which systematically neglect or ignore the fundamental human character of those individuals under its care. At worst, these processes rob the offender of personal history insofar as the act of criminality now becomes synonymous with individual existence, evoking a perpetual derogation of human possibility and becoming.

In an attempt to address these fundamentally dehumanizing processes related to the various disciplines of corrections, we have included in our reflections, various aspects of day-to-day practice and the way in which these theoretical concerns are played out in the prison yard, parole office, or therapy session. The reason for this connection is simple and straight-forward: There is no practice without theory and no theory without practice. Regardless where one enters this conversation, the issues before us remain the same. The practice of corrections or criminal justice is indeed a human enterprise and requires human solutions to the problems addressed rather than systematic excuses or rationalizations for those policies or actions undertaken in the name of restoration, rehabilitation, or justice. As Anthony Farley (2002) forcefully argues, "We take monstrous pleasure in creating monsters. Our monsters, to the surprise of no one, behave monstrously. Sometimes they even kill. For this, their monstrous behavior, they are monstrously punished" (p. 1493). The creation of monsters legitimizes the need to punish them monstrously, and by so doing, allows us to ignore those other all-too-human qualities, which these offenders also share with us.

References

Arrigo, B., Milovanovic, D., & Schehr, C. (2005). The French connection in criminology: Rediscovering crime, law, and social change. Albany: SUNY.

Berger, P., & Luckmann, T. (1966). The social construction of reality: A treatise in the sociology of knowledge. New York: Anchor.

Farley, A. P. (2002). Amusing monsters. Cardoza Law Review, 23, 1493–1517.

Toch, H. (1997). Corrections: A humanistic approach. Guilderland, NY: Harrow and Heston.

About the Authors

Christopher M. Aanstoos received his Ph.D. in phenomenological psychology from Duquesne University. After having previously taught at The Pennsylvania State University, he became a member of the graduate faculty at the University of West Georgia, where he has been a professor of psychology since 1982. He is a fellow of the American Psychological Association and has been on the executive boards of APA's Divisions 24 and 32, including having served as president of Division 32, and as editor of its journal, *The Humanistic Psychologist*. He has edited two books on humanistic and phenomenological psychology and has more than a hundred publications in those fields.

Kenneth Adams is a professor in the College of Health and Public Affairs, Criminal Justice and Legal Studies at the University of Central Florida. He has also taught at the Indiana University-Purdue University Indianapolis School of Public and Environmental Affairs. He is co-author of *Acting Out: Maladaptive Behavior in Confinement* (2002), *The Disturbed Violent Offender* (1994) and *Incarcerating Criminals* (1998).

Bruce A. Arrigo, Ph.D. is a professor of criminology, law, and society in the Department of Criminal Justice and Criminology at the University of North Carolina at Charlotte. In the College of Liberal Arts and Sciences he holds additional faculty appointments in the Department of Psychology and the Public Policy Program. In the College of Health and Human Services he holds a faculty appointment in the Department of Public Health Sciences. He is also a faculty associate in the Center for Professional and Applied Ethics and a senior member of the University Honors College. Professor Arrigo began his career as a social activist and community organizer for the homeless, persons with mental illness, survivors of sexual assault, recovering substance abusers and at-risk youth. He is an internationally acclaimed social theorist and research scientist having co-authored or co-edited 26 books and more than 150 peer-reviewed articles, book chapters and scholarly essays. Selected recent books include, *Philosophy, crime, and criminology* (2006) and *Revolution in* *penology: Rethinking the society of captives* (2009). He is presently completing the book, *Madness, citizenship, and social justice.* Among his numerous awards and recognitions, Dr. Arrigo is an elected fellow of the Academy of Criminal Justice Sciences, an elected fellow of the American Psychological Association, and the recipient of the Bruce Smith Sr. Award (for distinguished research contributions). In 2005, his book, *The French connection in criminology: Rediscovering crime, law, and social change,* won the book-of-the-year award in crime and juvenile delinquency from the Society for the Study of Social Problems.

Michael Braswell is a former prison psychologist, who has taught ethics, human relations and other criminal justice courses for more than 30 years. He is Professor Emeritus in the Department of Criminology and Criminal Justice at East Tennessee State University. He has authored/co-authored/co-edited books on ethics, counseling, human relations, peacemaking and a short story collection (*Morality Stories*, Carolina Academic Press).

Matthew Draper is an associate professor of behavioral sciences at Utah Valley University. He is the former Director of Training of Mental Health Counseling at Indiana State University. Matthew completed his doctoral work at the University of Texas at Austin in counseling psychology. His research interests focus mainly on psychotherapy theory and process, with an emphasis on moral and dialogical theory and philosophy. In his clinical practice he has worked in correctional, university and hospital settings and currently maintains a private practice in Orem, Utah.

Ginger Faulkner is a doctoral student at Indiana State University. She completed her undergraduate work at Arizona State University and masters degree in counseling from Eastern Washington. Her research interests entail personality dynamics in psychotherapy as well as psychotherapy process. She works clinically both in hospital settings and in the counseling center of a small Midwestern college.

John Randolph Fuller is a professor of criminology at the University of West Georgia. He is author of several textbooks and is currently writing a new book on criminology.

Mark Green is a doctoral student at Indiana State University. He completed his undergraduate work at Brigham Young University where he found an affinity for theoretical psychology. His research interests include hermeneutic and interpretive approaches to psychotherapy and the philosophy of the science of psychology. He currently directs mental health services at Southwest Youth Village, where he provides bilingual psychotherapeutic services.

Catherine A. Jenks is an assistant professor of criminology at the University of West Georgia. Her research areas include courts, sentencing, and survey research methods. In 2009 she received an "excellence in teaching award" from the College of Arts and Sciences.

Terry A. Kupers, M.D., M.S.P. is an institute professor at The Wright Institute, and a Distinguished Life Fellow of the American Psychiatric Association. He provides expert testimony as well as consultation and staff training regarding the psychological effects of prison conditions such as crowding and isolated confinement, the quality of correctional mental health care and the effects of sexual abuse in correctional settings. Dr. Kupers has published extensively, including the books *Prison Madness: The Mental Health Crisis Behind Bars and What We Must Do About It* (1999) and *Public Therapy: The Practice of Psychotherapy in the Public Mental Health Clinic* (1981). He is co-editor of *Prison Masculinities* (2002). He is a contributing editor of *Correctional Mental Health Report* and received the Exemplary Psychiatrist Award from the National Alliance on Mental Illness (NAMI) at the American Psychiatric Association meeting in 2005.

Lana A. McDowell is an assistant professor at Georgia College & State University. Professor McDowell has taught introduction to criminal justice, ethics, corrections, and white collar crime as well as other criminal justice courses. She is currently working toward her doctor of philosophy degree in administration of justice at The University of Southern Mississippi. She received a master of arts degree in criminal justice and criminology from East Tennessee State University as well as a bachelor of science degree in political science, criminal justice and criminology. Her research and teaching interests include restorative justice, peacemaking criminology, ethical issues in criminal justice, corrections, media influences within criminal justice and experiential learning within criminal justice.

David Polizzi is an assistant professor of criminology and criminal justice at Indiana State University. Prior to his arrival at Indiana State University, he worked as a forensic psychotherapist both within the Pennsylvania Department of Corrections and with offenders in a variety of community mental health settings. He has also worked as an adjunct professor at a variety of local colleges and universities in the Pittsburgh area from 1990 through 2005. He has published articles on restorative justice, suicide by cops and a variety of theoretical articles focusing on Lacanian psychoanalysis, humanistic psychology, social construction and existential phenomenology. He is also co-editor of *Surviving Your Clinical Placement: Reflection, Suggestions and Unsolicited Advice* (2010) published by Carolina Academic Press.

John S. Ryals, Jr. is a licensed marriage and family therapist, licensed professional counselor and clinical supervisor. He holds a bachelor's degree in psychology, master's degree in marriage and family therapy and a Ph.D. in counseling and was appointed by Louisiana Governor Bobby Jindal to the state Juvenile Justice Advisory Board. Dr. Ryals' diverse experience includes program implementation, policy analysis and development, evidence-based practice implementation, juvenile justice reform and collaboration building. Dr. Ryals has authored several publications concerning juvenile justice, with topics ranging from restorative justice to comprehensive planning and has presented at many local, state and national workshops and conferences.

Drake Spaeth is a faculty member with The Chicago School of Professional Psychology; he teaches gradute courses in the clinical and forensic psychology programs. He currently serves as coordinator of The Chicago School Adult Blended Learning Program at the Grayslake, IL campus. He also teaches courses in humanistic-existential psychotherapy, trauma and crisis intervention and others. His interests include spirituality, existential issues and violence risk in adult and adolescents.

Hayden Smith is an assistant professor at the University of South Carolina Department of Criminology and Criminal Justice. His principal focus of study is the intersection of the criminal justice and public health systems. Current research topics include self-injurious behaviors by inmates, jail diversion programs and prisoner reentry.

John Whitehead is a professor in the Department of Criminal Justice and Criminology at East Tennessee State University. He is the co-author of *Juvenile Justice: An Introduction* (6th ed.) with Steven Lab and of *Exploring Corrections in America* (2nd ed.) with Mark Jones and Michael Braswell. He has written articles on the death penalty and corrections.

INDEX